An Hachette-Vendome Book

THE CHATEAUX OF FRANCE

by the Editors
of Réalités-Hachette
and Daniel Wheeler

The Vendome Press
New York   Paris   Lausanne

Design by Marlene Vine,
adapted from the layout of the Hachette-Réalités
collection « Merveilles des châteaux de France »
by Pierre Faucheux.

Copyright © 1979 by Librairie Hachette, Paris
Copyright © 1979 English adaptation by The Vendome Press, New York
This edition first published 1979 in Great Britain by Octopus Books,
59 Grosvenor Street, London W. 1.

Distributed by Rizzoli International Publications, Inc., 597 Fifth Avenue, New York City 10022
Distributed in Canada by Methuen Publications

Library of Congress Catalog Card Number: 79-5095
ISBN 0-86565-036-5
Printed and bound in Italy

Contents

Introduction

The châteaux of France! Like "the pyramids of Egypt," the very words have a rare and evocative power, capable of seizing the imagination and filling it with visions utterly beyond the mundane. And in the case of *château*, the term itself is special, in a way that lies close to the mysterious core of fascination that many of us feel for châteaux, with their venerable stones, their patrician interiors and superb settings, their intrinsic historicity.

Dictionaries usually give "castle" as the direct synonym of *château*, but while "castle" seems entirely adequate for describing the feudal architecture of Britain, Germany, or Spain, it fails to ring true when applied to structures of the same period and general type built in France. For English-speaking people to employ *castillos* in referring to the castles of Spain or *Schlösser* for the castles of the Rhine would not only risk affectation but possibly even rob these medieval marvels of their legendary and romantic qualities. Paradoxically, the opposite is true in regard to France, for—except where verbal variety demands—to call a château anything but a château is to violate common usage. No other word has ever served so well to evoke an essential and distinctive feature of country life among the French aristocracy. But like everything old and richly inflected by time and experience, the essential distinctiveness that makes châteaux what they are evades capture in a sharp and simple characterization. Still, a key to some meaning can be found in the fact that *château* is used by the French, as well as by everyone else, whether the dwelling in question is an austere, thick-walled, battlemented fortress dating from the Dark Ages or an airy, Rococo villa of the 18th century, its gracious interiors and radiant gardens suited to nothing more bellicose than the sweet strife of pleasurable living. It remains a château as long as it is a rural dwelling with the scale, the style, and the setting to make the occupant *seem* to partake of the ancient feudal tradition of power and privilege based upon land tenure.

Quite by itself, this uniformity of nomenclature distinguishes châteaux from their counterparts in, for instance, England, where once the hereditary magnates had begun to build more for comfort and courtly display than for the military defense of strategic sites, they no longer erected what they considered to be castles, but rather "halls," great houses, mansions, villas, or even palaces. The French, of course, made the same functional and stylistic transition from the Middle Ages to the modern world; indeed, they led the way and set the fashion for the whole of Europe outside Italy. In doing so, however, the French themselves were following Italy, and herein lies the real key to the peculiar nature of châteaux.

The Ancient Origins of the Châteaux

It was France's lasting destiny to be the nation, of all those north of the Alps, most decisively shaped by the humanistic culture of classical, Mediterranean Europe, with its irresistible conception of the world as an earthly paradise reigned over by a godlike humanity. Julius Caesar conquered Celtic Gaul in 58–51 B.C., which made the region the first to be affected by Roman imperial expansion into the Transalpine world. Five centuries later, Gaul, or what is modern France, was the last colony to be evacuated as

Roman power waned and its forces withdrew into the Italian peninsula. Behind them, however, the departing governors and their garrisons left the first monumental, stone, secular architecture that barbarian Europe had ever seen. Foremost among the monuments were *castra* ("fortresses") and *palatia* ("palaces"), many of them substantial and impressive enough to survive and generations later to serve as models, or even foundation stones, when native northerners determined, at last, to save themselves from their age-old migratory and marauding practices. The Romans' *castra* were rebuilt, bigger, tougher, and more impregnable than ever, and renamed in the vernacular, first *castels* (for *castellum* or "small fortress") and then *châteaux*, or *châteaux forts* since they were in fact more military strongholds than domestic abodes. Even so, domestic life filled these bastions, for only behind defensive walls could it flourish in an era of prolonged, universal anarchy. And those few who enjoyed such security reinforced it by adopting the style and symbols of the former officials of imperial Rome. Consequently, from the beginning, even the rudest of medieval France's *châteaux forts* could on occasion be invested with some element of the old *palatia*—of beauty, comfort, and grandeur for their own sakes.

In the course of French history, those who "defended" their estates by crowning them with châteaux never ceased to make the dwellings ever more palacelike. At the same time, however, the builders took pains to preserve, if only in token or ceremonial form, a thread of continuity with the old military or chivalric past, whence arose their claim to all the titles and prerogatives of feudal lords. Thus, while Germans would never give up altogether building true medieval castles and while the English gave them up totally in favor of Palladian country houses, with not so much as a turret in sight, the French evolved progressively in their own tradition of châteaux—structures as proud and secure as fortifications, yet almost as elegant, luxurious, and civilized as palaces.

The process that created châteaux was one of assimilation and integration of opposites, and it could only be accelerated by the Italian Renaissance, itself a conscious revival of humanistic Greco-Roman civilization. As if in self-recognition, France embraced the Renaissance virtually upon contact, even while its own native Gothic dominated Europe as the first true International Style since the collapse of the antique classical world. But a manner as profoundly indigenous as Gothic could not be given up so much as reabsorbed and then transformed into something else. It survives in châteaux as their famous picturesque, enchanted, or "fairytale" quality, which lingered all the while that châteaux assumed the clear, rational, and harmonious volumes of Italian *palazzi*. But if châteaux are not castles, they are also not palaces, which, as the Louvre, Fontainebleau, Versailles, and Compiègne clearly demonstrate, have a sovereign scale and an unrestrained luxury that mere land-holding châtelains could never afford—or would never dare afford, as the hapless Fouquet might say.

The Feudal Order

The present Duc de Brissac traces his ancestry back to the Roman consul Cocceius Nerva, and at least two châteaux represented in this volume rise upon sites first fortified by the Romans of Cocceius Nerva's time—Castries (the name alone reveals the château's origins) and Chinon, one of the oldest and greatest of the royal châteaux in the Loire Valley. While Chinon is a ruin, Castries continues to shelter the descendants of the seigneurs who built there centuries ago. It is just such continuity of claim upon precedent and property that produced the châteaux of France, and the

continuity itself was made possible by an institution that medieval Europe inherited from Rome and then transformed into the only agency, other than the Church, potent enough to give life some sense of order, at least on the local level, at a time when anything resembling a centralized state had long since disappeared. This was feudalism, an economic system involving a complicated series of interpersonal relations, obligations, and services based upon land tenure. He who acquired land held a **fief** and paid for it, not in money, which, in the absence of a national treasury, was nonexistent, but in service, usually military. The holder of land was considered a lord, and from him feudal obligation led downward from vassal to vassal and ultimately to the lower orders until the process reached the lowest level, occupied by the serf, who was bound to the land in total, abject service to the lord. As for the lords or nobles themselves, they held their fiefs from one another or from a higher suzerain, such as a king, who considered himself the direct vassal and fiefholder of God. In the darkest years of the Middle Ages, before Charlemagne (r.768–814) and in the century after him, the landowners became so powerful that they could ignore their obligations to the monarch, thereby complicating the problems that made government on a broad scale impossible. But to protect or increase their own holdings, the seigneurs spent considerable amounts of time in petty wars, which required that châteaux, the seats and symbols of feudal authority, become ever larger and more solid, the better to make a powerful show, to resist attack, and to provide shelter for the lord's own family and vassals.

The Medieval Château Fort

When feudalism reigned supreme, the château was truly a *château fort*, with its effectiveness based upon massive masonry and ingeniously contrived difficulties of access. It had to rest upon a height, either natural or constructed, and have as its chief feature a heavy, often square tower—a **donjon** or "keep"—which housed the seigneur and his family, signaled his power, and then became the last resort in the event of real danger from without (pp. 24–25). Radiating from this pivotal core was a complex system of defenses. An **enceinte,** or outer encircling wall, permitted an advance guard to hold off assailants until the château's own ramparts and towers could be fully manned. But in the event the *enceinte* was overcome, attackers would have great difficulty setting up the battering ram needed to breach the château's main walls, for between them and the *enceinte* was the all-important defense of the **moat** (p. 16–17), whether filled with water or left a deep and steeply inclined dry pit. Above the moat rose high, round towers, only slightly less heavy than the *donjon* and linked by thick walls, which, together with the towers, formed an inner, and often the principal, *enceinte* (pp. 26–27). The summits of these fortifications supported a **chemin de ronde** (pp. 22–23). Built as **machicolations**—that is, as a stone parapet or gallery corbeled or projected outward upon small supporting arches—this passageway provided a high, continuous vantage point along the full perimeter of the château enclosure (pp. 30–31). The *chemin de ronde*, whether roofed over or opened at the top by **battlements** (a kind of square-notched edge also known as **crenellations**), protected the guard while also giving them a full view of the exterior.

Needless to say, the most thoroughly defended part of a *château fort* was its entrance, so fortified that it constituted a **châtelet**—a "little fortress" or "barbican" (pp. 24–25). From the outside the portal could be gained only by way of a **drawbridge** (a narrow one for pedestrians and a much broader one for vehicles), which, of course, would be quickly elevated away from the outer bank of the moat whenever an unfriendly approach was sighted. Massive towers, typically twin, flanked the entrance, which, by passing through double walls linking the paired towers, formed a kind of trap. There surprise attackers who had made it across the drawbridge could be stopped by lowering a **portcullis,** or heavy timber grille, to close off the entrance on its courtyard side. Now, to finish off the assailants, the guard had only to crush them with a heavy stone or bludgeon (an *assomoir*) suspended through the vault above and always ready to be cut loose and dropped. But not only were the château's outer features made defensive, so too was the entire structure. In the *donjon* and in the towers the upper stories could be reached only by narrow, left-turning, spiral stairways built into the thickness of the walls or in slender corner towers added to contain them. So as not to weaken the cyclopian walls, windows cut through for air and light or for taking aim were limited in number and width (often no more than slits) and were never disposed one on top of the other.

The seigneur and his family pursued their indoor lives mainly in the largest room on the *premier étage* (the *étage noble* or second floor) of the *donjon,* eating there on portable tables and sleeping together in a large bed covered with furs and enclosed by wooden panels. The same "hall" might also serve as a council chamber where, seated upon a throne, the lord, with his lady enthroned at his right, dispensed justice to the assembled knights and other vassals, all resting upon cushions, furs, or straw spread over the floor. Gourmet cuisine had yet to be developed in France, since the only facilities for cooking were in the great open hearths or in a huge brick oven built in the open air of the lower court. The greatest comfort and convenience of the medieval fortress-château was its plumbing, which consisted of wells dug in the courtyard floors and conduits to convey water elsewhere. Latrines took the form of a small chamber (a *bretèche*) corbeled outward from a main wall and suspended over the moat below. Like everything else in a medieval château, it too could be used for defensive purposes.

Between sieges and battles, the seigneurs of medieval France hunted constantly in the dense forests that still covered much of the land. Women managed the household, cultivated needlework, remained long at prayer, and, during their lords' absences on crusades and other campaigns, took command of the entire fiefdom. In time, they also mastered the arts of courtly love, making themselves the objects of devotion on the part of chivalrous knights, who, to gain their ladies' favor, became lyric poets, all the while that they sought out and engaged in prodigies of heroism, if not in actual war, then in jousts or tournaments. In the evening the great hall could be the scene of feasting, cardplaying, dancing, and performances by traveling *jongleurs* or minstrels.

The Middle Ages, of course, were the great era of faith, and nowhere was the Church stronger than in France, which gave itself completely to the cult of the Blessed Virgin—*Notre Dame* or "Our Lady." This helps to explain the early date at which civility, personal refinement, and even courtly love developed among the French. Spiritual aspiration had its expression throughout architecture, especially in the chapel that no château could be without and where the entire population of the château attended Mass daily at sunup. As earlier stated, sheer, brute mass dominated the forms of châteaux in the dark times of the Middle Ages, but as the light of civilization gradually returned throughout the Romanesque (1050-1150) and Gothic (1150-1500) periods, the natural tendency of a highly spiritualized existence to reach upward resulted in ever more vertical, attenuated, and graceful lines and proportions (p. 40). Chambers, halls, and certainly chapels had high, arched ceilings created either by open timberwork or by stone

vaulting (p. 42). Until the advent of the Gothic, arches had the round-headed form favored by the Romans; thereafter came the **ogive** or pointed arch, which, through efficient control of the load from the upper structure, made possible still higher and steeper forms and spaces. This upward thrust was expressed everywhere, even in the weightiest towers, which received tall conical roofs that resemble witches' caps and are called *poivrettes* **("pepper pots")** by the French (pp. 38–39). Turrets particularly were peaked and came to resemble rockets even more than pepper pots (pp. 52–53). The elegance implicit in all this elongation had its counterpart in leafy or even lacy, carved-stone embellishments that eventually spread like vegetation over arches, dormers, gable ends, and wall sections (pp. 20–21). French masons and stone-carvers have never been less than sensitive artists, and in Gothic châteaux the smooth ashlar of interior walls received the added refinement of huge tapestries that drew off chill and damp and replaced them with warm color. Tall, light-transmitting, stained-glass windows did the same for chapels as soon as greater security and building techniques permitted dense, militaristic walls to be opened, turned outward, and transformed into exterior buttressing (p. 43).

The 10th and 11th centuries constituted the great age of the feudal lords, the most powerful of which were the counts of Flanders, Toulouse, Blois, and Anjou, and the dukes of Aquitaine, Burgundy, Brittany, and Normandy. The latter, as the name would suggest, were Norsemen whose fierce drives had first brought them to northern France as raiders and then made them among the greatest builders—of châteaux, cathedrals, and abbeys—in the Romanesque period, a time when monumental stone architecture returned to Europe in true glory and on a Roman scale. The châteaux of Chinon, Falaise, and Gaillard, not to mention Caernarvon Castle and the Tower of London, were all constructed by the ancestors or descendants of William of Normandy, who invaded Britain and claimed the throne in 1066. When Henry II of England married Eleanor of Aquitaine (1152), he became not only Duc de Normandie but Duc de l'Aquitaine as well, thus twice over a vassal of the French King, but a vassal more puissant than the suzerain himself. It was only a matter of time before this would lead to open conflict the Hundred Years War (1337 1453) which became the central event of France's Late Middle Ages. Further complicating the century of turmoil was the expansion of the duchy of Burgundy into a separate state. Concurrently war broke out between the Burgundians and the Armagnacs, all the while that royal France found it necessary to bring armed suppression to the heretical Albigensian majority in the county of Toulouse. Endless and pervasive warfare meant that incalculable amounts of energy had to be expended upon châteaux, besieging and destroying them, only to build new ones in greater numbers and with still more unbreachable defenses. It also taxed the ingenuity of Europeans to develop new weaponry, including cannon and gunpowder, which rapidly made the seigneurial residence so outmoded as a means of defense that châteaux were liberated to become increasingly more palatial.

The Renaissance Château

If in 1458 Charles VII of Valois ruled a France free of foreign occupation, it was thanks less to the arms of the feudal nobility than to the inspired courage and military leadership of Joan of Arc, a peasant maid from the Lorraine, and to the financial genius of Jacques Coeur, a bourgeois banker of Bourges. With the rise of the middle and lower orders to positions of power and prominence, France had left the Middle Ages and entered the Renaissance. This became a matter of royal policy, from the moment the French monarchs, in 1492, began a series of invasions of the Italian peninsula, ostensibly to recover the throne of Naples (lost in 1442 by René of Anjou to Alfonso II of Spain). Italy was then at the very zenith of its great cultural flowering, moved by the ever-present example of ancient Greece and Rome but powered by the practical discovery that individual genius counted for as much or more than advantageous birth. It would be long indeed before such a notion could destroy feudalism in France, or anywhere else, but meanwhile, Charles VIII, the first of the French kings to march south over the Alps, returned to the Loire Valley with an entire atelier of Italian artisans whose assignment was to transform Amboise from a *château fort* into a royal château. Under François I (r. 1515–47) the flood gates were opened wide so that Italian ideas and artists began simply pouring into France. Leonardo da Vinci became the King's personal guest in the Loire, while at Fontainebleau, in the Île-de-France, Rosso Fiorentino, Primaticcio, Cellini, and Serlio all worked to make the royal hunting lodge the Versailles of the 16th century. Back in the Loire Valley, which the Valois had learned to love while exiled there during the English occupation of Paris, François commissioned Chambord from scratch, making it the region's largest château, the first structure in northern Europe to reflect in its plan and elevation the symmetry and balance of true classicism (pp. 56–57). But while Chambord made a significant departure from the defensive, mazelike irregularity of the old medieval fortress, the château's tall, slender proportions and its graceful, attenuated lines speak powerfully for the survival of the native French sensibility, and they would remain constants in French architecture and design. Meanwhile, France produced its own Renaissance genius, Philibert Delorme, one of the first northerners to study the great monuments of Rome and master the "orders," using them with ease and authority as well as with independence. If classicism triumphed in France, it was because architects like Delorme reinvented it so as to make Greco-Roman forms native rather than alien to French soil.

The Renaissance had scarcely got under way in France when the nation was again torn, this time by the Religious Wars that pitted French Protestants—the Huguenots—against the forces of reaction, the Catholic League. A vicious conflict, it had a significant effect on the form that châteaux would take during the 16th century. First of all, the troubled times made it necessary to emulate the luxury of the Valois mainly by modifying existing châteaux or by building upon the foundations of old ones. It was just such a procedure that, when continued through the centuries, caused many châteaux to become veritable textbook surveys of the entire history of French architecture. Typically, the Renaissance château emerged when one wing of an old quadrilateral *enceinte* was reconstituted as a taller, more sumptuous **corps de logis** or main wing. The better to make this block the focal point of a true Renaissance perspective, the unit opposite the new *corps* would then be demolished and the units on either side of the original enclosure treated as side wings, with their ground floors opened on the interior side to give the effect of Italian-style arcades or loggias (pp. 138–141). Together, the *corps de logis* and its projecting wings would join at right angles, thus making a U-shape and forming a **cour d'honneur** open to light, air, and the new Italian garden beyond. Often, however, the Middle Ages governed the corners, which remained defended by fat, round towers, complete with their machicolations and high, pepper-pot roofs. Balance and equilibrium extended to the windows, cut large in the stout old walls, stone-mullioned, and ordered one over the other in a gridlike arrangement that, along with intervening friezes and moldings,

would bring a new emphasis to the horizontal dimension, itself so symptomatic of a society freshly in love with the potential of human life on earth (pp. 46–47). Ornamentation, however, would, if possible, be even richer than in Gothic times, albeit in formal themes derived from the classical repertoire—columns and pilasters, shell-headed niches, and dormers pedimented like temple fronts and crowned with candelabra (pp. 74–75).

While a left-turning, helical stairway might be allowed to linger in one of the corner towers, the Renaissance châtelain would certainly have wanted to boast of a new monumental stairway *à l'italienne*, a series of straight, right-turning ramps, rising under coffered barrel vaults, rather than under vaults groined and ribbed in the Gothic manner (p. 72).

No less monumental, classical, or architectural were the great fireplaces with their Italian marble mantelpieces richly decorated tier upon tier, like stories, with sculptural reliefs and even freestanding statues, many of them displaying an heroic nudity never before seen in Christian France (pp. 132–133). Now, however, eroticism reached unprecedented heights, and this had full or even prurient play in the frescoes that were painted, again after Italian prototypes, over as much wall space as the new windows would allow (pp. 118–119). Overhead, ceilings exposed their beams (pp. 72–73), an arrangement so favored that it lasted until well into the 17th century and became known as the "French ceiling" (*plafond à la française*).

In their greatest splendor, all these features would have appeared in the gallery or long hall fitted out the entire length and width of one wing and perhaps the full height of two stories. Other rooms now had specific purposes, such as bedrooms, but no space had yet been set aside for dining. Cavernous kitchens were built into basements, and the art of fine cooking arrived with the chefs brought from Italy by Catherine de'Medici. Once prepared, however, meals could be served in any room, upon extension tables of a type invented in Tuscany. The rest of the furniture tended to be heavy and medieval, modified only by classical decorative motifs. Small antechambers, where personal servants slept on pallets, made bedrooms more private, but the convenience of closets or armoires did not exist, and clothing had to be stored in chests. In the age of humanism, personal hygiene seems to have been left behind in the age of greater godliness. The old *château fort* had its well and its latrine, but both of these vanished from the Renaissance château, and bathrooms belonged to a distant future. With all its cleverness, the Renaissance invented the *chaise percée* ("pierced chair"), a portable chamber pot that could be used anywhere, even in public.

Where the Middle Ages remained unchallenged by pagan antiquity was in the chapel, which often took on the beautiful elaborations of the late, "flamboyant" phase of Gothic. Renaissance households, for all their worldliness, attended Mass daily. This was part of the widening range of experience, which enabled Renaissance men to hunt, go to war, make passionate love, read deeply in poetry and philosophy, appreciate the new drama based on classical models, and become collectors and connoisseurs. The latter interest often resulted in rooms set aside in châteaux for a library and a cabinet, where choice, precious objects could be kept and lovingly savored, not only rare books but also bronze statuettes, cameos, curious shells, and jewels.

The measure and harmony of the architecture embraced the gardens, which in peaceful areas could spread beyond the moat and entirely around the château, all geometrically ordered **broderies** (embroiderylike arrangements) of flowers and clipped hedges, vegetables and fruit trees, the whole studded with fountains and marble statuary imported from Italy (p. 87). There at the twilight hour, along manicured paths, in grottoes and nympheums, men and women dressed in pearl-laden costumes met, played ambiguous games of the heart, and frequently engaged in Machiavellian intrigue, one of the least efficacious of the recent lessons learned from the renascent south.

The Classic Châteaux of the Grand Siècle

When the three reigning sons of Henri II and Catherine de' Medici died without producing a male heir, the long-lived Valois dynasty finally died out. In 1589 Henri de Navarre mounted the throne of France as Henri IV, the first of the Bourbons—not, however, before he had abjured his Protestant faith in favor of Catholicism. With the tolerant Edict of Nantes (1598), he settled the religious crisis, and with the enlightened aid of his prime minister, the great Sully, he transformed France into an economically prosperous and competitive nation. Thus auspiciously launched, the French were ready for their *grand siècle*—the Baroque 17th century—when France achieved an ascendancy, in both politics and culture, that returned the nation to the dominant position it had held in the Gothic age. Now Paris began to replace Rome as the generative center of art in Europe. Now, too, the French language—all polish and perfection—gradually spread as the true *lingua franca* of every court in Europe, from Madrid to St. Petersburg. Art and architecture entered into service under the monarchy as once they had been in the service of the Church. A remarkable unity of style developed, the consequences of the regulatory power granted to the academies set up by Colbert, Louis XIV's trusted and trustworthy minister. In this time of absolutism, the taste favored was inevitably and quintessentially French, a stately and rather severe, although strong and full-bodied, classicism that stood in sharp contrast to the lavish and extrovert Baroque produced in Italy and most of the rest of Europe. Through its training and discipline, the academic system produced a host of creative geniuses: Descartes and Pascal in philosophy; Poussin and Claude in painting; Corneille and Racine in drama; Lully and Couperin in music; La Fontaine, Bossuet, Fénélon, and La Rochefoucauld in literature; and, of course, Mme de Sévigné and the Duc de Saint-Simon, those irrepressible letter-writers and diarists who have left us such vivid impressions of what life was like under Louis *le grand.* Most important for our purposes, it also yielded, beginning with François Mansart, a series of master designers and architects from whose drafting boards came what for many are France's classic or definitive châteaux.

Until after 1682, when Louis XIV moved to Versailles and forced the feudal nobility to give up their independence and join him as subservient courtiers, the *grand siècle* was a great age of châteaux. Louis's policy—of radical centralization under an absolute, divine-right monarch—seemed the only means available to curb the anarchical drives inherited from the past and to consolidate and expand the gains made by the early Bourbons. After all, the much-loved Henri IV had perished in 1610 of assassination by a religious fanatic. Moreover, both Cardinal Richelieu and Cardinal Mazarin, the astute ministers who governed France through much of Louis XIII's reign and on into the minority of Louis XIV, had to contend with serious rebellions (the Fronde of 1648–53 being the most critical) fomented by nobles disgruntled over the power increasingly granted by the throne to the rising bourgeoisie. These were the bankers, tax collectors, army suppliers, manufacturers, merchants, jurists, and bureaucrats who, since the time of Jacques Coeur, had been doing the practical, quotidian work of making France function. Earners of money, rather than inheritors of land, the bourgeois soon exceeded all but the greatest grandees in wealth, and very often it was they—Choisy at Balleroy, Fouquet at Vaux, Ruellan at Le Rocher-Portail—who in the 17th century built some of the finest châteaux outside the royal properties.

A Louis XIII château by or influenced by François Mansart would, in all its grand, bilateral symmetry, seem nothing so much as an eloquent, three-dimensional demonstration of Gallic logic and the Cartesian method (p. 105). The unity, clarity, and triadic balance of the conception would be fully stated in the overall plan of a central *corps de logis* set at the bottom of a *cour d'honneur* on either side of which stand, facing one another in mirror image, an identical pair of low service structures or outbuildings called **communs** (p. 179). Independent blocks, rather than wing extensions as in the Renaissance château, the *communs* are nonetheless perfectly integrated, through style and perspective lines, with the main building. Further clarifying and unifying all the forms is the separate but identical roof for each unit, even in the *corps de logis,* which typically consists of a tall central pavilion flanked by a pair of lower, slightly recessed blocks. The roofs, meanwhile, have the familiar and ever-popular hip angle invented by Mansart; they enclose attics lighted by trios of windows, all grouped as round *oeil de boeuf* ("bull's eye") openings on either side of tall pedimented ones (pp. 142–143). A crowning lantern and majestically tall chimney stalks, or stacks, add further dignity, as does the *enceinte,* now formed as a platform "defended" by a balustrade and a moat. These features, like the toy turrets at the outer corners of the *communs,* serve merely as ceremonial reminders of the feudal tradition through which the châtelain could justify his claim to such a sumptuous country house and to the estates that supported it. Then, just as all this formality threatens to turn cold and overly severe, it is warmed by the color of the materials: the rose of the brick walls contrasted to the blue of the slate roofs, with the whole lighted by the white of the windows' wooden mullions and the limestone "chains" of masonry that articulate, and thus clarify, every corner and edge (p. 110).

In the second half of the 17th-century the château would very likely have been enhanced both inside and out with the formal and decorative ideas introduced at Vaux le Vicomte by the masters who went on to create Versailles for Louis XIV. These were the painter Charles Le Brun and the garden architect André Le Nôtre. The truly exalting feature of a salon decorated in the manner of Le Brun is its ceiling, painted over with an immense, illusionistic scene of classical personages soaring aloft in heroic confrontation against a cobalt sky streaked with pink-lined clouds (p. 127). Abetting this colorism would be the gilt of richly carved moldings, the dazzling white of stucco relief sculptures, and the polychrome of the marbles (or wooden paneling painted to simulate veined marble) inlaid as wainscoting and window-door enframements (p. 113).

In his compositions Le Nôtre transformed geometry into high art and so extended and elaborated the patterned Renaissance garden as to make nature seem utterly subdued by human intelligence (pp. 124–126). After Le Nôtre, French gardens were no longer mere gardens but vast parks, composed of terraces, or **parterres,** planted *en broderie* or watered with mirrorlike ponds and basins asplash with high-jetting fountains. Long, straight *allées* lined with clipped trees lead to starlike conjunctions with other perspectives, some of which conclude in the inevitable forest or turn back to the climactic focal point occupied by the château, along the way treating the stroller to bosky dells and grottoes populated by marble nymphs and gods. The château gardens of Le Nôtre must be counted among the supreme glories of French art.

The 18th-Century Château

With the death of Louis XIV in 1715, after a reign of seventy-three years, much of the aristocracy that had been drawn to Versailles returned, as if released from captivity, either to their estates or, more often, to town houses in Paris. Weary of grandiloquence, the French would now cultivate intimacy, comfort, and elegance. In the time of Louis XV (r. 1715–74), it was not the monarch who dominated, but his mistresses, especially Mme de Pompadour, a clever, educated woman with an active interest in the world of arts and letters. The Marquise held her position largely because in an age positively jaded with sophistication, she had a gift for combating boredom, doing so by replacing heavy, masculine heroics with feminine artifice and a light, discriminating touch. The Baroque remained the coin of the realm, but flipped to its reverse side, where ponderous solemnity gave way to wit, charm, and exquisite taste.

Through the Regency and the reigns of Louis XV and the doomed Louis XVI, France remained the richest country in Europe, but a nation constantly on the verge of bankruptcy. A paralyzing paradox, it came mainly from a fear of modifying the moribund but sacrosanct institution of feudalism for the sake of much-needed socioeconomic reform. But if the French failed in this respect, it was not for the want of ideas, which the intelligentsia produced in prodigal abundance. To cite Montesquieu, Fontanelle, Diderot, d'Alembert, Voltaire, Helvétius, and Rousseau is merely to name the brightest stars in a veritable galaxy that, quite justifiably, caused the period to be called the Age of Enlightenment. No less prodigious were the arts, which brought forth Rameau in music; Marivaux, Le Sage, and Abbé Prevost in drama and romance; Watteau, Boucher, Chardin, and Fragonard in painting; and Boffrand, Gabriel, and Ledoux in architecture. Encouraging the creative ferment and the whole cosmopolitan character of life were the salons, often held in châteaux and invariably hosted by ladies of style and intelligence, vying with one another to attract the most famous and the most accomplished persons of the time. Conversation, which constituted the very food of life, had to be quick, deft in repartee, and sparkling with fresh aphorisms. But country existence could also be quiet and reflective; at the Château de Maisons, for instance, Voltaire wrote much of *La Henriade*, while his host, the Marquis de Maisons, performed scientific experiments in his own laboratory.

Everything in the French sensibility that tended toward measure, harmony, and balance received its ultimate refinement in the châteaux of the 18th century. Shifts in wall plane from one pavilion to another were so slight and shallow that the *corps de logis* came to resemble a smooth-surfaced, rectangular block, its subdivisions acknowledged mainly in the variations of the roof line over the low, dormered attic (pp. 144–145). Sometimes, the distinctions proved even more subtle, when a balustrade *à l'italienne* replaced the usual Mansart. Instead of a grandiose portico, designed like a temple front or a triumphal arch, the entrance could be an open vestibule discreetly recessed into the volume of the building and screened by a one-story colonnade. The uniform use of light-colored stone reinforced the effect of utter unity, while iron grillework, wrought in the graceful lines of the Rococo style, lightened the ensemble, once added as handrails over story-high windows and, with gilded pinnacles, formed into gates at the entrance to the park (pp. 154–155). A sense of airy spaciousness was preserved by placing the *communs* at greater remove from the *corps de logis*, all the while integrating them stylistically with the whole.

The surrounding park could well have been transformed into a garden *à l'anglaise*, for this was an age of eager anglomania, as well as a generation encouraged by Rousseau to return to the simplicities of pastoral living. Rather than geometric and formal, the English garden is "natural," a picturesquely random arrangement of reedy ponds, flowering meadows, and shaggy trees linked by pathways meandering past such "surprise" features or "follies" as sham classical ruins, Dutch mills, tiny dairies, or Chinese pagodas.

For the first time almost as much attention would be given on the interior to comfort and convenience as to décor. Now was introduced a true dining room, heated by an Austrian-style ceramic stove and served possibly by means of a dumbwaiter from a kitchen in the basement directly below. Upstairs, an innovative disposition of space allowed boudoirs to have closets and, at last, *cabinets de toilette*, even if these were utilized more for applying perfume and makeup than for washing. Another logical development came when the main stairway, formerly so triumphant and prominent a feature, moved to the side, freeing the entrance space to become a real reception room leading to the salon, now on the ground floor rather than on the *premier étage*. This placed the salon on the garden side, where tall windows give full view onto the infinite vistas of the park. Back at the stairway, the ramp rises along an extended and graceful curve enhanced by the wrought iron of the handrail that, here too, replaced the masonry balusters of the former century.

The curve, and even more the reverse curve of the arabesque, dominated the design vocabulary of the 18th century, just as it had that of the 17th century, but emphatic Baroque plasticity would be supplanted by delicate linearity. This was the Rococo, whose name appears to be a contraction of the French words for rock or pebble (*rocaille*) and shell (*coquille*), natural forms that, along with those of leaf branches, flowers, and bamboo, became stylized into ingenious and engaging compositions. Like trendrils, these wove themselves into cartouches and friezes and could be worked in any material—wood, plaster, or fabric. All of it was to be found in the salon, whose very form—the oval—was likely to be governed by the curve principle (p. 165). Walls bore beautifully carved fruitwood paneling (*boiseries*), sometimes finished in clear wax, often painted cream and then highlighted in gilt, but also colorfully decorated with *singeries*—scenes of monkeys playfully performing human acts. The Orient enjoyed scarcely less popularity than England, and to imitate it, the Martin brothers invented a hard lacquer (*le vernis Martin*) that in cool or brilliant monochrome brought sheen and color to the paneling of many rooms. Paintings appeared mainly over doors, set into the paneling (p. 161), while mirrors filled the spaces over the small marble mantels that framed the fireplaces (p. 147). The furniture, with its cabriole legs, its caning or silken upholstery, its satinwood inlay and ormolu or gilded fittings, sets the standard, even today, for charm, grace, and beauty.

The 18th century was a skeptical age, wrapped in ease and luxury while awaiting—almost with bated breath—the Revolution that had to come. God remained in the château, but neatly tucked away, not in a chapel, but in an oratory, which was barely larger than the *cabinet de toilette*, and hardly more endowed with Christian symbols. Although feudalism lingered, its martial past seemed distant indeed, and this was acknowledged more in the arms carved upon pediments and worked into iron grilles than in the "defenses" of decorative turrets.

It is in the very nature of the arts that they sense and anticipate the trends that culture in general is destined to follow. Thus, some twenty-five years before the Revolution, French architects and designers began to reform the Rococo and to reconstitute classicism as a highly abstract or a purified, almost archaeologically correct style (p. 182). But the Revolution destroyed feudalism in France and with it the whole raison d'être of châteaux, with the result that Neoclassicism, which climaxed under the Napoleonic Empire, touched few châteaux except in the form of furniture and interior décor brought to structures put up before 1789 (pp. 190–193). No country house built after this date, however large and sumptuous, would ever be imbued with the old feudal spirit that makes a château what it is—a proud, seigneurial residence that, at the center or edge of an ancient, game-filled forest, remains romantically alive with the memories of an aristocratic and chivalrous past.

The Preservation and Restoration of Châteaux

While feudalism survived as a living institution there was never a great concern for preserving and restoring châteaux, since the very need of feudal lords to have proper country abodes meant that old dwellings would be kept up or new ones built. But with their lifelines cut, châteaux had to be given artificial support if they were not to disintegrate and perish from age and neglect. And emergency care became essential at an early date, for most châteaux were sacked by the Revolutionary mob—especially those belonging to titled gentry who emigrated abroad after having long abandoned their estates and peasants for life at court. Many were also burned and the great medieval keeps blown up. But worse was to follow, when properties fell into the hands of speculators who stripped the interiors of their gilt and marble and sold off the structural brick as raw building material. Such vandalism has left us with nothing but fragments of Philibert Delorme's Anet, one of the great masterpieces of the French Renaissance.

The first conscious attempts to restore châteaux came during the Restoration period (1814–30), when Louis XVIII and Charles X unwisely did all in their power to reverse the Revolution and bring back the *ancien régime*. Indeed, the Restoration collapsed in large measure because of an 1825 law that indemnified the émigrés whose property had been confiscated by the Revolutionary government. If many of the old families still hold their châteaux, it is owing to this legislation, which at the time created such resentment among those whose interest income from government securities was reduced to pay the indemnities.

In 1830 the royalist government took the innovative measure of establishing the post of Inspector General of Historic Monuments, whose responsibility would be to make an inventory of such assets and to recommend for or against their conservation. In 1834 the appointment went to Prosper Mérimée, distinguished novelist and author of *Carmen*. Once a château was deemed worthy of salvage, the issue arose whether simply to preserve it in its present state, thus preventing further deterioration, or to rehabilitate and rebuild it according to what the restorers believed the structure to have been in its prime. With Eugène Viollet-le-Duc, the architect-engineer

and passionate medievalist who also served as Mérimée's principal collaborator, the second approach was the only one to take. In the instance of Pierrefonds, what the method produced was less an authentic 14th-century *château fort*, than a realization of what a gifted scholar imagined such a place should have been. Still, if Pierrefonds tells us little about the real Middle Ages, it reveals much about the Second Empire, and that in itself is of immense value. However, in lesser hands, which usually had control, such aggressive restorations could do more harm than good. The lamentable consequences are to be found everywhere, from the great Château de Blois on the Loire to Burgundy's La Rochepot.

Today, with all the knowledge of advanced archaeology, with the techniques of sophisticated science, and with the support of republican governments fully conscious of France's great heritage, restorations of the most sensitive and remarkable sort have been accomplished and are always in progress. Vast sums, in fact, have been spent to bring Versailles, the Louvre, Fontainebleau, Chambord, and Vincennes back to the state they enjoyed just before the Revolution mutilated them. Now funds are being spread more broadly and thus more thinly, in the hope of at least staving off the irrevocable loss of literally thousands of châteaux, manor houses, and *gentilhommières* that still, after all the depredations, proliferate over the French countryside.

Appropriately enough, the châteaux that survive best—such as the almost indescribably magnificent Champ-de-Bataille—are those still occupied and cared for by the titled descendants of the feudal lords who built them. A lived-in château is a living château, and no one is likely to repair a leaky roof with greater dispatch than the person whose head is there to be dripped upon. But the low value of agriculture (as always, the chief product of land), the high cost of labor and materials, the unavailability of the armies of servants formerly required to maintain great houses and estates, and the heavy burden of taxes of every sort—all work against private ownership. Paying visitors and such special events as *son et lumière* performances help to defray the onerous expenses and keep life's blood pumping through a château's aged arteries. Thus, more than the late 20th century might think or deserve, châteaux continue to stand, splendid anachronisms yet welcome reminders of the human capacity to strive for the earthly paradise.

Most of the châteaux illustrated and discussed in this volume are accessible to the public, either on a regular basis or on proper application to the occupants. To verify which châteaux may be visited, as well as the hours and seasons at which visits are possible, the interested traveler should communicate with the Caisse Nationale des Monuments Historiques, 62 rue Saint-Antoine, Paris IV. Often, the information available there can also be obtained from the various outlets of the French Government Tourist Office, as well as from the local *syndicats d'initiative* throughout France.

Daniel Wheeler

Chinon

High upon a rocky escarpment above the Vienne, a tributary of the great Loire River, loom the battered but noble ruins of one of the oldest and most historic châteaux in France—Chinon. This heavy medieval redoubt, its bristling feudal defenses never once touched by the soft, humanizing hand of the Renaissance, stands in marked contrast to the surrounding countryside, so sweet and salubrious, so lush with green meadows and game-filled forests, that from the earliest times it was known as "the garden of France." The richer the land in natural produce and beauty the greater the need to fight for and defend it. And so by the 5th century the strategic site at Chinon bore a battlemented crest—a Gallo-Roman *castrum*—sufficiently fortified and threatening to incite siege in 446 by the Roman General Aetius. Reconstruction and repeated assault brought history again and again to the ramparts and towers of Chinon, until events climaxed toward the end of the Hundred Years War (1337–1453), when the French royal court, denied Paris by the occupying English, found their principal refuge in the great castle at Chinon. Now came forth a savior—Joan of Arc, the divinely inspired peasant maid from the Lorraine—who by torchlight marched into Chinon on the evening of March 9, 1429, and persuaded the Dauphin, the uncrowned Charles VII of France, that it was her destiny to lead him and his beleaguered nation to victory under God. This was Chinon's moment of glory, and following the treachery that brought *la Pucelle* to the stake at Rouen, the old *château fort* entered upon a decline that was arrested only in the 19th century.

Chinon, even in its reduced state, consists of three different fortresses, strung out from east to west and linked by walls and bridges over deep moats. The intermediate edifice, the Château du Milieu, and that at the western extremity, the Château du Coudray, date back to the 10th and early 11th centuries, when Chinon belonged to the powerful counts of Blois. In 1044, a shift in command occurred, following the defeat of Thibaud III de Blois by Geoffroy Martel, Comte d'Anjou. The Anjou counts proceeded to consolidate Chinon's *enceinte* and to reinforce its towers. By 1154 the Anjou domains had devolved upon Henri de Plantagenêt, who now mounted the throne of England as Henry II. Taking Chinon as his preferred residence, Henry added the castle's westernmost unit, the round Tour du Moulin, which served as the château's principal *donjon* or "keep," and the square-based Tour du Trésor. He also made the bastion more habitable by endowing it with a proper *logis*.

Having spent much time at Chinon, but little of it in the company of his Queen, Eleanor of Aquitaine, who preferred her own court—the legendary "court of love"—at Poitiers, Henry II died at Chinon in 1189, as did his son and successor, Richard the Lion-Hearted, in 1199. Affronted by the English presence in France, King Philippe Auguste laid siege to Chinon for an entire year and finally, in 1205, won the stronghold and the whole of the fief for the French crown. Soon the château would be further enlarged and reinforced, which gave the complex its definitive shape. Then in the early 14th century Philip the Fair erected the Tour de l'Horloge, an entrance *châtelet* on the east and the only one of Chinon's many towers to survive intact. A century later Charles VII, to distract himself and the court from the worries of war, built the Grande Salle, a handsome Gothic hall, and there staged many desperate festivities. It was in this chamber that Joan of Arc found the throneless King, hiding incognito among his courtiers.

After 1477 Louis XI left Chinon in care of a governor, the chronicler Philippe de Commynes, who added the powerful Tour d'Argenton, designed to prevail in the age of artillery. With royalty rarely drawn to Chinon, Cardinal Richelieu took possession of the château in 1633, mainly to prevent its falling into the hands of rebellious nobles. Thereafter neglect and accelerating deterioration were the fate of the castle on the Vienne. Systematic demolition came during the Revolution and Empire, a process that ceased after 1855, once Prosper Mérimée, the author of *Carmen*, had entered a new office, that of France's inspector general of historic monuments.

Spread out like a great carcass upon the rocky cliff above the Vienne, a tributary of the Loire River, Chinon has a social and military history that can be traced back to the 5th century, when the site was fortified with a Gallo-Roman castrum. Throughout a millennium, it was besieged, rebuilt, and enlarged, by the counts of Blois and Anjou and then by the kings of England and France. And even in its reduced state, the castle consists of three fortresses separated, within the enceinte, by deep moats and connected by bridges and high ramparts. At the western extremity is the Château du Coudray, whose walls date back to the 10th and 11th centuries. Equally ancient are the foundations of the middle fortress—the Château du Milieu—upon which rise the ruins of the logis built in the 12th century by Henry II of England and those of the Grande Salle erected in the early 15th century by Charles VII of France. Eastward of the huge square base of the Tour du Trésor and beyond the tall 14th-century Tour de l'Horloge—the castle's entrance châtelet—lingers what little remains of Henry II's late-12th-century Fort Saint-Georges. By torchlight on the evening of March 9, 1429, Joan of Arc, with her six male companions, strode through the Tour de l'Horloge and in the Grande Salle revealed to the apprehensive Dauphin—the uncrowned Charles VII—her plan to lead France out of the Hundred Years War. Shortly thereafter Chinon fell into disuse and then into a decline that was arrested only in the mid-19th century.

La Brède

The Middle Ages produced no château more delightful than La Brède, a feudal site so ancient that Charlemagne is believed to have slept there following the loss of Roland at the Battle of Roncevalles. But however Gothic its form—a small though heavily fortified, polygonal complex afloat in the middle of a lake at the edge of the forests south of Bordeaux—La Brède is vital with the spirit of one of the most modern-minded human beings who ever lived. Indeed, it could be said that the Enlightenment itself and the essential concept of democratic government, as embodied in the American Constitution, had their inception at La Brède, for here lived, reflected, and wrote Charles-Louis de Secondat, Baron de La Brède et de Montesquieu—better known simply as Montesquieu (1680–1755). Avid traveler, jurist, political philosopher, and satirist, Montesquieu loved life with a rare devotion and was comfortable everywhere in the world as only the most civilized people can be. La Brède, however, claimed him even more than Paris could. Thus, it was at home on his ancestral estate, actively involved with the vineyards and with the making and sale of wine, that Montesquieu spent most of his life. While happily speaking the local *patois* to his fellow Landais, he would return to the library at La Brède and, with witty brilliance, compose in a French that became the very model of classical clarity and perfection. The satiric *Persian Letters* came forth in 1721, bringing the author instant notoriety. In 1734 Montesquieu produced *Considérations sur les causes de la grandeur des romains et de leur décadence,* a scientific, historical study of the rise and fall of Rome. Much more influential, however, was the political treatise *De l'esprit des lois,* which appeared in 1748. Meanwhile, the landed aristocrat reserved his fondest words for La Brède. To a great friend, the Abbé Gausco, Montesquieu wrote in 1744: "I treat myself to the pleasure of inviting you to my country place, La Brède, where you will find a château Gothic to the T but enhanced by a park whose charm was inspired by an idea I discovered in England." Eight years later he wrote to the same correspondent: "I can say that just now La Brède is one of the most agreeable places in France, so completely does nature thereabout seem just out of bed and still wearing her dressing gown."

Little wonder that Montesquieu had such a strong sense of place at La Brède, since the estate had remained, and remains today, in the same family—the lords of La Lande—that first fortified the site in the 11th century. A reconstruction occurred between 1300 and 1309. Then with the outbreak of the Hundred Years War (1337–1453) the Landes, like most of the nobility of the region, sided with England, which had held the Aquitaine in fief ever since 1152, when Eleanor of Aquitaine married Henry II Plantagenêt. The conflict required stronger defenses, and resulted in a new building campaign in 1419. Except for a few 16th-century modifications, which on one side replaced the *enceinte* with a terrace and elsewhere perforated the outside walls with mullioned windows, the château's overall appearance has scarcely been altered since. But as France regained its territories, the dissident Lande family fled to Britain, leaving their property to be confiscated by the French crown. Restitution and return took place after the general amnesty granted by Charles VII in 1453.

Montesquieu was born at La Brède by virtue of his mother's descent from the original Landes. After a childhood on the estate, he went away in 1700 to study under the Oratorians at Juilly, near Meaux. By 1711 he had returned to Bordeaux and become counselor to the local parlement, only to assume the presidency of that body in 1716. Considering himself less than a distinguished jurist, Montesquieu departed on a series of long journeys, which took him to Italy, Germany, Holland, and England. In the last country he developed many affinities, among them a taste for English gardens, which, as the letter above confirms, he soon applied to the grounds around La Brède. Once back in France the great man settled upon his domains and thereafter left them only for brief annual visits to Paris, during one of which he died at the age of seventy-six.

below: Rising upon foundations that date back to the 11th century, La Brède at the edge of the forests of La Lande, south of Bordeaux, has changed little since its reconstruction in 1419. To enter the château one must cross a drawbridge over the wide moat (actually a lake), traverse an islet forecourt defended by a stout tower, cross a second drawbridge, this one protected by a tiny **châtelet**, and then, beyond another, flat-ended tower (where Charlemagne is supposed to have slept), pass over a third drawbridge. Thereafter the visitor arrives upon a terrace created when, in the 16th century, one side of the polygonal, asymmetrical **enceinte** was removed to open the inner court to light, air, and a view upon the park. Dominating the whole complex of turrets, buttresses, peaked summits, half-timbered upper stories, and flat, red-tile roofs is the tall **donjon**, crowned by a machicolated **chemin de ronde** (an enclosed lookout passage for sentinels) and a slate-covered "witch's cap." Having become an Anglophile in Britain, the great Montesquieu, La Brède's 18th-century châtelain, redesigned the park as an English garden, one of the first of its kind in France.

left: The only large room within La Brède is the former guard hall, a long, barrel-vaulted space that Montesquieu transformed into a library. There, the 18th-century **philosophe**—and ardent lover of life upon his ancestral estate—wrote treatises whose advanced ideas on despotic, monarchic, and republican forms of government traveled far and even found their way into the main body of the United States Constitution.

Josselin

On the exterior Josselin turns to the world a solid, grimly Breton front, its massive stone walls and towers climbing like a cliff high above the Oust River. But what this fierce and defensive structure protects is an interior court façade that is as refined, flamboyantly Gothic, and welcoming as the outside ramparts are tough, Romanesque, and forbidding. Thus, Josselin—half-fortress, half-palace, and long a seat of the historic Rohan family—offers in its architecture a split personality that perfectly reflects the genius of its masters for alternately selecting losing and winning sides in some of France's major political disputes.

Josselin, Brittany's most famous château, took its name from the son of Guéthenoc, Vicomte de Porhoët, the medieval knight who in 1008 put up the first fortification on this site. The original château lasted no more than a century and a half, for in 1168 it was razed during a conflict between Eudes II de Porhoët and Henry II of England. In 1173, however, Eudes obtained a pardon and the permission to rebuild Josselin, traces of whose second keep can still be found on the south edge of the present *enceinte*.

Eudes II's first son, Josselin II, inherited the château, while Alain, the second son, received the title of Vicomte de Rohan, thereby founding the long line of proud, even haughty aristocrats who would bear this name. In 1307 Philip the Fair confiscated Josselin, which made it a French stronghold when, at mid-century, war erupted over the succession to the duchy of Brittany. The commandant of the fortress was Jean de Beaumanoir, whose fate it was to lead thirty French knights against a comparable force from England in the terrible *combat des trente*, which the French won, but without winning the war.

Olivier de Clisson married Beaumanoir's widow, Marguerite de Rohan, and, although a vassal of the dukes of Brittany, proceeded to transform Josselin into a formidable outpost supporting France. It had high, stout walls connected by a series of nine cylindrical towers, the intimidating character of which can still be appreciated in the three that survive (in restored state) on Josselin's "public" side. After the death of Bertrand du Guesclin, Olivier de Clisson succeeded this great hero of the Hundred Years War as constable of France. He died at Josselin in 1407, not however before marrying his daughter to Alain VIII de Rohan, who thereupon received the Josselin fiefdom.

Still loyal to France, the lords of Josselin once again incurred the wrath of the Duc de Bretagne, who in 1488 ordered a new dismantling of the château and its defenses. But Rohan steadfastness received its reward when Charles VIII, whose marriage to Anne de Bretagne united the long-divided interests of Brittany and France, financed a full restoration. This enterprise continued from 1490 to 1505 and, even after the arrival of the Renaissance, imposed upon the old fortress a new and exquisitely domestic Late Gothic structure.

No longer caught between contestants in an old medieval rivalry, the Rohans soon became powerful at the French court. Henri de Rohan married Marguerite de Béthune, daughter of the great finance minister Sully, and in 1603 received the title of Duke from Henri IV. Trouble, however, returned to the family in the time of Louis XIII (r. 1610–43), for the Duc de Rohan had assumed leadership of the Protestant party. Cardinal Richelieu, the King's first minister, could not tolerate this and ordered the demolition of Josselin's fortifications, including the great keep built by Olivier de Clisson. The Prince de Condé interceded with the King to save Josselin from total destruction, but from that time on the Rohans increasingly abandoned the château in favor of their considerable domains elsewhere. The towers commanding the first gate and drawbridge were pulled down in 1750. By 1776 the château had been made to shelter a cotton mill, established to provide work for poor children. During the Revolution, the Duc de Rohan did not emigrate, thus never lost his estates. In 1824 the Duchesse de Berry, mother of the four-year-old heir to the throne of France, visited Josselin, then in a ruinous state, and recommended its restoration. This was undertaken in 1866. The château remains a possession of the Rohan dukes.

opposite: First built in 1008, the Château de Josselin now visible in the thick Romanesque walls and towers of the clifflike façade rising over the Oust River dates from the late 14th century. It was then that Olivier de Clisson transformed Josselin into a powerful stronghold for France in Brittany, still a fief of the English king. Originally, Clisson's great fortress boasted a huge keep and nine towers linking battlemented ramparts that provided a continuous parapet completely around the area secured by the enceinte. *The tall, two-story dormers, with their refined Late Gothic style, suggests the markedly contrasting architecture that the tough outer bastions protect within.*

overleaf: The façade of Josselin confronting the cour d'honneur *dates from 1490–1505 and offers a late Flamboyant Gothic style as light and lacy as the outer bastions are rude, massive, and Romanesque. Despite the hardness of the granite in which the carving has been done, the open-work gallery, the struts, crockets, and finials of the high dormers all seem more the product of the jeweler's art than of stonemasonry. Intertwined with this delicate fretwork are the ermine of Brittany, the* fleur-de-lis *of France, the "A" for Anne de Bretagne, and À plus—the device of the Rohans, long the lords of Josselin.*

Cherveux

The great beauty of Cherveux is the unity—rare for a medieval château—of its Late Gothic style. This aesthetic delight derives from the need to rebuild rapidly in order to defend a site so strategic that the fortifications established there since the earliest times had invariably been destroyed almost as soon as they were thrown up. The present château dates from the second half of the 15th century, when it was erected in a single campaign under the sponsorship of Robert de Coningham, a Scotsman who served as captain of the royal guard under both Louis XI and Charles VII. But long before, Cherveux had been commanded by some of the most illustrious names in the whole of the French Middle Ages, beginning with the Lusignans. The Poitou house of Lusignan claimed ancestry from the fairy Melusine and, after active participation in the Crusades, produced a long line of kings in Jerusalem, Armenia, and Cyprus. In 1200 Hugues X de Lusignan figured large in the unification of France when King John of England abducted his fiancée, Isabelle d'Angoulême. The misdeed gave the French monarch, Philippe Auguste, an excuse to annex the Continental fiefdoms held by the English—Normandy, Maine, Anjou, Touraine, and the major part of Poitou, which includes the domain of Cherveux.

Also associated with Cherveux were the Mellos, the Craons, and the Chalons. In the 16th century, when the Reformation arrived, the châtelain was Charles de Saint-Gelais, who made Cherveux a Huguenot stronghold. This brought sieges in 1569 and again in 1574, the latter commanded by the Duc de Montpensier. Today Cherveux is owned and beautifully maintained by M. Lucien Redien.

opposite: Occupying a militarily strategic site, long fortified and often destroyed, Cherveux enjoys a rare stylistic unity—Late Gothic. This virtue arose from the need to rebuild for defensive purposes in a single campaign, which took place in the second half of the 16th century. Access is across a stone bridge and through a tall châtelet. To the right looms up the stone mass of a great square donjon, a robust form made elegant by the crisp angles of its buttresses, which rise from the water and continue right through the machicolated summit, adding a fold to the steep, pointed roof. The quality of the stonework can be seen on the interior of the chemin de ronde **(left)**, where even in this enclosed passageway the upper corners have been ornamented with sculptured heads.

Vitré

Like Fougères, and for much the same reasons, Vitré is a tough feudal fortress on Brittany's easternmost border facing France. It is, however, all but unique among French castles in preserving its original *donjon* or "keep." Set upon a rocky promontory above the surrounding town, high, thick walls and stout towers come together to form a large triangular *enceinte*. Emphasizing the continuous, circumscribing linkage, as well as the defensive character of the whole, is the machicolated upper walkway *(chemin de ronde)*, which provides a protected passage and an exterior vantage point completely around the fortified enclosure. Recessed summits and elongated pepper-pot roofs assure Vitré of a richly varied silhouette, while the drawbridge and portcullis entryway make the stronghold seem a realization of some ancient medieval romance.

Vitré was founded in the 11th century by Robert I, Baron de Vitré, thought to have been a close relative of the counts of Rennes. In the 13th century the barony passed by marriage to Guy VII de Laval. A century later Guy XII became regent of France when Duke Jean IV accompanied Charles VI on a campaign in Flanders. Despite a second marriage, to the widow of Bertrand du Guesclin, hero of the Hundred Years War, Guy XII left no male heir, with the result that his daughter Anne conveyed the estate in marriage to Jean de Montfort, who styled himself Guy XIII de Laval.

In the 16th century Vitré passed to the Rieux family and then to Paul de Coligny, with each heir assuming the Laval arms and dignities. During this period Vitré became the scene of a brilliant court, alive with the new ideas of the Renaissance then pouring into France from Italy, their architectural impact falling mainly upon the chapel. In 1564, 1582, and 1583 the great château sheltered the parlement of Brittany, which left Rennes to escape a succession of plague epidemics. It also became a Protestant redoubt surrounded by Catholic Brittany. In 1589 this invited a five-month siege laid by troops of the Catholic League under the leadership of the Duc de Mercoeur.

In the 17th century, from 1655 to 1706, the Breton *états* met at Vitré. On several of these occasions Mme de Sévigné attended, mainly to participate in the festivities designed to win votes for the taxes requested by the royal authority. As always, she left us an unforgettable impression, finding "Mesdemoiselles de Kerqueoison, de Kerborgne, or de Kerlouche as gaudy as the King's candle."

After the Trémoilles inherited Vitré in the 18th century, they abandoned the château and finally sold it in 1820 to the *département*. Now, considerably restored, the old outpost houses a public library and museum.

above: Situated on the old medieval border between Brittany and France, the château fort *at Vitré bristles with all the defensive militarism that such a strategic location required. The high walls linking still higher towers date from the 14th and 15th centuries, but they rise from foundations first laid in the 11th century. By following the contour of the rocky promontory that supports Vitré, the pre-Romanesque builders realized an* enceinte *with a nearly perfect triangular shape.*

opposite: Access to the interior court at Vitré is by way of a drawbridge over a moat, now dry, and through a portcullis protected on either side by flanking twin towers, immensely tall and linked at the top by the overhang of an enclosed and continuous, machicolated walkway (chemin de ronde). Above, the summits are recessed and crowned by steeply attenuated "witches' caps."

Fougères

"You must see Fougères," wrote Victor Hugo in 1836 to the painter Louis Boulanger. "Imagine a spoon. . . . The château is like a spoon, with the town its handle. On this château, all red and sprouting verdant growths, place seven towers, each different in form, height, and age. Onto the spoon's handle pile up a jumble of towers, turrets, ancient crenellated walls, literally bristling with thatch, notched gables, pepper-pot roofs, stone bridges, open balconies, machicolations, and terraced gardens. Join the château to the town and arrange the whole upside down upon a slope in the largest and deepest of valleys. Then cut through the maze with the running waters of the narrow Vilaine, whose four or five watermills thrash away both day and night. Make smoke pour out of chimneys, girls sing, children cry, anvils ring—and you have Fougères!"

Although largely untouched by the tampering hands of restorers, this vast fortified ensemble in northern Brittany is virtually complete, except for the inevitable loss of the great Romanesque *donjon* ("keep"). The only thing of its kind to surpass Fougères is the much-restored castellated town of Carcassonne in southwestern France. Such remarkable survival is owing, perhaps first of all, to the geographical location, a strategic point in the long medieval contest between the French and their colonial brothers across the Channel, the Norman English. Here the very toughest defenses were needed, and if the ramparts of Fougères eventually succumbed to siege, they have proved magnificently resistant to the ravages of time. But so remote is Fougères that once history had passed it by—with the marriage of Anne de Bretagne first to Charles VIII and then to Louis XII, which made Brittany an integral part of France (1532)—the château and town were easily forgotten, left to preserve themselves like an enchanted realm sealed away under a bell jar.

The ancient bastion that sheltered Victor Hugo during a beautiful romance, and then served as the picturesque setting for his novel *Quatrevingt-treize,* was first established in 1024 by a feudal lord named Méen, Baron de Fougères. In 1166 this stronghold was razed by Henry II of England, to punish his vassal, Raoul II de Fougères, for acts of rebellion. Gradually rebuilding got under way and continued until the end of the 15th century. Marriage conveyed the domain to the Lusignans in 1256, but in 1307 Philip the Fair confiscated it for one of his sons, the future Charles V. By 1328 the Duc d'Alençon was at Fougères, in the process of enlarging the *enceinte* ("walled enclosure") virtually to its present dimensions. Some fifty years later, during the Hundred Years War, Bertrand du Guesclin secured the outpost for France. After being sold to Jean II d'Alençon in 1428 and then retaken by François de Surienne for the English, Fougères entered the royal domains when Anne de Bretagne became Queen of France. In the 16th century Diane de Poitiers, among others, received a life interest in Fougères, which, under the Duc de Mercoeur, remained loyally Catholic throughout the age's religious disputes. In 1715 the barony went to the Duc de Penthièvre, and in 1784 the château to M. de Pommereul. Mme Gilbert de Pommereul was hostess to Honoré de Balzac when the great writer, then still very young, arrived at Fougères in 1828 to prepare *Les Chouans,* a novel about the Breton insurgents who attempted to liberate royalist Catholic Brittany from the atheistic republican government imposed by the French Revolution.

Offered for sale in 1836, as a "topographical position . . . highly favorable for the establishment of an industrial plant," the château was finally acquired in 1892, from the last Baron de Pommereul, by the town of Fougères.

The medieval romance of Fougères, the Carcassonne of Brittany, captivated both Victor Hugo and Honoré de Balzac. A great fortified château and town nestled in the valley of a branch of the Nançon River, Fougères dates from the 12th century but acquired its present aspect mainly in the 14th and 15th centuries. It is a red masonry mass softened by the green growths of time, lacking only the huge original Romanesque keep at the center of a picturesque jumble of high, machicolated walls and heavy, defensive towers, topped by crenellated parapets and pepper-pot roofs.

Commenced in 1470 and concluded in 1510, Chaumont is almost entirely a Late Gothic château, even though its owner during the final campaign, Charles II d'Amboise, knew the Renaissance well from his long governorship of Milan. Still, the structure is a fine one, with an unrivaled site on a bluff overlooking the Loire River. Originally, four substantial logis and fat, round corner towers closed the quadrangle, but in the 18th century the north wing was removed so as to open the cour d'honneur to the superb view beyond. The entrance gate embodies an unusual and striking concept—a châtelet set diagonally across the southeast corner, flanked by twin heavy towers and approached over a double drawbridge leading to an arch for carriages and a separate, smaller one for foot traffic. The tall, massive donjon projected from the southeast corner is windowless and purely feudal, but the château's late date can be told from the large windows and high dormers of the logis and from the slightness of the chemin de ronde—the machicolated galleries—at the top of the defensive towers. In one of the high bell turrets Catherine de' Medici is thought to have practiced sorcery before forcing Diane de Poitiers to exchange Chenonceaux for Chaumont.

Chaumont

Chaumont, whose name means "hot mountain," is a fine, large 15th-century château splendidly sited in the Touraine on a bluff overlooking the Loire River. Yet, so many of the famous who lived there seem to have done so only because the places they preferred had been denied. Perhaps some negative spirit entered the very stones of Chaumont when the counts of Amboise erected it in compensation for the Château d'Amboise itself, the magnificent residence from which they had been evicted by order of Louis XI. That these lords built an almost purely Gothic structure even as the Renaissance was arriving in France suggests a fundamental lack of enthusiasm for the project. Then, when Catherine de' Medici acquired Chaumont, she used it mainly for sorcery and finally as a ploy in the bargain she forced upon Diane de Poitiers, Henri II's mistress, whose romantic, almost Venetian Chenonceaux the Queen Regent had long coveted and now, with the King dead, insisted upon having. As for Diane, she merely posted her arms at Chaumont and immediately decamped for Anet in Normandy, there to make the Renaissance still more triumphant than at the castle on the Cher. Even as late as the Napoleonic era, Mme de Staël took Chaumont principally as a place of exile, living sumptuously but never ceasing to prefer the trickle in the street behind her house in Paris to that beautiful river, the Loire. All this does little justice to a majestic, albeit somewhat old-fashioned, Château de Chaumont, with its high, square enclosure, massive, cone-capped *donjon,* and superbly feudal entrance *châtelet.* Nor does it speak for the gorgeous site, at the very heart of the "garden of France."

In 1039 the counts of Amboise acquired through marriage the *château fort* that Eudes I, Comte de Blois, had established in the previous century at Chaumont. But in 1465, by raising a rebellion against Louis XI, Pierre d'Amboise lost his ancestral estate and caused Chaumont to be dismantled. An early pardon permitted the malefactor to rebuild Chaumont, if not to repossess Amboise. By the time of Pierre's death in 1473, half the quandrangle had been erected. The second half came in 1500–10, during the tenure of Charles II d'Amboise. Long absent in Milan, where he served as governor, Charles probably left most of the decisions at Chaumont to his uncle, the Cardinal premier of France under Louis XII.

The year 1560 brought both Catherine de' Medici and Diane de Poitiers to Chaumont. It was here, high up in one of the bell turrets, that the Queen Mother consulted her magic mirror, which foretold the disasters that lay in store for the house of Valois. In the early 17th century the châtelaine of Chaumont was Isabelle de Lineuil, the wife of Scipio Sardini, Marie de' Medici's banker from Lucca. The beautiful and cultivated Isabelle had received from Pierre Ronsard the dedication of his *Nouvelles poésies* (1564).

Around 1740 Chaumont became a more civilized and livable place when Nicolas Bertin de Vaugien, tutor to the royal Duc de Bourgogne, demolished the north wing and thus opened the *cour d'honneur* to the Loire Valley below. Between 1772 and 1786 the ceramic sculptor Nini worked at Chaumont, in a pottery established by châtelain Jacques-Donatien Le Rey.

After the Revolution, which bypassed Chaumont, the château had what many would call its most illustrious occupant—Germaine de Staël. Exiled from Paris by Napoleon, who feared her searching, educated, highly influential mind, Mme de Staël sought refuge in the Loire, closer to the center of the life she loved than was her Swiss estate. There the author, surrounded by children, servants, lovers, and a brilliant circle of friends, finished the manuscript of *De l'allemagne,* that blueprint for the whole Romantic movement in France. Once the book had been published in 1811, the imperial police appeared at Chaumont's twin-towered gate, ready to escort Mme de Staël to exile beyond the frontiers of France.

The Prince and Princesse de Broglie, descendants of Mme de Staël, brought to Chaumont a radical, 19th-century-style restoration and an opulent manner of living. The château now belongs to the French state.

Tarascon

Made famous in modern times by the unforgettably picaresque exploits of Daudet's Tartarin, Tarascon could long before that boast one of the glories of the Late Middle Ages—the 15th-century fortress-château built and lived in by the unlucky but cultivated and festive King René of Naples. Still centuries earlier the Romans had recognized the strategic possibilities of Tarascon's spectacular site. This is the point on the Rhône where Provence, the land of *langue d'oc,* could stand vigil against the land of *langue d'oïl*—northern France—on the opposite bank of the great river. But it was in the southern air of Provence that flourished the dulcet life of courtly love and *troubadour* poetry. Thus, while the Château de Tarascon towers above and dominates all that it surveys—a powerful and crisply defined cubic block with pale masonry walls, defensive corners, and a battlemented terrace completely around the summit—it also has accommodations suitable for a civilized and comfortable life. Open loggias and galleries, winding stairs, and tracery vaults in Flamboyant Gothic create a palatial interior, the approach to which is through a forecourt sweetened by cypresses, oleanders, and flowering shrubs. For a moat, Tarascon has the rushing, ever-fresh waters of the Rhône.

Tarascon already had its foundations in the last decade of the 14th century, laid by Louis II d'Anjou, Comte de Provence. It was René d'Anjou, however, who gave the château its essential character and brought it to conclusion in 1450. The second son of Louis II, René inherited the duchies of Lorraine and Bar in eastern France, but found it impossible to hold them. Then in 1434 he inherited Anjou and Provence from his older brother, and a short while thereafter the Kingdom of Naples from the Angevin Queen, Jeanne II. Four years later, however, in 1442, Alfonso of Aragon proved stronger than René and succeeded in enforcing his claim to the throne in southern Italy.

From that time on, the crownless King René stayed within the domains of Anjou and, most of all, Provence. Debonair and good-hearted, René gained the affection of his subjects and cultivated the arts with a passion matched only by the princes of the Italian Renaissance. But not only did he collect illuminated manuscripts, he also created them himself, all the while pursuing an active interest in agriculture and horticulture. With a taste for public as well as private pleasures, René wrote a treatise on tournaments and initiated Tarascon's annual feast of *la Tarasque,* exuberantly observed to this day. The occasion celebrates Saint Martha, the sister of Mary and Lazarus, who, according to legend, came to Tarascon to save the citizenry from a terrible monster, the Tarare, intent upon devouring the community's young men. The very presence of the Saint transformed the monster into a docile pet. To commemorate this miracle, the Tarasque, a model of the monster originally made by order of King René, is paraded through the streets on the final Sunday of every June. The legs inside the creature's mouth symbolize the devoured youths, while eight young men walking outside represent those saved by Saint Martha.

At René's death in 1480 the French crown took possession of both Anjou and Provence, which deprived the Château de Tarascon of its purpose and importance. Still, several monarchs stayed there in the course of their travels in Provence—François I in 1516 and Charles IX in 1564. Richelieu made it his headquarters in 1642 when he went south to arrest those conspirators against his power—the Marquis de Cinq-Mars and his friend François de Thou.

Tarascon suffered much abuse once it was made to serve as a prison in the 18th century, with particularly great damage occurring at the time of the Revolution. Appropriately, it was from the castle's upper battlements that the outraged Tarasconnais hurled the revolutionaries after the fall of Robespierre brought an end to the Reign of Terror. Thanks to a campaign by the writer Prosper Mérimée, the château was classified in the 19th century as an historic monument. Then massive restoration returned Tarascon to its original state. The French government has been the châtelain since 1926.

below: *From its spectacular site on the Rhône River, the early 15th-century château-fortress at Tarascon served as a defensive outpost for the counts of Provence—mainly René d'Anjou—on the frontier facing France. The walls and corner towers all rise to the same height, thus making a smooth-surfaced, crisply defined block with a machicolated terrace completely around the summit. The tall, massive form simply dominates the surrounding plains.*

left: *A palatial residence as well as a military stronghold, Tarascon is honeycombed with loggias and galleries, chapels and vaulted chambers, all worked in Flamboyant or Late Gothic tracery as delicate as lace. Here the Good King René anticipated the Renaissance in the festiveness and refinement of his court.*

Anjony

Although sited for defensive reasons, feudal Anjony upon its perch above a green valley in the Auvergne Mountains could hardly seem more romantic to modern eyes. There is also something almost incredible in its history, for after an uninterrupted succession, from generation to generation, Anjony has passed, beautifully intact, to the latest descendant of the family that built it between 1435 and 1440. To complete a substantial *château fort* in such a brief period was remarkable, and it endowed Anjony with a rare stylistic unity—all late military Gothic. Probably only royal patronage could have made this possible, and the Anjony family had it, along with a tragic and interminable vendetta with a neighboring clan, the Tournemires, who supported England in the Hundred Years War, while the Anjonys aligned themselves with France.

The story of Anjony—well known because of the completeness of the ancient archives maintained at the château—provides a telling insight into the struggle of the late medieval French kings to forge a modern nation unified under royal authority. Such a goal meant curbing the power of the old and truculently independent nobility and of ejecting those most untrustworthy of vassals, the English, whose vast French fiefdoms included the Aquitaine in the southwest. The Tournemires, with a lineage and landed estate going back to the 10th century, had good reason to resist the growing centralization of the French government. They therefore made cause with the English monarchs, who, while in control of nearby Aquitaine, resided in Britain, too far away to threaten vested local interests. The French sovereigns, meanwhile, pressed their policy by creating and favoring a new, more loyal nobility, selected from the energetic and rising, recently wealthy bourgeoisie. This is where the Anjonys entered, increasingly benefitted at the expense of the older, prouder, and fundamentally more entrenched Tournemires.

Originally, the Tournemires were among France's richest families, but prolonged participation in the Crusades reduced their means. Thus, Marguerite de Tournemire found herself married in the second quarter of the 14th century to Bernard d'Anjony, whose fortune came not from land but from trade—skins—pursued in the city of Aurillac. Tensions mounted among both the Tournemires and the Anjonys when the bride's parents found it necessary to borrow from their daughter's in-laws. Eventually the debts accumulated until the Tournemires had to forfeit much of their estate, bit by bit, to the Anjonys, thereby fostering resentments that royal attitudes could only worsen. Thus, when Bernard d'Anjony commenced, with the approval of Charles VII, to build his own fortress on land originally claimed by the Tournemire clan, a quarrel erupted that lasted almost two centuries. Sometimes as much comic as tragic, the dispute was at all times appalling, involving as it did mutually exchanged and repeated insults, assaults, and even acts of murder.

Still, the Anjony family continued to rise, while the house of Tournemire, ill served by its own excesses, continued to decline. Symptomatic of this social dynamic was the marriage in 1557 between Michel d'Anjony and Germaine de Foix, daughter of a branch of the sovereign counts of Foix. Finally, after much more bloodshed, the ancestral struggle ceased with another marriage. In 1643 Michel I d'Anjony took as his wife Gabrielle de Pesteils, who for the want of a male heir, carried with her the entire estate of the senior branch of the Tournemire family. This at last united the warring factions into a common, indissoluble interest.

In the 16th century Michel II became Marquis de Mardogne and *gentilhomme de la chambre du roi*. In 1739, after a long and distinguished military career, Claude d'Anjony made the family château more comfortable by adding a wing whose form is that of an 18th-century manor house. Dying childless, Claude left Anjony to a nephew, Robert de Léotoing, whose wife saved the estate during the Revolution by carefully hiding the archives and furniture. The present châtelain is the Marquis de Léotoing d'Anjony.

above: *This room, because located at the top of the* corps de logis *at Anjony, has ribbed Gothic vaults overhead, rather than a flat ceiling. It was from here no doubt that justice and other affairs of the estate were administered. The chests contain archives and land registers complete and continuous from the time of the château's construction.*

opposite: *From its perch on a ridge overlooking Auvergne's Doire Valley, Anjony displays a rare unity of style—late feudal Gothic—thanks to the royal patronage that permitted it to be constructed, whole and complete, within the brief period spanning from 1439 to 1540. The only significant modification is the manorlike wing added in the 18th century for more comfortable living. The form of the old* château fort *is that of a cubic mass reinforced at the corners by tall, round, cone-capped towers, with every unit terminating at the top in a machicolated* chemin de ronde, *that defensive device of an enclosed walkway or gallery. Three large, superimposed halls fill the* corps de logis, *while a chapel occupies one tower and stone stairs spiral their way up another.*

above: *Another choice feature of Anjony is the chapel, a hexagonal, groin-vaulted chamber located in one of the corner towers. Completely frescoed, by a 16th-century workshop of primitive, itinerant craftsmen, the walls tell the story of the Passion. To the right of the altar, a niche contains a statuette of the Black Virgin of Anjony, an archaic work of the School of Auvergne.*

right: *In 1570–80 Michel II d'Anjony, to honor his marriage to Germaine de Foix, prepared the second floor of the Château d'Anjony as a grand, formal hall. Beneath the heavy ceiling beams, all supported by stone corbels, appear frescoed murals relating the histories of nine valiant "knights": Hector, Alexander the Great, Julius Caesar, Joshua, Judas Maccabaeus, David, King Arthur, Charlemagne, and Godefroi de Bouillon. The cycle of heroic figures, with accompanying inscriptions, constitutes a rare and precious example of monumental, secular painting as it was practiced in the provinces of Renaissance France. In complete harmony with the decorative scheme is the handsome furniture dating from the early 17th century.*

The Renaissance origins of Gordes are best revealed on the château's interior, where a magnificent chimney-piece constitutes a monumental sculptural composition embracing an entire wall, doors included. Almost every architectural or decorative motif of the classic revival can be found here—pilasters, shell-headed niches, triangular pediments, scrolls, vases, acanthus leaf friezes.

Gordes

Crowning a hilltop village like some Cyclopian acropolis, Gordes surveys its valley in the Vaucluse with all the serenity of a monument that has survived the centuries unsullied by either modification or restoration. For its pristine condition, the château must thank the almost Romanesque toughness of its materials and construction, rather than its history, since the lords of Gordes were active participants in the religious wars that racked France during much of the 16th century. Where the château reflects the past is in its form, for while built around 1525, well after the arrival of the Renaissance, Gordes resembles a medieval stronghold, complete with thick, defensive walls and machicolated watchtowers. Inside, however, the new humanism made itself felt in decorative touches inspired by classical motifs imported from Italy, then at the height of its Renaissance.

Although the Gordes site was fortified as early as the 11th century, the date 1541 on one of the fireplaces confirms that the present edifice was first undertaken about 1525. The initiating châtelain was Bertrand de Simiane, who at age seven had become the page-companion of Pierre de Bayard, the brilliant military commander and hero of François I's Italian campaigns. The Simiane family counted among the oldest in Provence, already well established in 1070 when Rambault d'Agoult, seigneur de Gordes, married and took the coat of arms of his wife, Sancie de Simiane. In the century following the château's construction Gordes was raised to marquisate for the benefit of Guillaume de Gordes-Simiane. The first Marquis's son, François, then became high bailiff of Provence and knight-in-waiting to the Queen of France. The last of the line was a young woman who married Émmanuel de La Tour d'Auvergne, Duc de Bouillon. The issue of this union was also a daughter, and with her marriage Gordes went to that great family of courtiers, the Rohans, in the person of Charles, Prince de Soubise. By the time of the Revolution the château belonged to the Condé princes, who were of the royal blood itself.

The Château de Gordes now serves as a town hall. The village, long in a semiabandoned state, has now been adopted by artists, who bit by bit are restoring the structures they occupy.

opposite: *Like a pyramidal mass of planes and cubes, the village of Gordes climbs to the summit of its rocky site, crowned by the château and church. The whole arrangement resembles the Provençale landscapes painted by the late 19th-century master Paul Cézanne.*

Although built at the outset of the Renaissance, the Château de Gordes—at the heart of the religious wars of the 16th century—has all the characteristics of a feudal redoubt, including high, thick walls defended at the corners by round, machicolated towers.

left: René de Chateaubriand (1768–1848).

below: Profoundly affected by the gloom and isolation of Combourg, the great Romantic poet René de Chateaubriand has provided the best description of the old medieval fortress in which he spent the most formative years of his childhood: "The château can be seen between two groups of trees. The curtain wall of its severe and melancholy façade supports the corbeled continuity of an enclosed and machicolated gallery. At either end towers of different periods and of different materials, heights, and thicknesses terminate in crenellations surmounted by roofs pointed like caps set upon Gothic crowns." Although its oldest parts derive from the 11th century— mainly the foundations and the keep (the huge tower on the right in the photograph below)—the castle was remodeled and enlarged in the 14th and 15th centuries and in the 19th century somewhat overrestored on the interior. During the latter period, Buhler designed the handsome English-style park that spreads out before the main façade. On the opposite side, the château faces a pond bordered by poplars along the road to Rennes.

Combourg

"At last we entered a valley at the far end of which, near a pond, rose the village spire," wrote René de Chateaubriand of his arrival at Combourg after a long absence. "At the western extremity of this village, the towers of a feudal castle loomed up from the midst of a wood struck by the light of a setting sun." After these lines, the great Romantic poet confessed: "I had to stop: my heart was beating to the point of pushing away the table where I sat. Memories rushed in and overwhelmed me. . . . Pervasive silence, gloom, and everywhere a surface of stone: that is the Château de Combourg."

It was in *Mémoires d'outre-tombe* ("Memories from Beyond the Tomb") that Chateaubriand evoked the Combourg of his childhood, which proved so formative for his dreamy, melancholic sensibility. Even now the old medieval stronghold is a brooding, dungeonlike place that could trouble the sleep of anyone who succumbed to its rather sinister charms. Dark and defensive, Combourg has thick, almost windowless walls and massive corner towers crowned by machicolations and "witches' caps." High in the tower called "La Tour du Chat," overlooking a primeval forest on the edge of a chilly lake, Chateaubriand had his room, an aerie complete with creaking doors, whistling wind, and flapping birds. There the boy found himself haunted by the ghost of a certain wooden-legged Comte de Combourg, then dead for a number of years: "Sometimes his false leg got up and walked all by itself, accompanied by a black cat!"

The foundations of Combourg go back to 1016, but the old *château fort* was gradually rebuilt, mainly in the 14th and 15th centuries, as the dwelling we now know. In the mid-17th century it served as refuge for Marie de Rohan-Montbazon, Duchesse de Chevreuse and one of the leading *amazones* who sided with the Fronde against the royal authority during the minority of Louis XIV. The son of the household, Malo-Auguste, Marquis de Coëtquen and Comte de Combourg, fought with distinction at Lille but lost a leg at Malplaquet, thereby releasing the curious ghost that haunted the young René de Chateaubriand. In 1761 his daughter sold Combourg to the poet's father, an impoverished descendant of old aristocracy who had made a fortune as a privateer on the high seas.

René-Auguste de Chateaubriand was a man who paced at night even more than the spectral wooden leg. "We dined and had supper at a far end of the [great hall]," wrote his son. "After the meal we repaired to the other end . . . in front of a huge fireplace. . . . Autumn and winter evenings I sat down near the fire with Lucile. . . . My father then began his walk, which would end only at bedtime. . . . Away from the fireplace he was perceptible only by his footsteps, which we could hear in the shadows. Then slowly he would reemerge from the penumbra, with his white robe and cap and his long, pale face. In a hushed voice, Lucile and I exchanged a few words while he was at the other end of the room, then stopped when he appeared. Even then he would say: 'What were you talking about?' Terrified, we made no reply . . . . The rest of the evening we heard nothing but the measured sound of his steps, my mother's sighs, and the rustle of the wind. In good weather, after supper, we would sit on the steps outside. My father, armed with a gun, shot owls as they flew out from the crenellations at nightfall. My mother, Lucile, and I would watch the sky, the forest, the final rays of the setting sun, the first stars. At 10 o'clock we went indoors and to bed."

Years later, in 1801, on a final visit to Combourg, the mature master wrote to Mme de Staël: "It was in the Combourg forest that I became what I am, that I began to feel the first attack of the boredom that I have carried with me all my life, the sadness which is both my torment and my happiness."

Pillaged during the Revolution, Combourg was subsequently reacquired by the Chateaubriand family. About 1848 the château's interior suffered a drastic revision in the contemporary "Gothick" manner. Through marriage Combourg went to the Comte de La Tour du Pin Verclause, whose descendants hold it today.

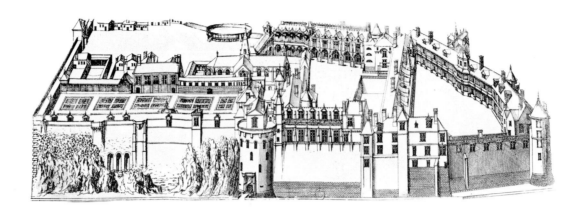

above: *"Proudly erected upon a rock" is how a contemporary described Amboise in its prime. Of the structures in the foreground, only the great, polygonal Minimes Tower and the tall, high-dormered logis du roi survive, all built in the last decade of the 15th century. Also remaining from this era is the Chapel of Saint-Hubert, located within the* cour d'honneur *on the right. The so-called Louis XII wing, a structure to the left of the* cour d'honneur, *was completed in the Early Renaissance style just after 1515. Foundations, ramparts, and the heavy, square-based* donjon *in the right foreground could date as far back as the 11th century.*

below: *In the last decade of the 15th century, Amboise became the principal residence of Charles VIII. The first of the French kings to know the Italian Renaissance first hand, Charles completed Amboise with the aid of imported Italian artists and artisans. But as the great Minimes Tower on the left and the sumptuous* logis du roi *at the center would suggest, the spirit of the northern Gothic still reigned supreme. Even so, the château's arcaded lower terrace, the niche-ornamented buttresses, the richly carved balustrades and dormers all represent a nonmilitary, domestic luxury that would have been unthinkable a generation earlier.*

Amboise

When first built upon its rocky cliff high above the Loire, the château of the counts of Amboise was one of the most heavily fortified in France. After 1434, however, the property rested with the crown, and from that moment forward the old stronghold—which dated back to the 11th century—gradually absorbed or shed its rude, thick-walled defenses and began to reexpress feudalism in terms more elegant and symbolic than real, signifying an age that found its security in peace and plenty more than in military prowess. At Amboise the Middle Ages meshed with the Renaissance, easily, gracefully, and well before this cultural interface could have occurred at any other site in France. If the Gothic remained overwhelmingly dominant in all the new architecture at Amboise, it was a Gothic ordered, clarified, proportioned, and, above all, humanized by the new ideas eagerly received from Italy. Alas, the spirit of civilization, revived in France only since 1453, after a century of barbarous conflict with England, suffered a new and fatal affront at Amboise a century later, when the terrible massacre of Protestants so blighted the château that reigning monarchs abandoned it virtually forever.

The house of Amboise came to the fore when it proved the strongest of the warring factions in this region of the Touraine. The *château fort* the Amboise family put up in the 11th century was trapezoidal in plan, with a collegial church, dedicated to Saint Florentin, situated outside the *enciente*. By the 14th century the clan had divided into two branches, the senior of which presided at the ancestral dwelling, while the junior built anew at Chaumont. In 1431, Louis d'Amboise, head of the elder line, managed to compromise himself in a plot against Georges de La Trémoille, whose royal patron, Charles VII, took revenge by arresting Louis and confiscating the whole of the Amboise estates. After 1434, when La Trémoille himself fell from grace, the Amboises recovered their liberty as well as their property, all save the Château d'Amboise itself, which Charles attached to the royal domains. This act both reflected and reinforced the taste the French kings had developed for the Loire Valley, the south bank of which had become their refuge during the Hundred Years War, when the English occupied most of France north of the river.

Louis XI soon began to modernize the old fortress, mainly as a dwelling for the Queen, who bore the Dauphin there in 1470. Having grown up at Amboise, this young man, Charles VIII, made the château his preferred residence once he succeeded to the throne in 1483. By 1492, Charles had begun to put into effect a plan designed to aggrandize the medieval bastion and to transform its militarism into a domestic luxury suitable to the monarch of a newly unified and secure France. An army of masons, under the supervision of Colin Biart, Guillaume Senault, and Raymond de Dezest, were swarming over Amboise when the King, inspired by tales of chivalric adventure, departed with an army to invade Italy, his purpose being to recover the throne of Naples lost in 1442 by René d'Anjou to Alfonso V of Spain. In the south Charles discovered and fell in love with the Italian Renaissance. Returning to France in 1492, he brought with him not only a hoard of art works but also an entire atelier of artists and artisans, whose assignment was to work at Amboise.

According to the contemporary chronicler Commynes, Charles VIII, in rebuilding Amboise, wanted to unite "all things beautiful . . . wherever they could be found, in France, Italy, or Flanders." Unquestionably, it was the Italian Renaissance that most impressed Charles; but with rare insight he saw that it was the spiritualized Gothic, more than the rational, humanistic forms of Italy, that would best serve the meditative purposes of the Chapel of Saint-Hubert, built at Amboise in 1493. While Italians applied themselves to the château's secular structures, Flemish masters carved the breathtakingly fine and delicate stonework of these vaults and decorations. The chapel is honored by the remains of the great Leonardo da Vinci, who at the end of his life, from 1516 to 1519, lived in the Loire Valley as the personal guest of François I. French royalty rarely visited Amboise after the demise of the Valois dynasty in the late 16th century.

41

This began the process of cultural transformation whereby France would eventually renounce its northern, Gothic traditions and replace them with the values and forms of Mediterranean classicism. At this early date, however, the native spirit remained too strong for the Renaissance to express itself directly at Amboise, even with the help of the imported Italians, other than in the interior décor, now lost, and in the Italian garden laid out by the Neapolitan horticulturist Pacello da Mercogliano. Gothic continued to reign, but with a new decorative and structural ingenuity, in the sumptuous *logis* named for the Seven Virtues and in the great *logis du roi,* whose low, arcaded gallery, immensely tall upper windows, and richly ornamented dormers still lord it over the Loire below. At the east end of this wing Charles also built what may be the château's most fascinating and structurally precocious feature—the Minimes Tower, a sixteen-sided form housing an ogive-vaulted, helical ramp supported by a single newel, yet strong and wide enough to be mounted by horses and carriages. This approach to the royal castle never failed to fill the King's guests with wonder and delight. For the jewellike Chapel of Saint-Hubert,

Charles wisely reverted to the age of faith and recruited not Italians but Flemings to carve the richly Flamboyant embellishments.

In 1491 Charles VIII had married Anne de Bretagne, which furthered the national consolidation of France, but the union, while a happy one, failed to produce a living heir. Consequently, when Charles died in 1498, of a head injury suffered while negotiating a low lintel at Amboise, the crown passed to his cousin, the son of the poet-prince Charles d'Orléans. The new King ascended the throne as Louis XII, taking Anne de Bretagne as his Queen. But Blois had become home to the Orléans family; thus, Louis XII retained his allegiance to that château and transferred the court to it. Meanwhile, at Amboise—not in the château itself, but in the little adjacent manor of Clos-Lucé, connected to Amboise by an underground tunnel—lived Louise de Savoie and her children, Marguerite (who became Queen of Navarre and the grandmother of Henri IV of France) and François d'Angoulême, Louis XII's heir apparent. When this Prince became François I, after marrying Claude de France, the daughter of Louis XII and Anne de Bretagne, he completed a short wing at Amboise commenced by Louis XII, and did so in the true Renaissance manner of the new *logis* at Blois. Nonetheless, he too favored other residences, mainly Chambord and Fontainebleau. What held great meaning for François was Clos-Lucé, and there he installed the elderly Leonardo da Vinci, the father of the High Renaissance and, by far, the most illustrious of the King's guests from Italy. And it was at Amboise that in 1539 François made peace with his archenemy, the Emperor Charles V, and received him in state.

Amboise had its most historic—and tragic—moment in 1560, during France's Wars of Religion. While the court was in residence there, led by the Queen Mother, Catherine de' Medici, François II, and his wife, the nineteen-year-old Mary Stuart of Scotland, an armed band of Huguenots, instigated by the Prince de Condé and the English ambassador, attempted to take possession of the castle and to seize the King. Behind walls no longer suited to withstand siege, terror reigned, but the attack was repulsed by the Duc de Guise, the powerful leader of the Catholic League. More than 1,500 Protestants were arrested and executed, many of them gibbeted upon the château's own balconies and battlements, in full view of the court, which assembled to witness the victims' final agonies.

After the so-called *conjuration d'Amboise* the great royal château entered upon its long decline. In the 17th century Louis XIII stayed there alone a few times in order to hunt in the neighboring forest; eventually, however, he gave the domain in appanage to his brother, Gaston d'Orléans. But when this unruly Prince staged a rebellion against the crown, he brought destruction upon Amboise, which suffered the demolition of the few fortifications that remained to it. In 1762 Louis XV gave Amboise to the Duc de Choiseul, then foreign minister. At this owner's death the property passed to the many-châteaued Duc de Penthièvre, who spent most of his time at Anet in the Île-de-France. The Revolution brought confiscation, and the Napoleonic regime still further destruction. Roger Ducos, a member of the Consulate, received the château in 1802 as a gift from his senior colleague, First Consul Napoleon Bonaparte. To save himself the cost of maintenance, Ducos demolished several structures, among them Charles VIII's *logis* of the Seven Virtues and the exterior collegial Church of Saint-Florentin. After Waterloo, in 1816, Amboise was returned to the Orléans family, in the person of the Duchesse d'Orléans, who was the daughter of the Duc de Penthièvre. When her son, King Louis-Philippe (r. 1830–48), inherited the château it again became royal property, only to be confiscated, once more, at the downfall of the July Monarchy. As a state prison, Amboise housed Emir Abd el-Kader, the leader of the Algerian nationalists. In 1863 the remains of Leonardo da Vinci, exhumed and desecrated during the Revolution, were recovered from the site of the château's old collegial church and reburied in the Chapel of Saint-Hubert. Finally, in 1872, following the exile of Napoleon III, Amboise returned definitively to the Orléans family, who soon initiated a restoration, a process that continues. Today the château belongs to the Fondation Saint-Louis, an organization representing the royal princes of France.

opposite: Two-aisled, rib-vaulted, and thoroughly Gothic, the Hall of the Estates General occupies the main floor of the logis du roi at Amboise. The great fireplace and the piers have been carved in relief with Charles VIII's fleur-de-lis and the ermines of the Queen, Anne de Bretagne. When this royal pair reigned, the room was no doubt made sumptuous with "tapestries from France and Flanders," Damascus hangings, and "deep-piled Turkey carpets," all of which are mentioned in an inventory made at Amboise toward the end of the 15th century. Amboise, however, entered upon a long decline after 1560, when the balcony outside the tall windows on the right was hung with the slaughtered bodies of the Huguenots arrested in an attack upon the château made while the court of François II— headed by his mother, Catherine de' Medici, and wife, Mary Stuart of Scotland—were in residence.

below: The marvel of Amboise in the time of Charles VIII was the ingeniously designed interior of the Minimes Tower. Here, a gently rising helical ramp, rib-vaulted and suspended from a single newel at the core, is, according to Commynes, "so spacious and cleverly made that carts, mules, and litters could easily ascend," along a smooth, stepless incline, from the town below to the very top of the castle ramparts. Lighting the way are numerous large windows cut through the immense thickness of the faceted outer walls.

Blois

No château is richer in the history of royal France, or in the symbolic counterpart that sheer architectural variety can provide, than Blois. Here in the early 15th century Charles d'Orléans wrote lyric poetry and sired Louis XII; here also came Joan of Arc, in search of a blessing as she departed to raise the siege of Orléans; here tall, ardent François I danced and loved; and here lived the two Medici Queens, Catherine the regent and Marie the captive of her son, Louis XIII. But the least quiet spirit at Blois is that of the Duc de Guise, stabbed to death in the King's own chambers and dragged bleeding and mutilated before an Henri III stricken with mock-disbelief. And here, too, Gothic secular architecture realized one of its great triumphs, only to be supplanted by the flowering of the Renaissance, which in no way prevented the advent of the Baroque as this was formulated by the masterful François Mansart. But as each style gave way to the next, it also lingered and prevailed in its own right, for however densely experience may have crowded in at Blois, the great château had the amplitude to accommodate all that came to it—events, personalities, and aesthetic forms.

In the 10th century the site in the Loire Valley was fortified by Thibaut *le tricheur* ("the trickster"). Of the successive buildings erected there by the powerful lords of Blois, Champagne, and Châtillon, only a few vestiges remain from construction undertaken in the 13th and 14th centuries: three cylindrical towers embedded in the François I wing, one of which is visible on the right exterior façade; and a large, two-bay, barrel-vaulted chamber called the Hall of the Estates General. In 1391 Guy II de Châtillon, the last of the counts of

At right angles to one another within Blois's cour d'honneur, *the Gothic of Charles d'Orléans (1440s) and that of Louis XII (1498–1503) confront another. An elevation of ground-floor gallery supporting a single upper story of large mullioned windows and a dormered attic characterizes both wings, as does the stone and red-brick construction, but the Renaissance has begun to express itself, if only timidly, in the newer wing. Here among the lavish sculptural embellishments, typically Flamboyant Gothic, an occasional Italian-style roundel or rosette makes its appearance. No less Gothic is Louis XII's corner stair tower, its top story corbeled over an octagonal plan and its ground-floor walls laid with a cross-diagonal pattern of blue and red brick.*

Blois, sold the estate to Louis d'Orléans, the brother of Charles VI. The buyer had been aided by the seller's enamored wife, Marguerite de Namur, which did not prevent the immense grief of the beloved's own wife, Valentine de Milan, when the Duc de Bourgogne had the Duc d'Orléans slain in the streets of Paris in 1407. As France disintegrated under the impact of the Hundred Years War, the widowed Duchesse d'Orléans died at Blois "of anger and pain." Her son, the poet Charles, became Duc d'Orléans, only to be captured at the Battle of Agincourt and then held prisoner in England for twenty-five years. During this period Blois suffered several sieges, until Joan of Arc arrived. There, before marching on beleaguered Orléans, she had communion distributed to her 3,000 soldiers by the priests of the Church of Saint-Sauveur, then at the front of the château. At the same time, the Maid received the *fleur-de-lis* standard from the hands of Renaud de Chartres, Archbishop of Rheims. At the conclusion of the century of hostilities, Charles d'Orléans returned to Blois, surrounded himself with poets, among them no doubt François Villon, and collected tapestries, fine books, and musical instruments. He also began to build a more comfortable *logis*. A fragment of this edifice clings to the courtyard side of the chapel—a two-story wing of stone and red brick with a flattened arcade on the ground floor, large mullioned windows on the second, and stepped dormers in the attic.

After the accidental death of Charles VIII, his nephew, Charles d'Orléans's son, became Louis XII. The new King, having been born at Blois in 1462, made the château his preferred residence. New and important building now rose, the only parts of which to survive are the chapel and the "Louis XII Wing" on the northwest side of the *cour d'honneur*, with its flanking stairway towers. Also arcaded and constructed of stone and red brick, and still Flamboyant Gothic, with steep slate roofs and *fleur-de-lis* pinnacles atop the tall

Of the oldest portions to survive at Blois, the most important is the Hall of the Estates General, so-called for the two sessions of that body held there in 1576 and 1588 at the climax of the Wars of Religion. During the second of these convocations the Duc de Guise behaved so insolently that Henri III determined to have him assassinated. A thoroughly Gothic space with two aisles, an ogive arcade, and high barrel vaults, the hall also witnessed countless festive celebrations and in 1559 a performance of Trissino's Sofonisba, *the first tragedy in the Greek manner ever rendered in French.*

With Jacques Sourdeau as his architect, François I undertook, from 1515 to 1524, to rebuild the northwest wing at Blois. The new corps de logis, although still Gothic in plan, disposition, and general elaborateness, became the point of departure for much of French Renaissance architecture. On the side of the cour d'honneur the new manner can be seen in the strong horizontal accent provided by the double moldings marking the division between stories, in the classical pilasters on either side of the windows, and in the shell motifs of the richly carved cornice. The great staircase, virtually the signature of the Renaissance under François I, follows the medieval pattern of a left-turning spiral within a tower projecting from the mass of the building. But the simplification of it all to a mere structural skeleton—whose ramps served as balconies from which the court could witness the pageant of life under the "Merry Monarch"— is a direct expression of the scientific-mathematical mind of Leonardo da Vinci, François I's personal guest in the Loire Valley. Here too the decorative scheme is largely classical, consisting of pilasters, balusters, and Corinthian capitals, mixed with the King's personal device, the salamander. To Balzac the stair tower seemed "carved like a Chinese ivory."

dormers, this new architecture acknowledges the contemporaneous Renaissance—which Charles XII knew from his military campaigns in Italy—only in an occasional roundel or rosette. More impressed by the gardens of the south than by its architecture, Louis XII engaged Pacello da Mercogliano to lay out an intricately patterned garden on the château's west front.

In this very year, 1514, Blois saw the marriage of François d'Angoulême, heir to the throne, and Claude de France, and then the death of the Queen, Anne de Bretagne. Louis XII died the following year. Unlike his predecessor, François I submitted totally, or as much as a Frenchman could at that time, to the Renaissance. Thus, it was now that Leonardo da Vinci, Rosso Fiorentino, and Andrea del Sarto, among other Florentines, found a warm welcome and rich commissions in royal France. On the side of the Italian garden François I immediately commissioned a new wing for Blois. Everywhere, this vast structure displays a decorative encrustation of classical motifs, but on the exterior the designers went further and introduced loggias and niches in the manner of Bramante, and at the attic level a terrace screened by an Ionic colonnade. For all this, however, François preferred other residences—Fontainebleau and Chambord—but whenever he was at Blois, the château came alive with festivity. On one of the brightest occasions the future Henri II married Catherine de' Medici. This was also the day when the poet Ronsard saw Cassandre Salviati at Blois and conceived an unhappy passion that would last a full twenty years.

Under Henri II and his sons Blois regained its importance. In 1559 Mellin de Saint-Gelais's adaptation of Trissino's *Sofonisba*, the first tragedy in the Greek manner ever rendered in French, was performed in the Hall of the Estates General. In 1572, Catherine de' Medici received the court at Blois to celebrate the engagement of her daughter Marguerite de Valois to Henri de

From 1635 to 1638 Gaston d'Orléans had François Mansart, father of French Baroque architecture, replace one of the Louis XII wings at Blois with a vast new corps de logis. Sober, grandiose, and immensely sophisticated in the utilization there of the Greco-Roman orders, it makes the classicism of François I's logis seem almost playfully naïve.

Navarre, the future Henri IV of France. But this was also the year of the Saint Bartholomew's Day Massacre, and shortly thereafter all festivities ceased, as the Wars of Religion climaxed in two separate gatherings of the Estates General and the assassination of the Duc de Guise, both of which occurred at Blois in 1588. Henri de Guise had been the powerful head of the League, the extremist Catholic party supported from without by the King of Spain. His nemesis, King Henri III, died the following year, himself a victim of assassination.

With the demise of the Valois line, Blois ceased to be the regular scene of the court. In 1617 the château gave shelter to Henri IV's widow, Marie de' Medici, sent by her son, Louis XIII, into exile after the murder of her favorite, Concini. In 1619 she escaped, in a comedy that had the corpulent Queen descend a rope ladder and walk across the town, where she was taken for a bonne femme (a "lady of light virtue"). In 1626 Louis XIII assigned Blois to yet another royal mischief-maker, his brother Gaston, who became Duc d'Orléans and received the county of Blois in appanage. A man of grandiose vision, Gaston commissioned François Mansart, one of France's greatest architects, to demolish much of the Louis XII structure and to replace it with a new corps de logis so large as to constitute a château unto itself. Shortage of funds saved what little remains of 14th-century Blois. Gaston died at Blois before his monument to the French Baroque could be completed on the interior. By now Louis XIV reigned, and the court would soon move permanently to Versailles, leaving Blois to deteriorate, a process that did not cease until Félix Durban undertook complete restoration in 1845–69. The Revolution had destroyed the Church of Saint-Sauveur and the heroic statue of Louis XII that originally filled the central niche on the exterior façade of the extant wing built by that monarch. The château is now a public museum owned by the town of Blois.

Ussé

above: Flamboyant Gothic in its structure, the 16th-century chapel at Ussé submitted to the Italian Renaissance in its decoratif motifs. Here the classic-revival spirit can be seen in the flattened arch of the main portal flanked by richly sculptured Ionic pilasters, which support a round-headed tympanum filled with an enormous stone scallop shell.

opposite: Secluded in its wooded, tranquil site overlooking the Loire-Indre Valley, Ussé seems a fairytale castle, a picturesque, many-towered pile composed of high, white walls crowned by machicolated galleries and blue-slate roofs sprouting red-brick and zebra-striped chimney stalks. It may well have inspired Charles Perrault to write Sleeping Beauty. Built mainly in the early 16th century, but defended by a large round keep from the late 15th century, Ussé was originally closed on all four sides and surrounded by a watered moat. The Renaissance entered the Late Gothic château on the façade of what is now the right lateral wing and in a new chapel built outside the defensive walls. The Baroque 17th century opened the cour d'honneur to the park, added a new front to the façade now facing the park, and a new, Italian-style, flat-roofed pavilion to the exterior side of the tower terminating the right lateral wing.

If Ussé seems like a castle materialized from a fairytale, it has always been so, for here Charles Perrault, the 17th-century fantasist, often stayed and found material for his stories *Puss in Boots* and *Sleeping Beauty*. And one might well expect to discover Princess Aurora and her court still spell-bound behind Ussé's high, white, many-towered walls, their summits crowned by machicolated galleries and steep roofs of blue-gray slate. The effect comes not only from the Late Gothic château but also from its wooded and tranquil site. Located on the lea side of the valley shared by both the Loire and the Indre, Ussé is so protected from harsh weather that palm trees grow in the garden, adding a note of exoticism to a realm already drenched with enchantment.

The construction of Ussé extended over a long period. The heavy round keep—extended out from the southwest corner like a separate building—dates back to 1480, when it was erected by Jean de Bueil, a great captain of the age who served under Joan of Arc. His son Antoine married the daughter of Charles VII and Agnès Sorel, then in 1485 sold Ussé to Jacques d'Épinay, chamberlain for both Louis XI and Charles VIII. It is to the d'Épinays, therefore, that Ussé owes most of its form, which originally was closed on all four sides and surrounded by a moat. The entrance occurred by way of the pavilion that now forms the terminus of the left lateral wing, with access provided over a bridge across the moat—once filled—and through a gate formerly open between the pavilion's paired towers. The whole of this unit—a *châtelet*—can be identified by its attic stories, which are recessed, and by the adjacent apse of what initially was the château's chapel.

Between 1520 and 1531 Charles d'Épinay redid the right lateral wing in the classicizing style of the Renaissance, then just arriving in France, and built a new and much larger chapel outside the château's own walls. Although structurally—and elegantly—dependent upon the principles of Flamboyant Gothic, the chapel too discloses in its decorative motifs the irresistible new influence from Italy.

In 1659 Ussé became the property of Louis de Valentinay, controller general to the royal family, and the father of Louis II de Valentinay, who married the daughter of the great Maréchal de Vauban, Louis XIV's military engineer and the masterbuilder of France's vast 17th-century scheme of bridges, waterworks, and frontier fortifications. It was at this time that Ussé lost its fourth side, which opened the court to the new park laid out just before the château's walled platform, and gained the Baroque front on what is now the main façade, that at the bottom of the court facing the park. Ussé also acquired a new wing, the low pavilion, with an Italian-style flat roof, extended beyond the terminating tower on the right of the *cour d'honneur*.

Mme de Valentinay, now Comtesse d'Ussé, died at age thirty-five, but not before becoming an intimate of Voltaire, who several times stayed at the Château d'Ussé. After belonging to the Duc de Rohan-Montbazon and the Prince de Guémenée, Ussé survived the Revolution to be acquired by the Duc de Duras, whose wife, Claire de Kersaint, brought new literary lustre to Ussé through her Romantic novels as well as through her friendship with Chateaubriand. The Duchess's great success in promoting the poet's diplomatic career was owing in large measure to the success of the Duke himself, who served as first gentleman of the privy chamber to all three of the last of the reigning Bourbons. In the 19th century the daughter of the Duras, the Comtesse de La Rochejacquelein, restored Ussé with the zeal characteristic of the age. The estate now belongs to one of her descendants, the Comte de Blacas.

Le Lude

Celebrated for the magnificent *son et lumière* performances held there during the summer, Le Lude is one of those châteaux in which the accumulation of period forms constitutes a veritable textbook in architectural history. And since Le Lude was built in Anjou on the banks of the little Loir, not far from the royal châteaux of the great Loire Valley in the Touraine, it reflects the best of the stylistic currents that flowed across aristocratic France from the late medieval period right through the 19th century. What greets the visitor from the entrance gate is a Gothic-Renaissance forest of fat, battlemented, cone-capped towers sprouting a thicket of lantern pinnacles, inlaid chimney stalks, and high, richly carved dormers and finials. The effect is uncannily evocative of Chambord, on a smaller scale. From the park, however, the aspect presented is that of the purest and most refined Louis XVI Neoclassicism, while the early Baroque from the age of Henri IV reigns on the main façade of the *cour d'honneur*. A comparable stylistic range prevails on the interior as well, but everywhere at Le Lude, both inside and out, the hand of the 19th-century restorer has borne down heavily, leaving the usual trail of historical anachronisms, some a good deal less charming than others.

The story of Le Lude as we know it begins in 1457, when the fief was acquired, through marriage to Renée de Vendôme, by Jean de Daillon, governor of the Dauphiné and life-long confidant to Louis XI. The foundations, however, which trace out a square *enceinte* with all four corners defended by round towers, survive from a 13th-century fortress. Only the northern wing—the most medieval part of the château—rose in the time of Jean de Daillon. Work continued under his son Jacques, bailiff of Anjou, but mainly on the south wing, where the resemblance to François I's Chambord is so striking. Jean II de Daillon succeeded Jacques, served as chamberlain to both Louis XII and François I, and saw Le Lude elevated to the status of county. At the end of the 16th century Comte François became an intimate of Henri IV and even received the King at Le Lude. In 1619 Louis XIII also went there. It was in this era that the chateau acquired its Early Baroque *cour d'honneur*.

In 1675, after the distinguished artillery service of Henri de Daillon, a grateful Louis XIV made Le Lude a duchy. But the first Duke died childless, leaving the estate to his nephew, the Duc de Roquelaure, who then passed it to the Duc de Rohan-Chabot. Joseph-Julien de Velaër, of the Compagnie des Indes, acquired Le Lude in 1785. His niece, the Marquise de La Vieuville, became the next châtelaine. During her tenure the architect Barré gave the castle its chastely elegant Louis XVI wing.

The daughter of the Marquise de La Vieuville married the Marquis de Talhouët. Not only did the Marquis win military honors under Napoleon; in addition, his grandson became minister during the Empire. Marriage conveyed Le Lude to the Nicolay family, and with them it remains today. The summer *sons et lumières* are performed by two hundred persons, all inhabitants of the château's pendent village.

below: *The great pride of Le Lude is its Early Renaissance wing, which bears such striking resemblance to François I's Chambord. Here, on a smaller scale, are the same fat, cylindrical towers, their summits rimmed by decorative machicolations and their conical caps sprouting thickets of high dormers, inlaid chimney stalks, and lantern pinnacles. Like the wide moat, now dry, these are all medieval features, but, as at Chambord, the Renaissance is also very much present in the pilasters flanking the windows and in the shell motifs on the dormer pediments. Equally "modern" are the della Robbia-like busts framed by roundels and the arcade-supported, balustraded terrace linking the corner towers.*

left: *A 16th-century mural representing the parade of animals, fabulous as well as real, going aboard Noah's ark adorns a wall in the chapel built into the tower at the right of Le Lude's François I wing. The charmingly naïve quality of the work suggests that it may have been done by a provincial craftsman.*

One of the most interesting of the interiors at Trécesson is a room with a Gothic vault whose groin ribs converge upon a sculptured keystone. The primitive murals date from the 17th century and depict scenes from Tasso's Jerusalem Delivered.

Trécesson

By reason of its highly irregular form and brutally thick walls, constructed of flattened but rough-hewn blocks of reddish schist, early 15th-century Trécesson is one of the most individual and fascinating châteaux, not only in Brittany, but also in the whole of France. If the "witch's cap" roofs on the towers give the medieval pile an air of enchantment, so does the surrounding moat, which spreads into a lake on one side, isolating the château and making its great, weighty mass seem, improbably, to float on a chilly sheet of dark water. The setting too is magical—the forest of Brocéliande, well known to King Arthur's knights and long the dwelling place of gnomes and fairies.

The bewitchment of Trécesson extends to a powerful legend, which holds that in the 18th century a poacher hidden in the woods near the château witnessed a scene worthy of a "Gothick" tale of horror told by Mrs. Radcliffe. In the dead of night a carriage suddenly stopped near a freshly dug ditch, and a young woman clad in wedding attire descended, followed by two elegantly dressed men. The latter issued an order, and, without a single protest, the woman lay down in the ditch. Her companions then proceeded to cover her with earth. As soon as they had filled the trench, the sinister pair returned to the carriage and drove off into the shadows. Shaken, the poacher rushed to the château, where he got help to save the poor woman from her living burial. The rescuers found her still breathing, but too weak to survive or explain. Never was it possible to identify either the criminals or their victim, which leaves us, three hundred years later, still ignorant of the reason for this ghastly deed. Until the Revolution the pitiful evidence of the wedding dress remained in the château chapel, the object of a pilgrimage made by girls who regarded it as a relic with the power to provide them with husbands!

The château was built in the second quarter of the 15th century by Jean de Trécesson, chamberlain to Duc Jean V de Bretagne. Through marriage to Jean's daughter the estate passed to Éon de Carné. By 1493 their son had taken the name of his mother's family. In 1681 Trécesson was raised to county. In 1773 it passed to the Le Prestre de Châteaugiron family, who sold the property to Nicolas Bourelle de Sivry in 1793. Further names entered the rolls at Trécesson when Bourelle's granddaughter, Alice de Perrien de Crenan, married first Baron Jean de Secondat de Montesquieu and then, upon his death during World War I, Comte Antoine de Prunelé. The château now belongs to Comte Michaël de Prunelé.

The strong, highly individual character of the late medieval Château de Trécesson derives from the busy irregularity of its forms, the rude elegance of the schist masonry, and the reddish reflection the whole casts upon the gleaming surface of a pondlike moat (actually the source of the little Oyon River). Polygonal towers, crowned by slate roofs shaped like witches' hats, defend every corner, while access to the cour d'honneur is gained through a tall, powerfully fortified gate (a châtelet) at one side of the asymmetrical mass. Here corbeled, rocket-shaped towers rise high on either side of the entrance arch, to be connected halfway up by a machicolated, gallerylike bridge.

53

Azay-le-Rideau

"A faceted diamond set in the Indre Valley" was how Balzac characterized Azay-le-Rideau in the 19th century, but people in every age have been inspired to poetic description by the lyric beauty of a château that seems created less by the labor of masons than by the touch of a fairy's wand. And indeed the structure is largely make-believe, a Renaissance dwelling replete with sophisticated Italian or Greco-Roman detailing, but one in which all the medieval features were added—moat, machicolations, and turrets—only to be reduced to the vestigial state of mere decoration. Instead of defense, their purpose was to evoke the seigneurial tradition and thus by association to benefit the château's bourgeois builder, a financier eager to rise in a society dominated by feudal privilege.

Important as aristocratic privilege was in the 16th century, it had nothing of the energy or pragmatism needed by kings intent upon securing royal authority with national prosperity. And so Gilles Berthelot could gradually advance from the relatively low position of a crown counselor to the all-powerful one of treasurer of France. While pursuing such a career, Berthelot could have spent little time cultivating a country estate, and so it must be to Mme

Sited in a green meadow edged by weeping willows and freshened by the lazy, lily-padded waters of the Indre River, Azay-le-Rideau would seem more conjured by a fairy's wand than built by masons. The sense of make-believe comes from the medieval elements, which, because incorporated into a Renaissance structure, are so vestigial and decorative as to be more symbolic of a feudal past than practical defense for the time of their construction. No sentry, for instance, could walk through the chemin de ronde, *for the space there has been incorporated into the rooms of the upper story. Meanwhile, the Renaissance abounds in the harmony and balance of the whole, as well as in the sculptural embellishments: classical pilasters flanking the windows, roundels embracing the corbeled turrets, shells and candelabra crowning the dormers.*

Berthelot, Philippe Lesbahy, that Azay-le-Rideau owes its gracious qualities. The lovely site—a green meadow edged by weeping willows and freshened by the lazy, lily-padded waters of the Indre River—had been host to an ancient stronghold that perished during the Hundred Years War. Two of the clans once established there were the Azays and the Ridels—hence the château's name. Based upon the old foundations, the new plan called for a quadrangle composed of four equilateral pavilions, but when the court began to question the dealings of its financial advisors, Gilles Berthelot thought it prudent to flee into exile. This left Azay-le-Rideau with its picturesque and celebrated L-shape, derived from the right-angle relationship of the only two wings ever constructed. Commenced in 1518 and abandoned in 1527, the château was confiscated shortly thereafter by François I, who gave it to Antoine Raffier, a hero of the King's Italian campaigns. In 1684 Henri de Beringhen, a courtier in the time of Louis XIII and Louis XIV, acquired the domain and gave the château its *communs* or service outbuildings. In the 18th century the property passed to the Vassé family, who kept it until 1791, when the Marquis de Biencourt became châtelain. The estate remained with the Biencourts throughout the 19th century. During their tenure the chateau suffered an overly aggressive restoration. In 1905 it became government property.

The bravura touch on Azay-le-Rideau's main courtyard façade is the twin-window, openwork stairway. Such emphasis places the stairs in the medieval tradition that climaxed in the great helical cage at Blois. In other respects, however, the ramps at Azay-le-Rideau are among the very first to follow the new Renaissance mode from Italy, for while they occupy a bay unto themselves, they are not in a semi-independent tower. And not only is the styling Greco-Roman, but, in addition, the steps turn to the right, instead of to the left, and rise along straight lines rather than a spiral.

Chambord

"From a distance the building is like an arabesque," wrote Chateaubriand, ". . . like a woman with wind-tossed hair. On closer inspection, however, this creature becomes the masonry and changes herself into towers."

Here the arch-Romantic of the early 19th century touched on an essential truth, for François I (r. 1515–47), the royal creator of the Château de Chambord, brought to his love of building something of the same passion he bore toward beautiful women. In this he anticipated Louis XIV, and indeed Chambord—with its 400 rooms and 70 staircases, its 365 chimneys and 100-foot-high central lantern towering above a 15,000-acre, heavily wooded park, all enclosed within the longest wall in France—could be called the Versailles of the 16th century.

One lyrical legend has it that François I chose the site and commissioned the château out of fond memory for a certain Comtesse de Thoury. More likely, the King was attracted by a forest particularly rich in game, and wanted to create an establishment suitable for the great hunts upon which the Renaissance princes liked to expend their energy, a resource that endless wars and amours seemed never to exhaust. The territory, originally part of the county of Blois, came into royal possession when its owner, Louis d'Orléans, succeeded to the throne as Louis XII (r. 1498–1515). Work on the present building began in 1519, the year François approved plans clearly inspired by the Italian Renaissance, which the monarch had so enthusiastically introduced into Late Gothic France. None other than Leonardo da Vinci, a guest of the Valois King and a Loire resident at the end of his life, may have contributed ideas. The final conception, however, is generally attributed to Domenico da Cortona, a pupil of the 15th-century Italian master Giuliano da Sangallo. But the superb workmanship came from the French, first under François de Pontbriand and subsequently under Denis Sourdeau of Blois and Pierre Nepveu, called Trinqueau. Except for the years 1524–25, when, following the French defeat at the Battle of Pavia, François I was a prisoner in Spain, the château continued to rise until in 1539 it was sufficiently advanced to permit the King to receive Emperor Charles V, the victor at Pavia, in a state visit. The occasion, marked by such gala festivities as ballets, concerts, and feasts, dazzled the Hapsburg dignitary, but so did the splendor of Chambord, whose central keep, Charles declared, obviously derived from "an epitome of human skill." Even so, the castle was little more than three-quarters finished when François I died in 1549. The King's son and heir, Henri II, continued the work, but upon his death in 1559 Chambord remained incomplete, and for almost seventy years it would rarely receive the royal household.

The arrival of the Renaissance is most evident in the plan of Chambord, where symmetry and balance replace the irregularity of the old French fortress. Still, a sense of the military stronghold, characterized by its impenetrable *donjon* or keep, lingers in the sheer strength and mass of the main elements at Chambord, despite the windowed openness permitted by the more peaceful times. The effect comes from a central cubiform block, which on the inside, however, is penetrated and subdivided by corridors intersecting one another in the shape of a cross. They focus upon a broad, circular staircase giving access to clusters of rooms so organized as to make them the prototypes of modern apartments. Further stressing the integration of old and new, the French and the Italian, are the round towers that punctuate the four corners of the square; also the echo of this arrangement in the surrounding *enceinte* and moat (the latter filled in during the 18th century). From the exterior, the first three stories of Chambord, with their levels separated by continuous moldings and with their windows placed precisely over one another, emphasize the horizontal, yet allow horizontality to be matched by verticality in a way distinctly reminiscent of the Italian urban palazzo. Above the third level, however, the skyline of this serene, rational structure suddenly sprouts a wild thicket of high dormers, buttresses, turrets, chimneypots, and lanterns, whose

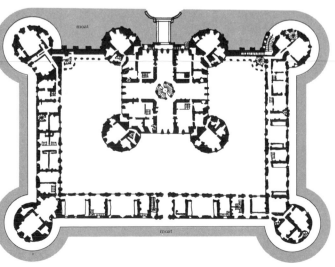

"... a royal château or rather an enchanted one," wrote Alfred de Vigny in his description of Chambord in Cinq-Mars (1826). "One would believe that, thanks to a magic lamp, an Oriental spirit had captured [the castle] during an episode in A Thousand and One Nights, stealing it away from the lands of sunlight so as to conceal it in those of fog, along with the loves of a handsome prince." Such indeed is the effect still produced by François I's Château de Chambord, as the great pile of Late Gothic and Renaissance forms emerges from the mists of the Loire Valley and rises high above a vast, surrounding forest. The Renaissance is most evident at Chambord in the plan (1519), where rational balance and symmetry replace the medieval irregularity of the old fortress-residence then traditional to the French countryside. The round towers and centralized massing recall the donjons or keeps of earlier, more bellicose times, but even here circles and squares are treated like ideal forms and are integrated through the laws of proportionality.

soaring, jagged silhouettes speak powerfully for the survival of the native French sensibility. It was among these fantastic forms, from a terrace above the third story, that the ladies of the court could look out over the forest of Blois and follow the progress of the King's hunt.

As a royal château, Chambord witnessed many historic events, amorous and cultural as well as political. It was there, for instance, that Henri II signed the treaty by which the former German bishoprics of Metz, Toul, and Verdun became part of France. Meanwhile, the Queen, Catherine de' Medici, used Chambord's tall lantern as an observatory, where with her astrologers she "could study at night the sky and the stars."

After the demise of the Valois line, Louis XIII (r. 1610–43) was the first of the Bourbons to take an interest in Chambord. Mainly, the estate became a place of exile for the King's brother, the charismatic but controversial Monsieur (Gaston d'Orléans), who lived there in a royal manner, along with his daughter, the celebrated Grande Mademoiselle.

At the death of Monsieur in 1660 the estate reverted to the crown in the person of Louis XIV (r. 1643–1715), who favored the château and commissioned Jules Hardouin-Mansart to make it a setting worthy of *le roi soleil*. Chambord, which Louis visited intermittently up to 1685, therefore saw the first performances of two works by Molière, *Monsieur de Pourceaugnac* and *Le Bourgeois gentilhomme*. On his last visit to Chambord Louis took the serious step of signing a number of ordinances against the Protestants, thereby completing the revocation of the Edict of Nantes.

Once again Chambord was deserted, this time until 1725, when it became the residence of Stanislas Leszczynski, the dethroned King of Poland who was also father-in-law to Louis XV (r. 1715–74). Later this monarch made a gift of the estate to the great Maréchal de Saxe, who endowed it with a life only slightly less sumptuous than that at Versailles. Even theatre returned to Chambord, and *Madame Favart* was performed there.

During the Revolution the citizens of Saint-Dyé-sur-Loire asked the Convention to destroy "the enormous mass of stone . . . to make this nest of vultures into dwellings for good patriots." Although the request was denied, the château suffered the loss of its movable contents.

In 1808 Napoleon offered Chambord to Alexandre Berthier, Prince de Wagram, but as early as 1815 the Marshal's widow, frightened by the cost of maintaining the château, decided to rent it, finally to part with it. The royalists then organized a national subscription to purchase the estate for the Duc de Bordeaux, posthumous son ("the miracle son") of the Duc de Berry and grandson of Charles X, the last Bourbon King of France (r. 1824–30). The drive was successful, which made possible a complete rehabilitation of the château and its park. The young pretender—and great hope of the legitimist party—took the title of Comte de Chambord, which he "bore proudly along the roads of exile." He saw his estate only once, however. This was on July 5, 1871, when following the expulsion of Napoleon III, the "honor mad" Bourbon prince signed the famous manifesto refusing to acknowledge the *tricolore*, the French national flag since the Revolution, in any form whatever. The act cost France and the monarchy a quiet and popular restoration. On the death of the Comte de Chambord (1883), the estate passed to his nephews, the princess of Bourbon-Parme, who in 1932 sold it to the French government.

The wonder of wonders at 16th-century Chambord is the grand, open-work staircase at the center of the château. A remarkable conception, with twin helical flights, it allows those ascending to proceed undetected by those descending. Double spirals inscribed within a single square posed just the kind of abstract, mathematical problem that Leonardo da Vinci would have delighted in solving. French masons, however, had the precedent of a similar arrangement in the double-landing staircase at Paris's convent of the Bernardins.

La Roche-Pot

La Roche-Pot fascinates not only by the extreme picturesqueness of its 19th-century restorations but also by its historical links with the Grand Duchy of Burgundy, that long-lost "middle kingdom" between France and Germany whose over-ambitious rulers made Gothic civilization burn brightly, for one last golden moment, even as the Renaissance was aborning south of the Alps. The flinty, vertiginous site attests to the château's feudal origins and also accounts for the first part of its name. The second part comes from Régnier Pot, who was lord of the fief and a leading figure in the Burgundian government just when, in the early 15th century, the dukes had become the most powerful monarchs in Europe. But while Régnier Pot gave the château its maximum dimensions, the most striking feature now to be seen at La Roche-Pot is the steep, multicolored roof of glazed tiles. Added in the late 19th century—when the foundations supported little more than exposed walls—the roof had its inspiration in neighboring Beaune, where the celebrated *hospice,* or "hospital," is an authentic monument to Burgundian largesse.

Always politically important and militarily strategic, Burgundy in the 11th and 12th centuries became a center of religious power all but equal to Rome, once the monks of Cluny initiated the universal reform of the Benedictine order. This was the great age of monasticism—the Romanesque period that produced the High Middle Ages and the first truly monumental stone architecture to be built in Europe since classical times. It should not surprise, therefore, that the oldest construction known upon the Roche-Pot cite was an oratory, replaced in 1128 by a chapel. The latter structure was incorporated into the present castle—originally a *château fort*—when it was erected at the end of the 13th century. The family in command bore the name La Roche.

In the 14th century the property—then called La Roche-Nolay—passed by marriage to Jean de Thil, who was constable of Burgundy; next to Édouard de Beaujeu et de Dombes; and finally to Jacques de Savoie, Comte de Piémont. In 1403 Louis de Savoie sold the domain to Régnier Pot, of an ancient clan long established in Berry southwest of Paris. By now the dukes of Burgundy could claim sovereignty over everything from Holland and Flanders through the Lorraine to their home province in southeastern France. Ruling from Bruges and Brussels in the north and from Dijon in the south, they controlled Europe's banking and shipping and its most important industry—textiles—and for the sake of these interests sided with England in the Hundred Years War. In the fabulous house of Burgundy Régnier Pot served as chamberlain and then as ambassador to Hungary.

A great dignitary of the 15th century was Philippe Pot, Régnier's grandson, who too became chamberlain—under Duc Philippe le Bon—as well as seneschal or bailiff of Burgundy and ambassador to England. Famed for his Ciceronian eloquence, Philippe Pot undertook many important diplomatic missions on behalf of the Burgundian court. But after the death of Charles le Téméraire ("the Bold")—at the hands of the Swiss in the Battle of Nancy (1477)—Philippe Pot aligned himself with Louis XI of France, which reclaimed its old province of Burgundy, thereby shattering the dream of a "middle kingdom."

Through a collateral line and marriage, La Roche-Pot passed in the 16th century to the Montmorency family. The Sillys acquired it in 1551, but in 1645 a cousin—the liberal and rebellious Cardinal de Retz, Archbishop of Paris—sold the fief to Pierre Le Goux de La Berchère, president of the Grenoble parlement. By 1751 it belonged to Philibert Blancheton, who was made Comte de La Roche-Pot.

The Revolution, which was especially destructive in Burgundy, deprived La Roche-Pot of its *donjon* and used what remained as a source of building materials. Afterwards the château lingered in an abandoned state until 1893, when Mme Sadi Carnot, widow of the President of France, acquired the ruins. Her son, whose distant ancestor, Lazare Carnot, came from the adjacent village of Nolay, devoted his life to the restoration of La Roche-Pot. Today the castle belongs to Mlle Lucie Carnot and her brother, M. Pierre-Sadi Carnot.

opposite: The Château de La Roche-Pot occupies a site that is strategic not only for the vantage point provided by the rocky height but also for its geographical location at the very crossroads from which the 14th- and 15th-century dukes of Burgundy spread their influence from Paris to Basel and from Dijon to Bruges, Brussels, and Amsterdam. After the French Revolution, which wrecked the château, La Roche-Pot remained an abandoned ruin until restoration got under way in the late 19th century. The steep roof, with its striking pattern of glazed, multicolored tiles, was copied from the great 15th-century hospice in nearby Beaune. But some of the most picturesque and evocative features of La Roche-Pot's medievalism, including the marvelously complicated drawbridge (above), are inventions of the highly romanticized archaeology practiced in the 19th century.

Le Manoir d'Ango

Dating from 1530–45, the large and luxurious manor house built near Dieppe by Jean d'Ango is a monument to the energy and acumen demonstrated by France's entrepreneurial class at the outset of the age of European expansionism. Here, in a masterpiece of rustic architecture, Jean d'Ango, governor of Dieppe and rich privateer, received relays of distinguished and powerful guests. And from here he sent the Franco-Italian Captain Verrazano on a voyage that resulted in the discovery of New York Harbor and the coasts of New Jersey, Delaware, Virginia, and North Carolina. It was Ango who called the newly found northern territories Arcady, a name whose mispronunciation soon transformed it into Canada. The essential grandeur of this celebrated bourgeois comes through in his behavior at the conclusion of a major contretemps with the Portuguese. After the forces of John III had seized Ango vessels off the coast of Portugal, to prevent their breaking the Portuguese monopoly on the maritime trade routes to India and the New World, the fearless Norman commander sent a new fleet and threatened to blockade Lisbon Harbor. Upon appeal to François I, John III found himself forced to treat directly with Ango, who, after obtaining suitable reparations, regaled the ambassadors with a splendid feast at the manor outside Dieppe.

Jean d'Ango was born in 1481 of a mercantile family important enough to be ennobled. The skill and courage of his activity in the ports of Dieppe, Rouen, Honfleur, and Le Havre, the last then quite new, soon made him the greatest shipowner of his time. To challenge his Spanish and Portuguese rivals, Ango chose captains with qualities comparable to his own. One of them, Jean Fleury, seized near the Azores three huge caravels that had sailed from Mexico, loaded with the fabulous, golden wealth stolen from Montezuma. From 1535 to 1545 Ango actively supported François I in his conflict with England, receiving the monarch in a lavish fashion at Manoir d'Ango and even contributing his personal fleet of fifteen vessels. After the victory at Boulogne, the privateer's favorite ship, *La Pensée*, flew the French admiral's flag and carried France's ambassador. A glorious moment for Jean d'Ango, but the expense of it brought ruin when Henri II, François's son and successor, proved dilatory about his father's debts. The jealousy of competitors and risky speculation also contributed to the decline, until in 1551 one of the glories of French naval history died impoverished at his great manor house, the scene of so much past splendor.

After long abandon, Manoir d'Ango has now been wonderfully restored by its present owner, Mme Hugot-Gratry.

Perfect in its rustic dignity, the Manoir d'Ango was built in 1530–45 by one of the great heroes of French overseas exploration, the rich privateer Jean d'Ango. The harmoniously varied ensemble is organized around a large interior court, here seen through the Italian-style loggia opened on the ground floor of one wing. The view is toward a corner dovecote, built in a mosaic of red and black brick and capped by an ogive roof. An attribute of nobility, the dovecote may well be the most beautiful thing of its kind in all of France. In another corner is a tower from whose top windows Jean d'Ango could observe his merchant fleet in Dieppe Harbor.

opposite: *A throng of distinguished Renaissance personnages, including François I and the Portuguese ambassadors, came through this broad portal at Manoir d'Ango to be opulently received by the governor of Dieppe, Jean d'Ango. For all the rusticity of the manor house, the gray sandstone and flint masonry, the classical decorations carved in relief, and the patterned mosiac of red and black brick represent a triumph for Norman artisans.*

below: Nowhere in France is the mollifying humanism of the Renaissance more freshly or perfectly expressed than at Chenonceaux. With male militarism isolated in the feudal remnant of an old tower on the far side of the drawbridge, beautiful Chenonceaux—the château built by a clever and commanding woman and coveted thereafter by generations of queens and royal favorites—submits totally to the caressing waters of the Cher River, in whose very bed it lies. The cubic mass of the corps de logis, erected from 1515 to 1524, rests on pilings sunk a century earlier for a mill, while the extended wing—really a galleried bridge built between 1547 and 1589 from designs by Philibert Delorme—spans the river com-

pletely. On one side of the forecourt spreads the garden originally planted by Diane de Poitiers, the great love of Henri II, and on the other side the smaller Italian garden laid out by the same monarch's adoring Queen, Catherine de' Medici. During Catherine's long regency, Chenonceaux witnessed truly fabulous festivities or "triumphs," with "nymphs" and richly decorated gondolas on the river and fireworks bursting overhead. One of the most extravagant celebrations was staged to honor the marriage of that ill-fated teenage couple, François II and Mary Stuart of Scotland. The château's poetic beauty and history held great appeal for the lions of the Romantic age, from Rousseau to George Sand and Flaubert.

opposite: At Chenonceaux medieval defenses linger only as decorative symbols intended to do nothing but identify the bourgeois builders with the old feudal aristocracy. The corner towers are mere "pepper-pot" turrets without foundations of their own. Meanwhile, the Renaissance has spread everywhere over the façade: in the classical pilasters flanking the windows; in the vertical alignment of windows as bays; in the strong, unifying horizontal of the double moldings marking the division between stories; in the balustrade crowning the wall; and in the scroll and shell motifs and the baluster finials that embellish the dormers. Such a transitional style is typical of France's Early, or "first," Renaissance.

Chenonceaux

Moated by the tranquil and poetic Cher—which it spans completely from one side to the other—Chenonceaux has a loveliness that must be called female. This delightful and unforgettably romantic château was built by a woman, developed and cherished by that legendary royal favorite, Diane de Poitiers, and then seized and completed by her rival, Queen Catherine de' Medici. Finally, it was so coveted by everyone that even crown prerogatives could not keep the dwelling, of all the great residences in the Touraine, from remaining almost consistently in private hands. Although founded on ancient pilings, Chenonceaux was constructed entirely in the 16th century, and even now it exudes a Renaissance mood so pure that however crass the circumstances of its ownership—or its accessibility to hordes of modern-day, motorized tourists—the château and its very special environment remain inviolate in their flowerlike freshness. Much of this feeling comes from the sheer originality of the conception and the delicacy of all the relationships. Azay-le-Rideau may be surrounded by the Indre River, but Chenonceaux rises from the very bed of the Cher in full course, its *logis* resting on the substructure of an old mill and its one wing borne up by the arches of a stone bridge. The river even separates the château from its forecourt, which can be reached only by a drawbridge. And the forecourt itself is like a platform suspended in a circumambient body of water, making it necessary to gain *terra firma* by yet another bridge. Guarding the access—at one side and also set in water—is the lone round, defensive tower that survives from the earlier medieval fortress. But even this isolated vestige of male militarism seems softened and humanized once seen in relation to the colored pattern of the Renaissance gardens that spread over the river banks on either side of the castle's entrance. Capuchin nuns now live at Chenonceaux, which in no way prevents the imagination from wandering back to the 16th century, when guests were welcomed by beautiful young women swimming in the Cher like classical water nymphs.

Beginning in the 13th century, the Chenonceaux fief belonged to the Marques family. The stronghold of that era having been dismantled in 1411 by royal order, Jean de Marques obtained permission in 1432 to rebuild on the

The entrance to Chenonceaux leads across a moated forecourt, past the remnant of an early 15th-century keep, and thence over a drawbridge. Along the way, left and right, the visitor would have savored the fragrance and colors of intricately plotted Renaissance gardens. Thus prepared was Henri II for the arms of Diane de Poitiers, the brilliant and beautiful lady who dwelled at Chenonceaux during its most poetic years, from 1547 to 1559.

right bank of the Cher and to complete the ensemble with a mill in the river. Overburdened by their expenditures, the descendants of Jean de Marques sold the estate in 1512 to Thomas Bohier, receiver general for Normandy under Charles VIII, Louis XII, and François I. The new châtelain had also served, and brilliantly so, in the French Kings' Italian campaigns. Thus, he knew the Renaissance first hand and, like all Frenchmen similarly exposed at this time, wanted to introduce its ideas into his own seigneurial residence. Bohier destroyed the Marques structure—all save the cylindrical *donjon,* which he revised with large windows decorated in the Italian manner—and commenced to rebuild, not on the foundations of the old manor, but in the river, on the underpinnings of the mill. With the lord often away on business, the character of the new construction was no doubt determined largely by the lady—Catherine Biçonnet, the daughter of one superintendent of finances and the niece of another, Baron de Semblençay. What emerged is a cubic pavilion in which heavy, feudal forms have been reduced or eliminated in favor of all the new classicizing features seen at Blois.

After the death of Bohier in 1524 and that of Catherine two years later, their son Antoine found himself obliged in 1530 to forfeit Chenonceaux to the crown in compensation for the public funds alleged to have been used to pay for the château's construction. Later he even had to flee into exile when a further judgment was made against him, in the course of which the royal representatives maintained that the Touraine estate had never been fully or properly conveyed to the crown. Ironically, the royal pretense saved Chenonceaux from violence during the Revolution three and a half centuries later.

Whether rightly his or not, Henri II gave Chenonceaux to Diane de Poitiers, the lady of Anet whom the King long preferred to his adoring and much-distressed Queen, Catherine de' Medici. Diane engaged Philibert Delorme, France's first great Renaissance architect, to throw a bridge across the Cher to its left bank, preparatory to adding galleries above. This gave the châtelaine access to both sides of the river, where she laid out gardens, planted not only with flowers of every variety but also with a boxwood maze, an orchard, and a *potager,* or "kitchen garden," filled with such rarities of the time as melons and artichokes. In 1559, however, Henri II died of a tournament accident, and after twenty-six years of sharing him with a brilliant favorite, Catherine de' Medici—now all-powerful as regent of France—took revenge by forcing Diane de Poitiers to accept austere, closed-in Chaumont in exchange for sensuous and light-filled Chenonceaux. The Queen Mother then proceeded to build the Delorme-planned galleries upon the bridge, and to add a library to the *logis,* like a bridge itself spanning the distance between the chapel and a second apse projected over the water from the main mass of the building on its upriver side. And she too planted a garden, a very Italian one, laying it out at the side of the forecourt opposite that taken by the "Garden of Diana." Now, Catherine de' Medici made Chenonceaux the scene of *fêtes*—or "triumphs" designed by the Italian master Primaticcio—the likes of which, for their splendor, had never been seen in France. Not only did the Cher have "nymphs" floating in it, the mirrorlike waters also reflected bursts from fireworks, a marvelous new import from Italy. One of the most extravagant celebrations was staged to honor the marriage of that ill-fated teenage couple, François II and Mary Stuart of Scotland. It was as if fabulous revels could dispel the horrors of civil war and the relentless decline of the Valois dynasty.

At her death in 1589 Queen Catherine left Chenonceaux to her daughter-in-law, Louise de Lorraine, who herself entered widowhood that very year following the assassination of Henri III, the last of the Valois. Plunging into deep morning, she draped Chenonceaux's suites in black and had its ceilings painted with skulls, bones, and gravedigger's tools.

The next *dame de Chenonceaux* was Gabrielle d'Estrées, the mistress of Henri IV, the first of France's Bourbon monarchs. To obtain the château, the King paid the debts of Catherine de' Medici, which were threatening to ruin Louise de Lorraine. By agreement, the bereaved former Queen made a will in favor of her niece, Françoise de Lorraine, then six years of age and engaged to César de Vendôme, the four-year-old natural son of Gabrielle d'Estrées and Henri IV.

For more than a century Chenonceaux belonged to the Duc de Vendôme and his descendants. Then, in 1733, the estate was purchased by Claude Dupin, another rich tax collector whose wife was the daughter of a still richer banker. The Dupins surrounded themselves with a brilliant society; they even took Jean-Jacques Rousseau as tutor to Dupin's son by his first marriage. "We enjoy ourselves very much in this beautiful setting," wrote the great Romantic. "The food is delicious; thus, I am becoming as fat as a monk. There is much music, and I have composed several trios to be sung. . . . I have done other small things as well, including a verse play whose title, *L'Allée de Sylvie,* is taken from the park bordering the Cher." During the Revolution the widowed Mme Dupin—possibly because of the royal chicanery in the late 16th century—was left undisturbed at Chenonceaux. The family still owned the estate when in 1845 the Comte de Villeneuve, a descendant, received his cousin, the celebrated novelist, George Sand, *née* Aurore Dupin. Her little son, Maurice, amused himself emptying his chamber pot into the Cher. Two years later Gustave Flaubert, Mme Sand's fellow novelist, also visited Chenonceaux and then wrote of its "strange suavity," its "aristocratic serenity." Indeed, Chenonceaux figured large in the heated imaginations of many Romantics. Eugène Scribe made the château's gardens the setting of a major scene in *Les Huguenots,* and they reappear in Meyerbeer's opera based on that play.

In 1887 the sleazy politics of the Third Republic came to Chenonceaux during the tenure there of Mme Pelouze, whose brother—Daniel Wilson, the son-in-law of President Grévy—created a scandal once exposed for selling Legion of Honor decorations. Still, the festivities prepared by Mme Pelouze all but rivaled those of Catherine de' Medici. Also at this time, the château suffered a typically aggressive 19th-century restoration, which deprived the *logis* of the Medici library suspended over the water on the upriver side. Since 1952 a more scholarly and conscientious restoration has been under way.

Chenonceaux's galleries above the bridge are extremely plain, little more than bare stone walls somewhat enlivened by medallion portrait busts flanking niches that alternate with the deeply arched recesses of tall windows. Exposed ceiling beams and diagonal checkerboard paving add to the sense of perspective pull toward the great triumphal arch of the fireplace. Such vast interior spaces were made to receive the throngs of brilliant company who over the centuries have arrived to rejoice in one of the most romantic and festive châteaux ever built.

Kerjean

One of the most remarkable and remote châteaux in Brittany is Kerjean, wholly feudal in plan but purely Renaissance in elevation. After passing over a moat, and through a fortified gatehouse, then over a drawbridge and beyond extraordinarily thick walls, one discovers a *cour d'honneur* set with a handsome, off-center, stone well and surrounded by a main *corps de logis* and side wings. Among these forms much medieval asymmetry reigns, but the styling of them is Italianate and classical—round-headed arches and triangular pediments— and of a quality to evoke the name of Philibert Delorme, the greatest architect of the French Renaissance. The entrance portal in particular—a triumphal arch tiered in its arrangement of Greco-Roman orders—recalls the comparable form created by Delorme at Anet. In scale, however, Kerjean, like most Breton châteaux, is modest relative to the grandiose pile erected in the Île-de-France for Diane de Poitiers. A garden asserts itself within the *enceinte* but on the other side of the principal building.

Kerjean dates from the reign of Henry II, when it was commissioned in 1545 by Louis Barbier, the fortunate nephew of the enormously rich Abbot Hamon Barbier. In 1617 the patent from Louis XIII raising Kerjean to marquisate stated that "the Château de Kerjean is so beautiful and so magnificent that it would be worthy of a royal visit should business summon the monarch to Brittany."

In 1710 a fire destroyed half of the *corps de logis,* leaving a romantically ruined façade pierced by blind and empty windows. Then, during the Revolution, half of the right wing perished. Flaubert visited in 1847 and found the château in a pitiful state: "In the large spiral staircase . . . I stumbled upon a wolf trap. Ploughshares, rusty spades, and dried gourd seeds lay scattered over the floors or filling the large stone seats in the window corners." Finally, in 1911, the French state acquired Kerjean and set about to restore it.

above: Ordered like a medieval château fort, *replete with moat, drawbridge, and immensely thick walls, Kerjean in elevation has all the styling of the French Renaissance at its most graceful. Exemplifying this is the triumphal arch, a tiered arrangement of classical orders crowned by a triangular pediment.*

opposite: Inside the cour d'honneur *the arches of the grand entrance portal are repeated laterly to become an arcade surmounted by a balustraded terrace. The photograph here illustrates the quality of Kerjean's Renaissance styling, carved in hard granite.*

Montal

An exceptionally beautiful Renaissance château in the Aquitaine's Quercy district, Montal is also one of the most poignant dwellings to be found in France. It was built between 1523 and 1534 by Jeanne de Balzac d'Entragues, the daughter of Robert de Balzac, bailiff of Gascony and Agenais and an administrator for Charles VIII in Italy, and the widow of Amalric de Montal, governor of the upper Auvergne. Her purpose was to create a home for her elder son, Robert, who too had gone to Italy, as a military leader under François I, and to make it ready in time to celebrate the hero's anticipated return. Once the young man perished during the French defeat at the Battle of Pavia (1525), Jeanne de Balzac completed only two right-angle pavilions of the four she had planned, and transformed Montal into a sanctuary dedicated to the memory of her dead men—father, husband, and son. Although a structure without serious pretense at self-defense, Montal—in a manner typical of the age—has an exterior whose appearance is quite feudal, the effect created by fat corner towers and intervening pepper-pot turrets. The Renaissance, however, is opulently present on the two façades of what would have been a fully enclosed interior court. To make certain she had the best, Jeanne de Balzac imported masons and decorators experienced in the work then being done for the royal patrons in the Loire Valley. What the artisans created at the top of the ground floor, which itself remains quite plain, is a frieze more than two-hundred feet long, carved in low relief and with an exuberantly rich and detailed sequence of mythological subjects, animals, and birds, all decoratively mixed with patterned arabesques and interwoven with the initials of the disconsolate widow and her son. Above this, the mullioned windows of the upper story alternate with stone tabernacles in which were inscribed medallions containing powerfully expressive busts. Executed in high relief, they portray the foundress and her family. Each subject, remarkably, appears in the dress of his or her generation, so that Robert de Balzac wears a Louis XII bonnet, while his fallen namesake is coiffed in the manner of François I. Completing the elevation is a blind attic of flat pilasters surmounted by sumptuously decorated dormers. No less refined, beautiful, and unexpected is the interior. There the stone stairs follow the new trend from Italy and rise upon straight, rather than spiraling, ramps. But while the continuous underside of the steps has been relieved in ornamental themes reminiscent of the Florentine Renaissance, the vaults overhead are structured with the ribbed, ogival arches and carved keystones traditional to Gothic France. Even more marvelous are the formal rooms with their monumental stone fireplaces, one of which bears a life-size recumbent stag, carved in the round and fully antlered.

When Jeanne de Balzac received back not her living son but only his bones, she blocked up the exterior dormer from which she would have waved him home and emblazoned the sealed space with a knight's banner inscribed with the words *plus d'espoir*—"no more hope." To perpetuate the family, this strong-minded lady obtained a papal release permitting her younger son, Dordet, to leave the priesthood and marry Catherine de Castelnau. The son of their union left Montal to his daughter, who in 1593 bore it through marriage to François de Pérusse des Cars, Marquis de Merville. In 1760 the des Cars ceded the château to the Plas des Tanes. When this family emigrated during the Revolution, their property was confiscated and sold. After passing from owner to owner, Montal was purchased in 1879 by a vandal named Macaire, who stripped the château of its sculptural decorations and sold them, piece by piece, to collectors and museums as far away as the United States. Incredibly, the great house survived this martyrdom to experience a resurrection, thanks to a new châtelain, M. Fenaille, who was the very antithesis of Macaire. Beginning in 1908, M. Fenaille reacquired, at terrible prices, every lost piece, from Paris, Berlin, and London, and restored them all to their original emplacement at Montal—with the exception of one dormer window, which remains in the collection of New York's Metropolitan Museum of Art. He then refurnished the château and gave it to the French state.

Montal, although purely a maison de plaisance *dating from the early 16th century, preserves the old defensive look in the pepper-pot turrets and round towers of its exterior, but gives way opulently to the Renaissance on the façades of its court side. Jeanne de Balzac, the château's foundress, left the court open, bounded by only two of the four right-angle* logis *originally planned. Instead of completing the quadrangle, she decided to honor the memory of her son, fallen at the Battle of Pavia, by embellishing the walls that stand on the Renaissance side with the richest sculptural program that could be obtained from artisans familiar with the royal projects in the Loire Valley. Among the most remarkable features are the stone tabernacles that, alternating with the second-story windows, contain medallions enclosing highly expressive portrait busts of Jeanne de Balzac (**opposite**) and members of her family.*

above: Among the many wonders of Montal, the greatest may be the stairway, which openly discloses the transitional period in which it was built. While the ramps, instead of spiralled, are straight, after the manner of Italy, the vaults overhead are structured by means of the ribbed ogive arches traditional to Gothic France. But the Renaissance reappears in the resplendent pattern of Florentine themes carved in low relief on the steps' continuous underside. Such sculptural sophistication is equally present in the château's main fireplaces, including the one that graces the guard room *(below).* In the dining room *(right),* a series of fine 17th-century tapestries are part of the sumptuous furnishings brought to Montal by M. Fenaille, who acquired the château in 1908 and restored it.

Fontaine-Henry

above: At Fontaine-Henry the extreme irregularity of the roof line—ranging from the conical "witch's cap" over a corner tower through the vast "bishop's mitre," which rises even higher than its supporting walls, to the flat balustrade atop the square tower of another corner—gives witness to the importance of this château as a compendium of medieval and Renaissance architectural styles. The various manners come together most dramatically on the near façade of the large square donjon, where, sandwiched between the medieval elements of moat and extravagantly steep "mitre" roof, the Renaissance appears in the classical "ordering" of the three stories. Doric, Ionic, and Corinthian columns flank the windows and supersede one another in an ascending series, just as they do on the Colosseum in Rome. Still little understood in the distant north of France, the orders here do not structure the wall—which rests upon 12th-century foundations—but rather serve as decoration applied to it.

Fontaine-Henry, lying in Calvados between Bayeux and the English Channel, is a château that could have evolved only in Normandy, where monumental stone architecture developed consistently and progressively from the primitive keeps of the Middle Ages to the gracious, classicized forms of the Renaissance. Indeed, Fontaine-Henry is often deemed the northern province's finest Renaissance domestic dwelling, but it is more than that, incorporating as the structure does parts bearing the stylistic imprints of several earlier ages. And whatever the shifts in manner, each was accomplished with a high order of taste and technical mastery. A sprawling, asymmetrical, and picturesque assemblage of dissimilar parts, Fontaine-Henry transcends its irregularity to achieve unity, and even grandeur, through the consistency with which its châtelains—five generations of Harcourts—unabashedly preserved the old while embracing the newest and the best available from a succession of great builders.

Fontaine-Henry takes its name from the numerous springs that well up on the terrain, keeping it fresh and verdant, and from Henri de Tilly, a son of the high bailiff of Normandy who participated in the Eighth Crusade and died in the *donjon* of the family château. The early 13th-century chapel dates from his tenure, but still older are buttresses and traces of vaults dating from the 11th century and cellars from the two succeeding centuries that resemble those at Mont-Saint-Michel. The absence of documents for these early works suggests that the château was destroyed during the Hundred Years War.

In 1373 the Harcourts—a remarkable clan that flourishes today—came to Fontaine-Henry through marriage with Jeanne de Tilly. Reconstruction then

From one part of Fontaine-Henry to another the Middle Ages become the Renaissance, as the flattened arches, ogee moldings, delicate relief tracery, and mullioned panes of the Flamboyant windows in the right pavilion change to the rectangular fenestration and decorative roundels of the adjacent "classicized" façade. The later style further asserts itself both above and below, in the semicircular arches and bulblike finials of the dormers and in the little Doric temple built over the courtyard well. The corner turret, however, remains a thoroughly medieval "defensive" form.

commenced and continued from the time of Charles VIII (r. 1483–98) through the reign of Henri II (r. 1547–59). From the last of the 16th-century campaigns a corner stair tower and its decorative sculpture are attributed to Blaise Le Prestre. Meanwhile, in 1530 Anne d'Harcourt married Charles de Morais. Thereafter building eventually ceased because the Morais lived mainly at court and scarcely ever came to Fontaine-Henry. In 1655 Nicolas de Morais married Marguerite de Sévigné, sister-in-law of the celebrated letter-writer and chronicler of the age of Louis XIV.

Although never sold, Fontaine-Henry passed from generation to generation through women, which meant that a series of different names became associated with the estate. In the time of Louis XV, François-Louis de Montecler, the husband of Marguerite Bouttier de Château d'Assy, modified a façade to make it conform somewhat better to contemporary taste. The granddaughter of the Monteclers, Louise-Marie-Henriette de Vassy, held the domain during the Revolution. Unmarried, she left Fontaine-Henry to a nephew, Henry de Carbonnel, Marquis de Canisy, who painted and also collected the works of important artists. During the Restoration he redecorated the château's interior and laid out the garden in the English manner. Canisy too died childless, but instead of leaving the property to his own family, with whom he had quarreled, he willed it to his wife, who then made her niece and an adopted daughter, the Marquise de Cornulier, her heirs. The daughter of the latter became Comtesse Pierre d'Oilliamson (which name is a French corruption of Williamson). With courage and energy this châtelaine continues to devote herself to the maintenance of a marvelous and historic house.

The beauty of the sculptural decorations in the main stairwell at Fontaine-Henry may have come from the hand of Blaise Le Prestre. Here the relief composition is labeled pourtraict de Judith.

75

Bailleul

The land of Bailleul, near Angerville in the Caux district of Normandy, was acquired in 1543 by Bertrand de Bailleul. A very old family, the Bailleuls participated in the 1066 conquest of England, and one branch even settled on the northern side of the Channel, where the name was soon simplified to Baliol. Having descended from mothers with forebears among the ancient kings of Scotland, John de Baliol and his son Edward succeeded in asserting their claim to the Scottish throne, but managed to hold on to it only for a short time.

In France, the 16th-century Bailleuls embellished their terrain with a handsome château that has survived as one of the finest remaining examples of the French High Renaissance, a monument that now is filled with an incalculably valuable collection of historic paintings, objets d'art, and furnishings. The building itself, an all-stone structure, is notable for its solid cubic mass, a compact arrangement that eliminates the usual interior court. Also, instead of round towers, the four corners are occupied by square, strongly projecting pavilions, each capped with a separate roof whose steep profile is slightly concave. A central, three-story bay, formed of superimposed Doric, Ionic, and Corinthian orders emphasizes on the main façade the château's overall symmetry. Gracing the lateral façades are beautiful relief carving, tall chimney stalks, and loggias in the Italian style. As its natural setting the château has a superb park studded with vases and statues.

The estate owned by the present Marquis de Bailleul is one that has never left the hands of its founder's descendants.

opposite: A solid, cubic mass with square corner pavilions and a steep, separate roof for each of its habitable units, Bailleul dates from about 1550 and is one of the finest surviving examples of French High Renaissance architecture outside the royal domains. While the all-stone masonry is set in horizontal moldings, quoins, and window frames to emphasize, after the French manner, the structure's various elements, the central bay on the main façade strikes a note new in the Renaissance. There the classical orders are superimposed three stories high and are crowned by a square-domed dormer supporting a lead statuette that is a rare, original work of the 16th century.

below: A few of Bailleul's treasures are exhibited in the grand drawing room, where Houdon's marble portrait bust of Louis XV is flanked by two small works of Lucas Cranach and to the left and right by Franz Hals's portrait of a child and a Hobbema landscape. A 17th-century Persian carpet, petit-point-covered Louis XIV armchairs, and Oriental porcelain mounted in 18th-century gilt bronze complete an unusually rich ensemble.

Château d'O

The Château d'O is as multiple and complex in its form and history as the name it bears is monosyllabically simple. Commenced in the 15th century, but built mainly in the 16th and enlarged in both of the two succeeding centuries, O is a compendium of styles united solely by their common disparity. Augment this irregular Norman pile with its reflection in the vast, encircling moat, and the effect is that of a fairy's castle, an improbable realm of checkerboard masonry, steep, many-silhouetted roofs, polygonal turrets, and tall dormers crowned by "flaming" stonework. As if Merlin himself were beckoning, the approach is through a high ogive portal flanked by mismatched towers and reached by the ghost of what was once a drawbridge.

Although short in name, the Os were long in noble lineage, tracing their forebears back to the 11th century, when the first *château fort* was erected on the domain north of Alençon. Great distinction accrued to the Os through Robert I, who accompanied Robert the Magnificent, Duc de Normandie, on a Crusade to the Holy Land. Robert IV died for France at the Battle of Agincourt (1415). Then, because of the destruction wrought by the Hundred Years War, Jean I d'O, counselor and chamberlain to Charles VIII (r. 1422–61), undertook to reconstruct the family château. Work continued in the late 15th century under Charles d'O, and then in the 16th century under Jean II d'O, who as captain of the Scottish guard and high bailiff of Normandy was close to the court of François I. The overall character of the Château d'O relates to the reign of Louis XII (1498–1515), but the fame, or notoriety, of the dwelling and its ancient clan come principally from François, the son of Jean II, born in c. 1535. Not only did François continue the courtly tradition of his family and achieve a whole series of high offices, among them superintendent of finances, lieutenant general of Normandy, and governor of the Île-de-France, but he also engaged the intimate affections of Henry III and became one of the King's *mignons*. If the French people were scandalized by François's personal comportment and flagrant self-enrichment at public expense, they were positively outraged when he was reappointed by the next monarch, *le bon* Henri IV! But this was not the only irony attached to the life of François d'O. "How curious," wrote the great Sully, finance minister under Henri IV, "that this man wealthy by more than four million—or, better yet, by the value of the entire kingdom, which he disposed of with all but absolute authority—had scarcely been examined by the doctors when his relatives, whom he had always held in great affection, his servants, and others claiming to be creditors simply vied with one another to strip their lord so totally of his possessions that long before he finally expired, François had only the bare walls of his room to die in. It was as if his fortune had determined to perish with him in some final act of justice."

François d'O died without issue, and his château was sold to satisfy creditors. It went to Jacques de La Guesle, attorney general to the Paris Parlement. His son, Alexandre, succeeded in having Louis XIII elevate the fief to marquisate in 1616, but from the 18th century onward, O passed through a great variety of owners. Finally, in 1878 speculators acquired the domain and broke it up, selling the furniture and dispersing the library. A new châtelain, General d'Aubigny, put a stop to the depredations, and, following restoration, the château now serves as a center for social and vacation activity.

above: *The Château d'O seems to float upon the surface of its vast, encircling moat. But the element of fantasy only begins there. It continues in the improbably speckled, random pattern of the masonry mixed of light stone and red brick. Also in the extreme irregularity and dissimilarity of the shapes and silhouettes on every façade. The entrance is approached over the ghost of a former drawbridge leading to a high ogival arch, flanked by towers, one relatively plain and the other equally polygonal but articulated with the thin, vertical tracery typical of late 15th-century Flamboyant Gothic. Yet the tall dormer is embraced and crested by a whole repertoire of ornamental forms—pilasters, shells, and candelabra— that speak for the early arrival of the Italian Renaissance. Comparably disparate are the extreme left and right wings, where the corbeled turret and lacey stonework on the one and the large windows and Mansart roof of the other place Late Gothic and 17th-century Baroque in direct contrast with one another. The cluster of steep slate roofs, especially the cropped-off "bishop's mitres," reveal O to be a distinctly Norman château.*

opposite: *Shaping the* cour d'honneur *at O are the pondlike moat and a balustrade on one side and on the other a façade not unlike that of the late 15th-century Louis XII wing at Blois. The corner tower contains a grand staircase, while the long pavilion opens on the ground floor to a flat-topped arcade resting on polygonal piers.*

The grand drawing room at Clères is two stories high, thanks to the removal of an intermediary floor, a pair of whose massive, ax-hewn beams still span the space. The 15th–16th-century ceiling of exposed rafters bears 17th-century decorations in the form of trompe l'oeil *coffers, which come together as a fascinatingly primitive arrangement of crosses, arabesques, interlacements, and floral motifs.*

Clères

An ancient château frequently at the center of great events in the history of France and of Normandy, Clères is best known in our time for the extraordinary garden created there by Jean Delacour, which he made a veritable Noah's Ark for the most wondrous species of the animal kingdom. "In Eden as at Clères," wrote Colette, "there were tiny gazelles so fragile that they could break their legs on the rocks. . . . I like to think that if I raised my hand skyward in this bosky realm, it would become a perfect perch for such winged marvels as the monal pheasant, the lace-crested goura, the Chinese pheasant in its golden armor. This would indeed be a sign of the miraculous." The creator of the Eden at Clères had to work his miracle twice, the first time between the two World Wars and then again after the devastations of a fire in 1939, followed by the German occupation of the early 1940s.

A phoenixlike château, Clères has often risen from the ashes of its destruction. Thus, the remnants of a keep can be traced back to the 11th century. Here, tradition has it, Joan of Arc spent a night, a prisoner of the English, who were conducting her to Rouen for trial and execution. The château itself had fallen victim of the Hundred Years War in 1418. Following the expulsion of the English, the Clères family rebuilt their country residence in the Late Gothic styles of the 15th and 16th centuries. During this period Georges IV de Clères married Anne de Brézé, granddaughter of King Charles VII and Agnès Sorel and a sister of Louis de Brézé, high bailiff of Normandy and the long-mourned husband of Diane de Poitiers, the celebrated châtelaine of Chenonceaux and Anet. Later in the 16th century, the Clères were hosts to the Valois, in the persons of Charles IX and Catherine de' Medici, and then to the first of the Bourbons, Henri IV.

The 16th century saw the estate divided into the marquisate of Clères and Pabilleuses and the county of Clères, which contained the château. After the Comte de Clères had taken part in the Fronde of nobles rebelling against the crown during the minority of Louis XIV, the château suffered seizure. The Fontaine-Martel de Clères family recovered the property, but by the 19th century it had passed through marriage and lateral kinship to the Béarn family. In 1865 radical restorations were undertaken that destroyed some of the original elements for the sake of replacing them with a Second Empire conception of what a Norman Gothic structure should be.

Clères remained a domicile of the descendants of the Princesse de Béarn until 1919, when it was acquired by its present nature-loving owner.

above: *Devastated by the embellishing hand of its 19th-century restorer—Parent—and then by a fire in 1939, a wing of Clères stands like a phantom château set in a huge park ripe with century-old trees and alive with deer, pink flamingos, and the many other marvelous creatures gathered here by M. Jean Delacour.*

opposite: *A portion of Clères strongly characteristic of old Norman manor houses is the* cour d'honneur. *Here timber structural elements reinforced by brick mixed, mosaic fashion, with flint reflect the rural taste of the 16th century, when these walls were raised upon vaulted cellars surviving from a 13th-century* château fort.

Anet

The warm, humanist spirit of the Italian Renaissance breathed freely at Anet as nowhere else in the chill air of 16th-century northern France. The liberating influence derived from the devotion linking a triangle of noble lovers, as well as from the genius that a young artist had for expressing this beauty of feeling in a purely French manner, all the while using the formal language of Mediterranean classicism. The chain of romance began to take form when Henri II, as a prince and still a child, gave his heart to Diane de Poitiers, a lovely and gracious widow twenty years his senior. It continued as this lady honored the gallantry shown her, but in a manner that seemed never to compromise her faithfulness to the memory of a beloved husband, Louis de Brézé. As for the artist, this was Philibert Delorme, one of the first Frenchmen to study the great monuments of Rome and master the "orders," using them with ease and authority. Indeed, by reinventing classicism so as to make it native rather than alien to the Gothic soil of France, Philibert not only excelled at a time when mainly Italians enjoyed favor; he also emerged as France's first professional architect in the modern sense. Like the Italian masters, he was even sure enough of his ideas to articulate them in a book. Unfortunately, only a few of the buildings created by Philibert Delorme survive at all, none of them whole and complete. But one of the best and most representative fragments is the majestic gateway at Anet, a château commissioned by Diane de Poitiers and dedicated to her husband, but made possible and shared by an ardent, ever loyal Henri II.

In 1445, after receiving the domain of Anet in gratitude for his service to Charles VII, Pierre de Brézé built a relatively modest manor house in brick and stone. By the early 16th century Pierre's grandson Louis had become high bailiff of Normandy, and in 1515, at age fifty-five, he married a sixteen-year-old Diane de Poitiers. The beauty and charm of Diane were such that they worked wonders everywhere. These qualities were fatefully present when Diane accompanied a royal party to Bayonne for the exchange whereby the two small Valois princes would go as hostages against the release of their father, François I, then humiliatingly imprisoned in Spain following the French defeat at the Battle of Pavia (1525). Moved by the evident fright of the second boy, Henri, the lady of Anet comforted him with a kiss. From that moment on the Prince was enchanted. In 1531 Diane assumed mourning for her husband and never again wore color. To the younger man, however, she would always be the ideal woman, a creature of eternal freshness, a radiance in pink. After Henri succeeded as Dauphin, his marriage was arranged to Catherine de' Medici, only for the union to confirm him in his attachment to Diane de Poitiers, who shortly thereafter became the acknowledged mistress of her royal suitor, still only fourteen years old.

At the death of François I in 1547, Diane—now Duchesse de Valentinois—eclipsed all in her power at court, yet had the wisdom and skill to maintain good relations even with the Queen. It was now that Philibert Delorme was commissioned to design a new château at Anet, a huge walled complex of main and side wings, a chapel, and a gateway in the form of a Roman triumphal arch, the tympanum of which incorporated one of the masterpieces of the Mannerist Renaissance: Benvenuto Cellini's bronze relief of a recumbent Diana, goddess of the hunt. With its utterly new conception of architecture, Anet became the most famous and admired château of its time, a repository of the works and workmanship of many of the finest artists then practicing in France. But the mutilations of the Revolution and its aftermath were so extreme that the quality of the achievement can be appreciated only in a few vestigial remains—the triumphal arch; the left wing much revised in the 17th century; a fountain decoration in the form of a life-size marble sculpture-in-the-round, also recumbent, of Diana the huntress; and the portal to the main *corps de logis*, a monumental form built up of the three classical

As faithful to God as she had been to the two men in her life, Diane de Poitiers seemed to do penance when she erected her funerary chapel outside the enclosure at Anet and independent of the château's own chapel. The tomb, with the effigy by Pierre Bontemps, has recently been restored by the Moreau family.

opposite: *The surviving masterpiece of Philibert Delorme, the greatest architect of the French Renaissance, is the entrance gate giving access to the* cour d'honneur *at Anet, the resplendent château built in 1547–55 by Diane de Poitiers to memoralize the devotion she shared with both her husband and her royal lover, Henri II. A three-portal, symmetrical pile built up of arches, Doric columns and entablatures, marble inlays, balustrades in filigree, niches, and scrolls surmounted by a stag and hounds, the gate offers a purely Gallic but remarkably authoritative interpretation of the Roman triumphal arch. A Latin inscription over the main portal reads: "This spacious dwelling has been dedicated by Phoebus to the good Diana, who in turn is grateful for every favor she has received." Phoebus, the Greek Apollo, or sun god, refers to Henri II, while Diane is symbolized in the stag and hounds and in the image of Diana, goddess of the hunt, depicted nude and recumbent in the bronze relief filling the central tympanum. The original cast of this work now resides in the Louvre, for it too is a masterpiece of the Mannerist Renaissance, and one of the finest works of its creator, the Italian artist Benvenuto Cellini. The chimney summits formed like sarcophagi reminded Diane, Henri, and the world that the châtelaine remained always the bereaved widow of Louis de Brézé, high bailiff of Normandy. Originally, the freestanding animals were automatons that kicked and barked as the clock struck the hour.*

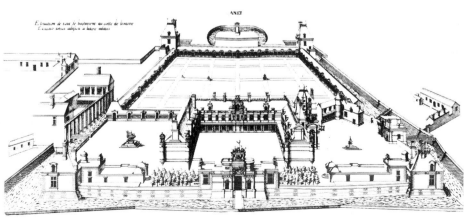

above: A melancholy vestige of the Renaissance splendor of Anet, the sole unit of the dwelling to survive is the left wing, which originally faced the cour d'honneur on one side and on the other the Cour de Diane. In 1681 the building received a high roof, while the windows lost their mullions and those on the lower level were enlarged to become doorlike "French windows." A restoration in the 1860s shortened the wing and finished the new end with corner turrets like those still standing from the original structure at the other end.

left: This 16th-century engraving provides a view of Anet in its prime, moated, walled, and approached through a great triumphal arch. At the bottom of the court on the right stands the château of the Brézés. To the left of the main château is the Cour de Diane, showing the original emplacement of the famous fountain statue of Diana the huntress.

orders superposed one upon the other. Here a culminating niche received a portrait statue of Louis de Brézé, for everywhere at the new Anet Diane de Poitiers honored her dead husband at the same time that she intertwined her initials with those of Henri II. At the death of the King in 1559, the former royal favorite retired to Anet, where she devoted the remainder of her long life to charitable works. Only a few years before her own death in 1566, Pierre de Brantôme could write: "I saw Madame la Duchesse de Valentinois at the age of seventy, still as beautiful, fresh, and charming as she was at thirty."

Diane's daughter, Louise de Brézé, Duchesse d'Aumale, inherited Anet and completed her mother's tomb, erected outside the *enceinte* and embellished with a marble effigy by the sculptor Pierre Bontemps. Then by legacy and by sale the domain devolved in the late 18th century upon Louis-Joseph de Vendôme, who transformed the Renaissance château into something approximating a Baroque one, with smaller suites instead of large rooms and a formal garden in the manner of Le Nôtre. Anet now became a gathering place for many of the age's creative lights, among them Jean de La Fontaine and Jean-Baptiste Lully. By 1732 various bequests conveyed the estate to the Duchesse du Maine, who at Anet as well as at Sceaux led a brilliant retinue, including Voltaire and Mme du Châtelet. After purchase by Louis XV and then resale two years later by Louis XVI, Anet in 1775 became the property of the Duc de Penthièvre, the grandson of Louis XIV and Mme de Montespan. This cultivated, generous grandee entertained such illustrious guests as the painter Jean-Baptiste Greuze, who may have painted *The Broken Pitcher* at Anet, using a gardener's daughter as his model. The revolutionaries left Penthièvre undisturbed, in recognition of his humane qualities, but seized Anet upon the Duke's death in 1793 and sold it—to bankers who stripped the château of its treasures, even scraping gold from the decorations. All that remained of the splendid pile were the few fragments mentioned above, with the portal to the main wing and the two sculptures deposited in Paris, the former at the École des Beaux-Arts and the latter pair in the Louvre. After several proprietors, Anet was acquired in 1860 by the Moreau family, who through four generations have endeavored to rehabilitate and preserve what they could of the noble conception brought to life by Diane de Poitiers, Henri II, and Philibert Delorme.

The genius of Philibert Delorme is fully evident in the chapel at Anet, where a giddy problem in geometry has been solved with true elegance, as the lozenge-shaped coffers rise and progressively diminish toward the oculus at the center. Like the dome, the surrounding sculptural program, where angels mix with personifications of fame, is typically Renaissance in the ease with which the Christian and the pagan classical have been integrated to express a new sense of the human potential.

Villandry

Set upon a platform bathed by the fresh, running waters of a system of canallike moats, Villandry is a handsome 16th-century château with a rectangular, U-shaped plan and a massive donjon *lingering in one corner from an earlier, more fortified dwelling. But the glory of Villandry, as well as of the Loire Valley and the whole of France, are the gardens. Works of scholarship and love, they are 20th-century re-creations of the intricately patterned, densely planted, and carefully trimmed flower-kitchen gardens that existed in the Renaissance. Such intimate arrangements disappeared in the 17th century once Le Nôtre had introduced his grandiose schemes of* parterres *and* tapis verts.

opposite: *Based on plans and descriptions left by the 16th-century engraver Androuet Du Cerceau, the garden extending before the main façade of Villandry consists of flowerbeds framed by paths and box hedges, studded with fountains and yew trees, all arranged like an iridescent carpet of intricately plotted geometries. A fresh-water moat, a grape arbor, and ranks of pollarded lime trees provide an* enceinte *for this fragrant domain reconstituted from the Renaissance.*

For its dulcet air and verdant, flowering banks, the Loire Valley, all the way up from the Atlantic Coast to Tours, has long been called the "garden of France." This consists of the old provinces of Touraine and Orléanais, whose "smiling" countryside was favored throughout the late Middle Ages and the Renaissance by French monarchs seeking to maintain themselves in an environment both safe and salubrious. Needless to say, the soil and the atmosphere encouraged gardens as much as it did kings, and the gardens laid out and cultivated around the walls and moats of the great châteaux were sweet-smelling worlds of rich color and intricate pattern. But the most remarkable garden now to flourish in the Loire is not a survivor from the pre-17th-century era, but rather a total re-creation, a work of love, skill, and vast scholarship carried on at the Château de Villandry by its owner, Dr. Carvallo, the founder of La Demeure Historique. By comparison with the unique character and beauty of Dr. Carvallo's Renaissance garden, the château itself—albeit a large and aristocratic dwelling—falls to a secondary level of interest.

Villandry as we know it dates back to 1532, when Jean Le Breton, secretary of state under François I, acquired a domain then known as Colombiers and built upon it a substantial château, rectangular in plan, open at one end, and completely surrounded by a moat. Incorporated into this structure are two elements from a 14th-century edifice formerly on the site: the exterior wall of the central *corps de logis*, and the massive, square *donjon* that forms one corner of the building. But to whatever extent Villandry may represent the Touraine of the Renaissance, it is thanks to the reconstructions made by Dr. Carvallo, for both château and garden underwent radical changes in the 18th century.

In the early 17th century Balthazar Le Breton, having inherited the Colombiers estate, had it raised to marquisate and then renamed Villandry. Almost a century later the last member of the Le Breton family, whom the Duc de Saint-Simon characterized as "a rich heiress," married Louis-François d'Aubigny. Villandry next went to the Marquis de Castellane, who set about, after 1754, restyling the château and garden to make them more consonant with contemporary taste. While the building was made to look more formal, the gardens were redesigned in an informal, "natural" manner then thought to be English.

During the Napoleonic Empire Villandry belonged to Joseph Bonaparte, then to the Hainguerlot family of bankers. The latter retained Villandry until 1893. Dr. Carvallo acquired the estate in 1906 and immediately began his research leading to restoration. The interior, with its paintings and period furniture, is fine, but the wonder of modern Villandry is the "old" garden, planted in the Renaissance way with vegetables as well as flowers, no variety of which could have been known only after the 16th century. Dr. Carvallo's principal source of authority was Androuet Du Cerceau (c. 1510–85), the famed engraver of châteaux and parks whose patron was Catherine de' Medici. Disposed on three different levels, the garden at its uppermost stage is a water terrace. Directly below it comes a terrace of box hedges, clipped yews, and flowers all arranged *en broderie*—like "embroidery." At the lowest level occurs a still more intricately designed terrace, but one planted as a *potager* or "kitchen garden." Here even the cabbages have been organized into geometric shapes and relationships, all framed and outlined by trimmed hedges, paths, and canals. Vines climb over trellises, while yews rise like sentinels on either side of entrances and intersections. The whole effect is as brilliant as stained glass and as abstractly decorative as a Persian carpet.

M. François Carvallo continues his father's work, and has even added a Renaissance "crown of fruit trees," a ten-acre orchard of rows perfectly aligned upon slopes overlooking the château, the garden, and the Loire below.

Saint-Germain-de-Livet

"A small gem for a child princess," is how the novelist La Varende charac-terized Saint-Germain-de-Livet, one of the most attractive fortified farm-houses still standing in Normandy's Pays d'Auge near Lisieux. In part a half-timbered manor house, and in part a Renaissance château constructed in a checkerboard arrangement of stone and brick, this charming residence rises above a moat formed by the running waters of the Touques River. Its longest association was with the Tournebu family, noted for feudal men so rough and combative that one lord of Tournebu was, according to legend, banned from court. Indeed, the King decreed that the offender should never again come before him "on foot, on horseback, or in a carriage." But not to be put off when a good fight was promised, Tournebu managed to join the royal forces for a great battle, yet without violating the interdict. Thus, the chief and his vassals fought not on foot, on horseback, or in a carriage, but on oxen, which frightened the enemy's horses and won the engagement—along with a royal pardon.

The first known seigneurs of Saint-Germain-de-Livet were the Tyrels in the 12th century. The Tournebus joined this clan through marriage and claimed the Norman estate in 1462. Eventually they added the Renaissance wing, which dates from 1561–78, during the tenure of Jean de Tournebu and his wife, Marie de Croismare. Saint-Germain-de-Livet remained in the hands of the Tournebus until the last heiress to bear this name married Pierre de Bernières, then Louis Louvel de Janville, president of the audit court in Normandy, but died childless in 1810. The estate passed to two nieces, the *demoiselles* de Foucault-Tournebu, who about 1850 restored the château in the overzealous and even destructive manner typical of the period. Finally, for the first time in the history of the domain, Saint-Germain-de-Livet went to a new owner not by legacy or marriage but by sale. In 1879 Mme Gobley purchased it, followed by M. and Mme Pillaut in 1920. A descendant of Riesener, the great 18th-century cabinetmaker, M. Pillaut rehabilitated the dwelling in the finest way. He also gathered there a whole collection of precious family memorabilia, some of which relate to the Romantic painter Eugène Delacroix, whose mother had been Riesener's daughter-in-law. In 1957 Mme Pillaut left Saint-Germain-de-Livet to the town of Lisieux.

above: A picturesque ensemble grouped to form a pentagonal enclosure, Saint-Germain-de-Livet has joined within it two typical Norman types of construction: the half-timbered manor house, dating from the 15th century, and a true Renais-sance château, modest in scale but complete with a galleried interior court, defensive towers, and a cincturing moat. Particularly charming is the masonry of the château, fabricated as a checker-board arrangement of white stone and bricks glazed red and green.

opposite: From the upper floor of the corps de logis at Saint-Germain-de-Livet the view is upon the cour d'honneur, which opens to the park on one side and is closed on the other by a subsidiary wing. The latter structure, as polychrome as the rest of this rustic 16th-century château, offers an arcaded gallery at the ground level and termi-nates in a round, cone-capped defensive tower.

Castries

The Château de Castries (pronounced Castre) rests upon a vantage point in the Languedoc—one of France's southernmost provinces bordering on the Mediterranean—and has been a bastion of power since antiquity, when the Romans there established a *castrum* for the surveillance of the *via Domitia* below.

In 1495, when Castries had long been an important medieval barony, the fief was acquired from Pierre de Ganges by Guillaume de La Croix, the governor of Montpellier, who now took the title of Baron de Castries and established a line that resides at Castries today. Between 1560 and 1570 Jacques de La Croix, the fourth Baron and the governor of Aigues-Mortes, rebuilt the château as a quadrangular arrangement of three *logis*, of which only that to the left of the entrance survives more or less intact. But the style then established prevails over all that presently stands, characterized by sobriety, emphatic horizontality, and a flat roof covered with Roman tiles. In 1622, the Duc de Rohan, head of the Protestant party, against whom Jean de Castries had won in the siege of Privas, took revenge by allowing his men to pillage the Château de Castries. The vandals set fire to the right wing, and all that remains of this *logis* are a colonnade of upright structural members and one wall of the main floor. Disgrace and loss of title came, however, in 1632, after Jean de Castries allowed himself to be drawn into the conspiracies fomented by Gaston d'Orléans and the Duc de Montmorency against the regime of Louis XIII. By 1645 René-Gaspard, Jean's son, had not only regained but also improved his family's status, doing so by virtue of outstanding military service during the Thirty Years War. Now Louis XIV elevated Castries to marquisate, which prompted René-Gaspard to restore the château, add the grand staircase, and create a park after plans prepared by Le Nôtre. This, in turn, called for the aqueduct, which, built by Riquet, conveys water from Fontgrand almost three miles away.

In the 18th century Charles de Castries earned a marshal's baton for distinguished military service, established the *code Castries*—France's maritime code—while naval minister, and aided the American War of Independence. For his role in the latter cause, Louis XVI created Charles' son—Armand—Duc de Castries. In 1828 the Castries reacquired their confiscated and devastated property. The Duchesse de Castries of this era—Henriette de Maillé—provided the model for the heroine of Balzac's *La Duchesse de Langeais*. In 1954, following return from the Battle of Dien-Bien-Phu, General de Castries took up residence in his ancestral home. "Thus [was] perpetuated," wrote the present Duke, "the continuity of a family that, for almost five centuries, have lived in a château that they built, whose name they bear, and that three times have been obliged to make rise from the ashes."

top: *Languedoc's Château de Castries, a vast Renaissance pile resting upon a vantage point first fortified by the Romans, retains only the left wing of its original 16th-century structure, thanks to the destructive effects of the Wars of Religion and the Revolution. Cleverly, the ruins of the right wing—a colonnade of piers—have been incorporated into formal gardens designed by Le Nôtre.*

above: *Castries's fountains are fed by an aqueduct almost three miles long, built in 1670–76 by Riquet, the engineer of the Canal du Midi.*

opposite: *Castries's Baroque staircase leads to a gallery fitted out a century after its construction in the 16th century as a hall suitable for meetings of the Languedoc états. The furnishings consist of boiserie bookcases, Renaissance tables, a magnificent ormolu desk attributed to Cressent, and a whole series of 18th-century chairs from the Régence, Louis XV, and Louis XVI periods.*

Ancy-le-Franc

Burgundy's Ancy-le-Franc, more than a beautiful château, is a capital work of architecture, one of the finest of the Late Renaissance in France. The author of the design is Sebastiano Serlio (1475–1554), the great Bolognese architect brought to Fontainebleau by François I. But Serlio functioned mainly as a theoretician, an intellectual who produced more literature than actual architecure. Thus, one of the marvels of Ancy-le-Franc is that—alone north of the Alps—it gives full, three-dimensional effect to a conception by one of the truly major exponents of the modern Greco-Roman revival, a movement that soon would replace the Gothic traditional to northern Europe with the humanist

right: Burgundy's Ancy-le-Franc, commenced in 1546 and structurally completed by 1574, was at that time the most thoroughly Renaissance edifice in France. Indeed, except for the high roof, the corner pavilions (which reflect the defensive towers of old), and the surrounding moat (now long filled in), visitors to Ancy often thought themselves, as one writer put it, "in Mantua, Parma, or Modena." So perfectly unified and balanced is the whole ensemble that a contemporary chronicler wrote that "it could have been built in a day." The reason for the rare authenticity of Ancy's Italianism is that the builders scrupulously followed the plans of Sebastiano Serlio, the great Bolognese architect brought to Fon-

tainebleau by François I. The absolute centrality of the square plan—which supports four rationally proportioned elevations offering almost identical façades—echoes the villas of the Veneto designed by the slightly younger Andrea Palladio. The plain exterior gives way on the inner court to richer, more intimate surfaces (**above** and **opposite).** In the courtyard at Ancy the Corinthian order, complete with pedestals and entablatures, marks the clear separation of each story, while the rhythm of arches (some opened into galleries) alternating with pilasters, paired on either side of square plaques in dark marble or shell-headed niches, recalls the Roman High Renaissance architecture of Donato Bramante.

The elaborate and extensive mural decorations at
Ancy-le-Franc were, for the most part, executed
by or under the direction of Primaticcio, one of
the most important of the Italian painters brought
by François I to work in the royal château at Fontainebleau. As developed in France, here is a
sumptuous example of the Late or Mannerist
Renaissance style flowing from the art of Michel-
angelo, Raphael, and Giuliano Romano. In a
room dedicated to Diana (**opposite**) one composition depicts the goddess surprised at her bath by
Acteon, under a ceiling ornamented in a manner
pioneered by Raphael in the Vatican loggias. In
the "Gallery of Sacrifices" (**above**) scenes painted
in grisaille represent legendary sacrifices made
in antiquity. The guard room (**below**) is so enormous that it takes the space of an entire floor of
one wing, an arrangement that allows illumination from two sides. Here, amidst the Italianism
of Ancy's painted decoration, the beamed ceiling
and patterned tile floor strike a native French
note. The fleur-de-lis upon the frieze recall the
visit made by Henri III to the château in 1574.

forms of Mediterranean classicism. The evidence of this lies not so much in
the pervasive presence of the "orders," which, after all, had long been known
and used in France, but rather in the total mastery of that usage, which
enabled the architect to speak with fresh, free expression as well as with
correctness. The simple unity, equilibrium, and horizontality of it all; the
rational proportioning; the wall sections that replace columns in the arcades of
the inner court; the orders complete with pedestals and entablatures that
mark the clear separation of stories; and the centrality of a square plan that
turns the same façade to the world on all four sides—such features could well
persuade viewers that they have crossed the French frontier and penetrated
deep into Italy. But on the interior Ancy-le-Franc seems even more the Italian
palazzo, where the stairways—hitherto always a focal feature in France—are
relegated to corners, the better to make long, unbroken wall planes for the
mural painting so fundamental to Italian decorative schemes. And what
schemes! To Ancy-le-Franc came a good portion of the King's own School of
Fontainebleau—Primaticcio, a number of his pupils, and Niccolà dell'Abbate.
Together these sophisticated practitioners of the Mannerist style covered the
walls with scenes from the epic Battle of Pharsala, waged entirely in classical
nudity; allegories of the muses and the liberal arts; serried panels of botanical
specimens; themes from the zodiac; and the image of Diana at her bath,
reminding us that the first mistress of Ancy-le-Franc was the sister of Diane de
Poitiers, the powerful favorite of Henri II. But for all its Italianism, the
château rests on French soil, and the roof it throws against the Burgundian
sky is tall as no Italian lord would ever have allowed. Too, the pavilioned
corners, while not heavily accented, still recall the defenses of old, as did the
waters of the encompassing moat, until eventually the trenches were filled in.

Ancy-le-Franc had its inception in 1537, when Antoine III de Clermont,
Comte de Tonnerre, acquired the land, a virgin terrain, with the idea of
erecting there a dwelling suitable to his status as lieutenant general of the
Dauphiné and France's chief minister responsible for forests and waterways. In
1546, just as his sister-in-law, Diane de Poitiers, was achieving full ascendency
at court, the Comte de Clermont-Tonnerre ordered that ground be broken in
Burgundy. By 1574 the château was ready to receive Henri III, who stayed at
Ancy on his way back from eastern Europe, where he had been crowned King
of Poland. The completion of Ancy's interior, however, remained to be done
by Charles-Henri, the second Duc de Clermont-Tonnerre. (The first Duke,
Count Antoine's son, had been killed in 1573 at the siege of La Rochelle.)

Soon Ancy-le-Franc acquired fame as a princely residence. The parade of
royal visitors continued, with Henri IV arriving in 1591 to relieve a siege
brought by the Catholic League. Charles-Henri gave dinner to Louis XIII as
the monarch passed through from Metz to Paris. Finally, in June of 1674,
following his conquest of the Franche-Comté, Louis XIV received the hospital-
ity of Ancy-le-Franc.

By then, however, the Clermont-Tonnerres found themselves crushed
with debt and forced to sell their estate in 1682 to Michel Le Tellier, Marquis
de Louvois and France's minister of war under Louis XIV. Mme de Sévigné
explained the sad situation to a friend who, having seen Ancy, failed to under-
stand how such possessions could be compromised: "You paint a mirror image
of the beauty, the magnificence, the extent of all these properties, and then you
cry out: How is it possible for the lords of such a realm to ruin themselves?
Alas. It is a story for balladeers. For a long time a public hospital was attached
to Tonnerre. Therein lies the single and true explanation, an explanation that
leaves us without a word to say. It shuts the mouth firmly, for the reason is one
to make the wolf come out of the woods, and that now signs over everything to
Mme de Louvois. We can only be happy that there is a minister rich enough to
take on such a sovereign responsibility."

While the busy statesman rarely visited Ancy, Mme de Louvois favored
the place and gave the château its handsome *communs*. The property remained
among the Louvois descendants until the last Marquis died in 1844. Then,
happily, the Clermont-Tonnerre family succeeded in reacquiring their ancestral domain. Now restored, Ancy-le-Franc belongs to the Mérode princes, the
heirs to the estate's founding line.

VANITAS · 1578 · NON NOBIS DOMINE SED NOMINI TVO DA GLORIAM · 1578 · FVGE NON PV

Cheverny

Favored by the Valois in the 16th century but abandoned by the Bourbons in the 17th century, the beautiful Loire Valley had few new châteaux to boast of when Cheverny was built between 1604 and 1634. Rare also for the time is the unity of the whole, a single oblong block, without right-angle pavilions or cour d'honneur. *Five separate roofs indicate the variety of the spaces enclosed, but unity triumphs through the dazzling whiteness of the masonry, the pervasive classicism of the styling, the flatness and strong horizontal coursing of the main façade, and the strict symmetry that governs every aspect of the organization. Dramatizing this last factor is the long perspective of the entrance drive. A certain provinciality—seen especially in the proportioning of the large lateral pavilions relative to the narrow central unit—simply adds to the mood of immutable, patrician reserve. Pedimented windows and dormers, Roman Emperor portrait busts alternating with the second-level windows, lanterns atop squared domes—all contribute to make Cheverny a major expression of the French Early Baroque.*

opposite: *Thanks in large part to the continuity of the Hurault family who built and still own Cheverny, the château retains virtually intact the whole of its original Louis XIII furnishings. In the so-called "Royal Chamber" they are almost too rich to believe, consisting as they do of mantel and ceiling paintings by Jean Mosnier; still more paintings by the same artist on the door and wainscoat panels; and, on every remaining inch of wall space, tapestries woven from a cycle of pictures painted by Simon Vouet in 1635 for the Hôtel de Bretonvilliers in Paris. Gilded moldings, heavily carved cabinets, tapestry-covered chairs, and a vast canopied bed hung and covered with 16th-century Persian embroidery complete an ensemble opulent enough for a King indeed.*

The serene aristocratic—but pleasantly provincial—beauty of Cheverny would scarcely divulge the domestic violence that brought about its construction. Here is a rare château indeed, a Louis XIII edifice consisting of a single oblong block without *cour d'honneur,* varied by its several, separate-roofed pavilions, but utterly unified through the dazzling whiteness of the masonry and the strict symmetry that reigns over the whole. Also rare is the intact state of the interior furnishings, for the most part all there from the time of the château's construction in the early 17th century. Completing the sense of immutable reserve and remove is the park, a vast perspective focusing upon the château at the center of a clearing in the circumambient forest. Amidst such quietude the anguish of an incautious young wife, suddenly confronted, becomes almost audible.

One of the reasons for the completeness and perfection of Cherverny is the remarkable continuity of the family that built the château and continue to live in it. The Huraults were there, in the Loire Valley, as early as 1338. The first structure of which any trace remains was a manor house erected in 1510 by Raoul Hurault, whose father had been governor of Blois and treasurer to Louis XII, and who himself was secretary to the King. Philippe Hurault, one of Raoul's seven children, became chancellor of France, keeper of the seals, and the first chancellor of the Order of the Holy Ghost, founded by Henri III in 1578. Philippe served both Henri III, the last of the Valois, and Henri IV, the first of the Bourbons. In recognition of this the latter monarch elevated Cheverny to the status of county. Succeeding the first Comte de Cheverny was his son Henri, who married Françoise Chabot, daughter of the Comte de Charny, Henri IV's grand master of the horse. Because of her husband's duties at court, the Comtesse de Cheverny, still young and very isolated on the Loire estate, sought and found solace in her page. This comfort turned into tragic grief when, inadvertently, Henri IV himself exposed it. "One day," the annals tell us, "the king, in a joking spirit, made the cuckold sign over his head. The courtiers all laughed. Unfortunately a small mirror on the wall . . . revealed to the Comte de Cheverny that he was the subject of the royal jest." The next morning at 5 o'clock the outraged husband was at Cheverny. He summoned the priest and went to his wife's room, "holding a goblet in one hand, a sword in the other. Promising to return within the hour, he left her to choose. Preferring the poison, the Countess expired as her husband reappeared. By nightfall, the Comte de Cheverny was back at court, in time to attend the King's retirement."

The page also paid with his life, and the avenged husband was exiled to his estate. There he immediately commenced to rebuild the château, as if to extirpate—or expiate—the sins of the recent past. The new edifice proved to be the region's most important and sumptuous dwelling built during the reign of Louis XIII. Commissioned from Jacques Boyer of Blois, it was completed about 1634, its classicism unsullied by the old château, whose medieval forms survive only in the altogether separate service buildings. Meanwhile, Henri de Cheverny had remarried. The daughter of this union, Cécile, inherited Cheverny in 1648. As Marquise de Montglas, she became the great friend of that noble scapegrace, Comte Roger de Bussy-Rabutin. In her *Mémoires* Mme de Montglas wrote that "nothing is more beautiful than Cheverny," but then she sold the estate to Comte d'Harcourt, who promptly abandoned it. By the time the Comte de Saint-Leu bought Cheverny, "the forecourt had wheat piled all the way to the steps . . . [and] this great château . . . had only five rooms that were livable." The new châtelain restored the place and introduced a brilliant era, which ended with the Revolution. But by continuing to live at Cheverny, he saved it from sack and confiscation. Still, Saint-Leu sold the property in 1799 after the death of his son. In 1825, finally, Anne-Denis-Victor, Marquis de Vibraye and heir to the senior branch of the Huraults, acquired Cheverny and thus returned the estate to its founding family. His descendants continue to maintain the château and park in impeccable condition.

Maintenon

Mme de Maintenon (1635–1719), as portrayed by Pierre Mignard. By professing virtue in an age of license, Mme de Maintenon achieved a career characterized as "transparent enigma."

With its robust towers, red-brick walls, dormers, and steep roofs, and with its moat freshened by the waters of the Eure, Maintenon stands proud and secure, but somewhat modest, like its great 17th-century mistress. This was Mme de Maintenon, the commoner-governess who raised the illegitimate children of Mme de Montespan, then reformed and morganatically married their father, Louis XIV. "A fine, substantial château at the edge of a fine, substantial village, and a site very much to my taste" was how the Marquise herself termed the domain at Maintenon. By the glittering standards of France's High Baroque age, the château seems rather austere and old-fashioned. And this too would have suited Mme de Maintenon, the *petite bourgeoise* who grew up in poverty, abandoned by a father imprisoned at Niort for fraud, but who, in an age of incredible license, built a great career upon the strong personal qualities of moral rectitude and devotion to duty. The extraordinary connection these gave to the royal household is physically evident in the park at Maintenon. There, like a monumental Roman ruin, the arches still stand from the aqueduct commenced by Vauban to convey water from the Eure to the great fountains of Versailles twenty-five miles away.

From 1505 until the end of the 17th century, the château in the fertile valley was so thoroughly rebuilt that only the corner fortifications remain from the original *enceinte*—a square stone *donjon* dating from the 13th century and round brick towers of a slightly later date. Originally the domain belonged to vassals owing fealty to the lords of Montfort, but in the early 16th century it was purchased by Jean Cottereau, treasurer under Louis XII and then François I. The new châtelain immediately undertook to rebuild two sides of the enclosure, creating a *corps de logis*, or main wing, and a secondary wing at right angles to it. Opposite these interior façades Cottereau retained the plain and simple walls, but elsewhere on the estate he had erected a chapel, dedicated to Saint Nicholas and still standing.

In 1526 the daughter of Jean Cottereau married Jacques d'Angennes, lord of Rambouillet, and took the château as her dowry. It was from a descendant of this union that Louis XIV bought Maintenon and offered it to governess Françoise d'Aubigné, evidently moved by the contrast she offered to the temperamental Montespan. Known as the "widow Scarron," from her early marriage to the libertine but paraplegic poet, Françoise soon became the Marquise de Maintenon, the King's chaste and discreet confidante. After building a second side wing, between the square keep and the main wing, and demolishing the last of the old walls, Mme de Maintenon so filled the place with her own spirit of prudent repose that it became a refuge for hard-pressed members of the court, especially the favorites seeking a quiet place in which to give birth to the infants sired by the King. Eventually this caused the châtelaine to complain: "I go to [Maintenon] for a breath of air, only to find myself stifled." It was there, however, that in 1684 Louis XIV secretly married Mme Scarron. And it was there that in 1689 and 1691 the great playwright Racine wrote *Esther* and *Athalie,* to be performed by the academy at Saint-Cyr founded by Mme de Maintenon to educate young women of good heart and slender means like herself. This charitable interest and the sovereign's own demands increasingly kept the good lady from her estate, until in 1698 she gave it to her niece, on the occasion of the latter's marriage to the Duc d'Agen, son of the Duc de Noailles.

During the Revolution the Noailles suffered dreadfully, but managed to regain their property, making it available to Charles X on the night of August 4, 1840, as this last of the Bourbon monarchs of France traveled into exile. Maintenon remains a possession of the Noailles dukes; one of them restored it in the 19th century, and imposed on the structure a Second Empire conception of what a Louis XIII château should look like.

At Maintenon the Eure River divides and then converges to freshen on all sides a park laid out by Le Nôtre. At one point the river is spanned by the remains of arches that the great engineer Vauban built in an aborted effort to convey water by aqueduct to the artificial lakes and canals of Versailles. Although useless, the arches are decorative and add a romantic touch to an otherwise formal and rather austere arrangement.

Rigaud's portrait of Louis XIV reminds us that here is where the sovereign slept during his rare visits to Maintenon. The painted wooden beams and a few pieces of furniture survive from that age, but otherwise the room is the product of a 19th-century restoration.

Le Rocher-Portail

Brittany's Rocher-Portail is one of those châteaux that stand as living monuments to the cleverness and enterprise, the ambition and pragmatism of the unprivileged individual, the sort so prevalent in France that it became a definable stratum of society and caused the French to invent a word for it—*la bourgeoisie*. And like the bourgeoisie, Rocher-Portail is plain and sober, but ample, solidly grounded, and enduring.

Tallement des Réaux's *Historiettes* relates the story of Rocher-Portail's builder, one Gilles Ruellan who was already of age the first time he put on shoes. Gilles made his living delivering sailcloth for a man named Ferrières and his partner, a widow of Saint-Malo. However, he soon had reason to wear shoes regularly, for after his master became tax collector for part of the Saint-Malo diocese, Gilles took a subcontract to work some of the hamlets. His performance was such that the widow, an astute businesswoman in her own right, suggested that the young man expand into the arms trade, then a lucrative opportunity, thanks to the Wars of Religion. With an initial capital of 300 *écus*, lent by the widow, Gilles earned a profit of 400 *écus!* This enabled him to marry the daughter of a Fougères fruitmonger, and even to launch a major career in finance. The *fermiers généraux* in Paris (the *ancien régime*'s principal means of tax collection), having heard that Gilles Ruellan "knew his way down to the slightest hamlets of Brittany's four dioceses," made an arrangement whereby, in exchange for a good tax harvest, Gilles could retain one-fifth of the profit and nothing of the loss—although he agreed to assume the cost of running down nonpayers! By his own admission a man of great "cunning" and one "who liked good food and was loved by everybody," Gilles soon made his presence felt at the royal court. He served as intermediary and brought Henry IV together with the Duc de Mercoeur, head of the Catholic League, even aiding the former to subdue Dinan and Fougères.

At the close of the Wars of Religion in 1596, Gilles had made his fortune and could now acquire style. He bought the domain of Rocher-Sénéchal, renamed it Rocher-Portail, and in 1608 arranged a barony. More titles followed—state and sword counselor, gentleman of the king's bedchamber, knight of Saint-Michel, and finally, in 1622, Marquis de La Balue. One daughter married the governor of Fougères (a man subsequently executed for high treason) and another the Duc de Brissac, whose family claimed direct descent from the Roman consul Cocceius Nerva.

Always a person with a good sense of the moment, the old Gilles Ruellan made arrangements in his will for the financing of a hospital in Rennes, a provision his widow and children contested until the Bishop had to effect a major compromise. Gilles's second daughter, Mme Barrin de La Galissonière, inherited Rocher-Portail and in 1653 left it to Jacques de Farcy. His descendants sold the estate to the Marquis de Saint-Brice in 1754. After long abandonment, the château was bought in 1866 by the Bourtray family. In restored form, it now belongs to the Baronne de Brugière.

opposite: Commenced in 1617 and built of quarried stone trimmed in granite, Rocher-Portail consists of four large, square corner pavilions sprouting tall chimney stalks and linked by three corps de logis. In the French fashion, each of the structural units has its own separate, steep roof, all of which are pierced by dormers. The arched pediments on the latter strike a classical note that is echoed in the château's most elegant feature—an Italianate arcade cut into the ground level on the interior façade of one wing. The vast cour d'honneur this confronts is entirely open on one side, protected only by a balustrade and a small drawbridge over a moat that elsewhere swells to the size of a lake.

The glory of Courances is its park, laid out in the harmonious manner of the 17th century and ornamented with sheets of water fed by thousands of springs welling up from deep within the terrain. The entrance drive here is bordered by two long canals, leading to a moat that surrounds the château. The view from that perspective is upon the mirrorlike surfaces of a rectangular lake and a round basin.

Courances

Courances takes its name from the abundant waters that spring from deep within the terrain, freshening the moats, canals, and mirror-surface lakes and basins that surround the château and brighten its park. A tradition held that the three wonders of old France were the flowerbeds of Cély, now disappeared, the woods of Fleury, and the streams of Courances. And it was the lord of Fleury—Cosme Clausse, secretary of state and superintendent of waterways and forests under Henri II—who around 1550 acquired the domain at Courances and commenced the château. However, the structure we know took form after its acquisition in 1622 by Claude Gallard, a royal counselor. The style is therefore typical of what had developed in the Early Baroque era under Henri IV and Louis XIII, with a massive main pavilion flanked by projecting side pavilions arranged to create a strongly centralized, symmetrical grouping in which each of the three units is crowned by its own steep roof. Also true to the style is the sober grandeur, warmed by rose brick walls and articulated in pale stone.

In the course of the 18th century Courances belonged first to the Novion family, relatives of the lords of Bélancourt, and then to the family of President de Nicolay. It was during this period that the entrance façade to the main pavilion received its double-ramp stairway, whose horseshoe form and undulating curves emulate the prototype at Fontainebleau. The 18th-century owners also fitted several of the château's interiors with handsome wood paneling decorated in the Louis XV manner. Other interiors retain marble inlays of the sort first introduced at Versailles in the time of its royal builder, Louis XIV.

After the Franco-Prussian War of 1870 the property was restored by Baron de Haber. His grandson, the Marquis de Ganay, now maintains the estate, sparing no effort to preserve the château, gardens, and art collection.

One of the many statues embellishing the park at Courances is the recumbent figure representing the nymph Arethusa. Originally it reposed in the royal gardens at Marly. Damaged by military occupation during and after World War II, Courances has now been fully restored.

right: This small salon at Courances is precious for its set of wooden panels decorated with paintings attributed to the early 18th-century master Claude Gillot. At the center of the delicately arabesque designs are scenes from contemporary comedies. Adding to the colorful Rococo setting are a painted-silk screen, Louis XV chairs covered in Aubusson tapestry depicting birds, and a corner chest, which is part of a series bearing the stamp of Cramer. No less rare is the early 18th-century carpet, patterned in ostrich-feather bouquets.

below: The château at Courances (a name meaning "running waters") had to be beautiful in order to serve as the centerpiece of a spring-freshened setting that long was considered one of the marvels of old France. Commenced in 1550, the present building took form mainly after 1622, during the Early Baroque age of Louis XIII. This can be seen in the symmetrical, highly centralized arrangement of three pavilions joined but distinguished by separate steep roofs. Also typical are the tall windows, high dormers, and the general air of great dignity, saved, however, from chilliness by the warm color of the brick walls and brightened by the articulations in pale stone. The 18th-century entrance stairway, a curvilinear double ramp, emulates the "horseshoe" prototype at Fontainebleau.

A rival architect, Claude Perrault, said of François Mansart's Maisons: "Its beauty is such that even foreigners want to visit the château as one of the greatest triumphs that France has ever produced." Here Mansart realized an early expression of French Baroque classicism at its most unified and balanced. The logic and cool rationality—those quintessentially French qualties—derive not only from the masterful handling of the Greco-Roman vocabulary, but also from the grand horizontality of the composition, the systematic repetition of all the structural and decorative elements, and the reflection in the steep roof line of the plan's every shift and angle.

Maisons-Laffitte

"Masterpiece," though debased by indiscriminate overuse, is a word that seems automatically to come forth whenever the subject is a building by François Mansart (1598–1666), the architect who, in the reign of Louis XIII and in the early part of the Louis XIV era, did so much to transform Greco-Roman classicism into an idiom uniquely and unmistakably French. And among the secular works by Mansart to survive, the genuine masterpiece must surely be the château that now bears the name of Maisons-Laffitte. Here some ten miles northwest of Paris and ten years after the publication of Descartes' *Discours de la méthode* (1637), Mansart put up a structure of such heroic harmony and equilibrium that it seems nothing so much as an eloquent, three-dimensional demonstration of Gallic logic and the Cartesian method.

The château was commissioned by René de Longueil, the scion of an old family of the *noblesse de la robe* that had held the Maisons domain for at least two centuries. The new power and wealth now commanded by René flowed from his steadfast loyalty to Mazarin and the crown during the Fronde rebellion. This made him superintendent of finances, host to young Louis XIV at the great Mansart château, and ultimately Marquis de Maisons. His brilliant great-grandson, the fourth Marquis de Maisons, succeeded him as chief magistrate of the Parlement of Paris. And before dying at age thirty-one, this young man had also become head of the Academy of Science and a staunch patron of Voltaire, who wrote *La Henriade* at Maisons. His heir, however, the Marquis de Soyecourt, did not have the fortune to maintain Maisons and in 1777 sold it to the Comte d'Artois, the younger of Louis XVI's two brothers. A passionate anglophile, this Prince went heavily into debt to gain access to Mansart's wonderful stables and there to establish a stud farm.

When the Comte d'Artois emigrated after 1789, Maisons was confiscated. From 1804 to 1809 it belonged to the Duc de Montebello, Napoleon's Marshal Lannes. In 1818 his widow sold the estate to Jacques Laffitte, a liberal-minded banker who made Maisons a center of opposition to its former châtelain—the Comte d'Artois, now Charles X. With the abdication of this last of the Bourbon monarchs of France, Laffitte became prime minister under Louis-Philippe, only to prove too liberal either to maintain law and order or to save himself from financial ruin. Once out of office, Laffitte tried to recoup his losses by selling off the Maisons park as building lots, which meant destroying the château's *communs*, among them Mansart's stables. Even after Laffitte, the destruction of Maisons continued, until 1904 when demolition seemed inevitable. But the state acquired what remained and instituted a process of restoration. Still magnificent, Laffitte nonetheless suffers from the loss of its proper environment, in consequence of which the château looks unnecessarily forlorn.

above: In the "summer dining room" installed about 1780 by the Comte d'Artois (the future Charles X), a distinctively 18th-century spirit invades Mansart's 17th-century Château de Maisons. Here the bacchantes surmounting the fireplace were designed by Bélanger and executed by the sculptor Lhuillier.

opposite: The most admired interior at Maisons is a relatively small circular room that culminates in a dome vault. Around the walls Ionic pilasters alternate with mirrored bays, but everywhere else the lower surfaces are embellished with a flat-pattern design composed of inlaid bone, pewter, rosewood, satinwood, and ebony. The result is of an extreme, decorative richness.

Sully

"The Fontainebleau of Burgundy" is how the inimitable Marquise de Sévigné characterized Sully in the late 17th century. But in regard to the inner court, she went still further and called it "the most beautiful . . . to be found among the châteaux of France." Alas, this marvel, which was probably inspired by the designs of Serlio at Ancy-le-Franc, is inaccessible to the public, being enclosed on all four sides and protected by the resident Mac-Mahon–Magenta family as a private domain. But from every approach, Sully is of a rare grandeur and magnificence. An immense structure dating mainly from the second half of the 16th century—with one outer façade rebuilt with true 18th-century elegance—Sully comprises four substantial wings that together form a quadrilateral *en-*

above and *right: The glory of Burgundy's Sully is the interior court, which Mme de Sévigné characterized as "the most beautiful . . . to be found among the châteaux of France." Enclosed by a set of four Renaissance façades, thought to have been inspired by the designs of Serlio at neighboring Ancy-le-Franc, the quadrilateral displays tall windows on two floors set within arcades punctuated by paired pilasters in the Doric order below and in the Ionic above. At the upper level the windows are mullioned and set behind balustrades, while the wall terminates in a frieze richly decorated with sculptural heads. The east wall illustrated here is also marked by a projecting entrance pavilion, which is steep-roofed and dormered like the wings themselves. A graveled surface and orange trees in tubs complete the scene.*

ceinte, defended at the corners by square, diagonally placed, lantern-coiffed towers and on all sides by moats filled with the living waters of the Drée River. From the center of one wing projects the apse of the chapel, while on the opposite, 18th-century side a monumental flight of steps descends to a broad terrace projecting into the moat, which here becomes a mirror lake wide enough for boating. Fully visible through an iron grille, Sully towers majestically over its dependent village, as well as over forests as game-rich as any in France.

The general plan of Sully must have been established in the 13th century, during the tenure of the family that gave the fief its name. In the 14th century Sully passed to the Montaigus, who formed a junior branch of Burgundy's ducal family. In 1470 it went to Hugues de Rabutin, when this lord of Épiry inherited the estate through his wife, the legitimatized daughter of Claude de Montaigu, a casualty of the Battle of Buxy. Less than a century later, in 1515, Christophe de Rabutin sold Sully to Jean de Saulx, husband of Marguerite de Tavannes. Now reconstruction commenced, in all likelihood from plans prepared by Nicolas Ribonnier, "architect for the King in the duchy of Burgundy." It continued, and was largely accomplished, under Gaspard de Saulx Tavannes, the son of Jean and one of France's great military men in the time of François I and Henri II. Named marshal of France and the King's lieutenant in Burgundy for his heroism at Pavia and Cérisoles, as well as for his victories over the Protestants at Jarnac and Moncontour, Gaspard de Saulx-Tavannes earned considerable notoriety from the instigating role he is supposed—perhaps unfairly—to have played in the Saint Bartholomew's Day Massacre (August 24, 1572). Brantôme, the chronciler of the age, described Gaspard as running through the streets of Paris shouting: "Blood! Blood! The doctors say that bleeding is as good for the health in August as in May!" Under Henri IV, Jean de Tavannes, Gaspard's younger son, espoused the Protestant cause as passionately as the father had the traditional Catholic party. Even after making peace with the French King, Jean refused to participate in the siege of Huguenot-held Amiens and was sent to the Bastille. Retired at Sully, Jean wrote his memoires, thereby providing historians with one of the period's most intimate portraits.

In 1716 Pierre de Morey, Marquis de Vianges, acquired Sully and gave the château its beautiful north façade, realized in the Régence style. By virtue of becoming the second husband of the Marquis de Vianges's daughter-in-law, Jean-Baptiste de Mac-Mahon, an Irish medical student in Autun, succeeded as châtelain of Sully. At the Revolution, which was especially destructive in Burgundy, an aged Mme de Mac-Mahon saved Sully in a marvelously macabre way. Whenever officials arrived to confiscate the property, the family claimed their matriarch was too infirm to be disturbed. The ruse was continued even after she had died—by pickling the corpse in alcohol and propping it up in bed each time a threatening knock was heard at the door!

Born at Sully in 1808 was the future Maréchal de Mac-Mahon, who earned the title of Duc de Magenta for his leadership at the battle of that name (1853). After the fall of the imperial government of Napoleon III, the Duc de Magenta also served as the first President of the Third Republic.

above: Built mainly in the second half of the 16th century, but shaped by medieval foundations, Sully is a quadrangular structure completely enclosed by logis on all four sides. Further defenses appear in the wide, encompassing moat and in the tall corner towers, lantern-crowned and diagonally placed.

overleaf: The Age of Elegance came to Sully after 1716, when the Marquis de Vianges bought the château and endowed its north side with the palatial Régence façade seen here. Below the two superimposed rows of tall windows separated by classical pilasters, a monumental flight of steps cascades from the pedimented central bay down to a broad terrace projected into the moat, which here spreads out into a mirror surface wide enough for boating.

Balleroy

A masterpiece of the early 17th century, Balleroy has traditionally been attributed to François Mansart (1596–1666), the greatest architect in the time of Henri IV and Louis XIII and a major formulator of French classicism at the dawn of its golden age. The château is the rural counterpart of that triumph of urban design, the Place des Vosges in Paris—grand without excess, clear, unified, and balanced in its forms and their arrangement, nobly proportioned, yet warmed by coppery-gray masonry and brightened with white stone articulations. At Balleroy the unity and bilateral symmetry of the conception extend even to the dependent village, which was reconstructed on either side of a long entrance *allée* leading straight to the château, placed like the climactic focal point in a vast system of perspective.

Balleroy was built by the Choisy family, which in the 16th century rose from modest origins to become powerful and property-owning in the 17th century. Jean II de Choisy, the son of a wine merchant supplying the court of Henri IV (r. 1518–1610), allowed himself to be checkmated in a chess game and thereby gained the friendship of François d'O, then France's superintendent of finance. Having entered the Marquis's service, Jean II was able, on April 16, 1600, to purchase the small fief of Balleroy for 5,500 *écus*. Jean's next move was to become *conseiller d'état* under Louis XIII and finally chancellor to Monsieur (Gaston d'Orléans, the King's brother). By 1626 he could afford to commission the château, the building of which took ten years, until 1636. Jean also married a high-born lady of the Hurault family. This was Olympe de Bellesbat, who, according to Saint-Simon, was "so ahead in the world and familiar with court intrigues." To the young Louis XIV Mme de Choisy said one day: "Sire, do you wish to become a gentleman? Well then, have conversations with me." The King agreed and paid her a pension of 8,000 *livres* for the regular service he received.

The son of Jean II to inherit Balleroy was the Abbé de Choisy, so infamous for the female attire he preferred—for the access it gave him to ladies' boudoirs!—that he was sent to serve the French ambassador to the King of Siam. In the end the Abbé acquired decorum, becoming an ordained priest, translating Thomas à Kempis's *Imitation of Christ*, writing an eleven-volume history of the Church, and gaining a chair in the French Academy.

In 1700 the Abbé de Choisy sold Balleroy to Françoise de Brancas, Princesse d'Harcourt. The following year Jacques de La Cour, a Choisy cousin and a counselor to Louis XIV, succeeded in exercising the right of lineal repurchase. By 1704 Balleroy had been raised to marquisate.

The second Marquis de Balleroy married a Goyon-Matignon, became first master of the horse to the Duc d'Orléans and then governor for the Duc de Chartres. But in 1744, having managed to incur the displeasure of Louis XV, he went into exile at Balleroy. There the Marquis busied himself with the coal

above: Unity, clarity, balance, and dignity—the very principles of French classicism—received early and triumphant affirmation at Balleroy, a Baroque masterwork with a rural setting in Normandy near Bayeux. Beyond a dry moat, concentric steps prepare the visitor for the absolute centrality and symmetry of the château, a pyramidal mass composed of a tall, three-story pavilion bracketed by lateral pavilions of two stories each. Clarifying the triadic nature of the conception are the lantern and gallery crowning the focal structure, also the dormers in which the middle window of each trio receives the accent of an arched pediment surmounted by a sculptural vase. Typically French are the steep slate roofs, with a separate one for each wing of the main assemblage.

opposite: Although grand and sober, French classicism in its early Baroque phase under Louis XIII was never dry or cold, and this can be appreciated at Balleroy. There a copper tonality warms the gray schist used for the masonry walls, while white Caen stone serves to articulate the noble forms and brighten the whole.

opposite: The main salon at Balleroy retains its decorations from the early 18th century, done in the rich manner of Versailles, including portraits of the French royal family and an allegorical ceiling composition by Pierre Mignard.

below: At Balleroy, even the dependent village was integrated into the overall scheme of a majestic, unified ensemble. Thus, the château is on axis with the only route leading to it, a long, straight *allée* that descends from a rise through the bordering village to a splendid wrought-iron grille, thence along gravel paths and formal gardens, and finally across a dry moat to a platform terrace flanked by a pair of sentry-box gazebos, wittily placed where defensive towers would have risen in medieval times.

pits at Littry and founded a stoneware pottery, an industry that flourishes today. During the Revolution his two sons, both military heroes of the Seven Years War, were arrested on their estate and executed in March, 1794. Their sister, the Comtesse d'Hervilly, escaped only through the devotion of a Dr. Vimard, who rolled her in nettles and pretended she was dangerously ill. Despite confiscation, Mme d'Hervilly managed to regain Balleroy, only to sell it to the Marquis de La Londe, but with a provision of repurchase by her son. Franz de Balleroy made his claim in 1827. In the next generation Albert de Balleroy, a popular figure, was elected deputy for Calvados in the French National Assembly. A painter of animals, he exhibited in the Salons of 1853 and 1864, and counted among his friends Delacroix, Baudelaire, and Manet. The seventh and last Marquis de Balleroy died in 1957, leaving a daughter, Myriam, who in 1964 married Hubert de Bénédic, a godson of Maréchal Lyautey.

In 1971 the Château de Balleroy was acquired by Forbes Investors Advisory Institute, Inc.

Grosbois

Grosbois, as the name should imply, rests upon a large and heavily wooded estate famed for the good hunting and riding it offers only twelve miles from Paris. This accounts for a history extending back to 1226, when Grosbois entered the records as a royal domain. The main mass of the present château, however, began to take form toward the end of the Renaissance, in 1580. It was commissioned by Raoul Moreau, a royal paymaster whose son-in-law, Nicolas de Harlay, Baron de Sancy, sold the property to Charles, Duc d'Angoulême, the hero of the siege of La Rochelle and a bastard son of Charles IX, the penultimate Valois King of France. About 1616, at the time of the Angoulême tenure, the château received its lateral wings, which, with their stepwise projections toward the curiously concave recess of the entrance façade, form a *cour d'honneur* that anticipated the much grander but similar arrangement at Versailles. Charles also redecorated the interior—to celebrate his marriage at age seventy-one to a fresh young woman of twenty-three! An important feature of this program consisted of a cycle of monumental wall paintings for the grand gallery, delightful period works that were rediscovered only in 1910 under several layers of old wallpaper.

After passing through a number of hands—including those of a wigmaker's son who had made a fortune speculating by means of "Law's system"—Grosbois reentered the royal domains when in the late 18th century it was acquired by the Duc de Provence. This was Louis XVI's younger brother who became Louis XVIII once the Bourbon dynasty had recovered the throne in 1815. Meanwhile, following the Revolution, Grosbois was the scene of brilliant and sumptuous life under the Directory and Empire, first during its ownership by the Comte de Barras, a great friend of Joséphine de Beauharnais, and then during the tenure of Alexandre Berthier, Prince de Wagram and one of the Emperor's most valued marshals. The latter filled the château with a complete and still intact collection of period furniture and decorations, including imperial portraits by Gérard, Gros, Prud'hon, and Canova. Only recently Charles de La Tour d'Auvergne, the Prince de Wagram's descendant, sold the estate to the equestrian society that presently owns it.

above: At Grosbois the stepwise projection of the side wings joins with the main façade to form a cour d'honneur *that anticipated the grander but similar arrangement at Versailles. The sense of active, dynamic forms is reinforced by the apse-like recess of the pedimented entrance façade, by the multiplicity of steep slate roofs, and by the way various structural elements are set off through their materials—stone, brick, and pebble-filled mortar. For centuries this courtyard received the great companies of brilliant society who arrived to ride and hunt in Grosbois's game-rich forest.*

opposite: The great gallery at Grosbois received its festive decorations in the second quarter of the 17th century, to celebrate and portray the union of seventy-one-year-old Charles de Valois with his twenty-three-year-old bride. Typical of the Louis XIII period are the ceiling beams exposed and polychromed, like the door panels, with curvilinear cartouches.

below: Guarding the cour d'honneur *at Tanlay are sentries in the form of rusticated obelisks, posted on either side of a narrow bridge leading over a wide, deep moat to a gatehouse designed as a triumphal, two-story arch. Here niches alternate with a colonnade whose Doric entablature supports a steep roof shaped like a truncated pyramid. Most of the greater forms at Tanlay date from 1643–48 and are the work of the court architect Pierre Le Muet. Typically Mannerist is the idiosyncratic handling of the classical vocabulary, as in the transformation of the vertical fluting on Doric columns into the stacks of horizontal rings seen here. Something equally maverick happens in the top two stories of the polygonal stair towers, where the lower windows sink well below the adjacent pilaster bases and the upper ones penetrate the entablature above.*

opposite: Access to the forecourt at Tanlay is gained through the "Petit Château" situated at right angles to the main axis of the great house itself. Commenced in 1568 but completed above the basement only in 1610, the edifice, with its heavily rusticated lower story—done in a technique called* vermicule *("wormy")—and its curious distribution of dentils throughout the pediments and cornice above, recalls the Mannerist phase of the Renaissance introduced at the Palazzo Pitti in Florence.*

Tanlay

Among Burgundy's many fine châteaux, one of the most fascinating and beautiful is Tanlay, a creation of the Louis XIII era in which the quality of ideas, materials, and workmanship remains high at every point. Tanlay is also one of the most civilized places in France, for if this marvelous dwelling remains perfectly intact, while all about the countryside is dotted with the fragments or restorations of former glory, it is thanks to the decency and humanity of the late-18th-century châtelains. Instead of abandoning their estate, as so many of the landed nobility did, either to live at court or to emigrate once the Revolution had broken out, the Marquis and Marquise de Tanlay chose to lead a country life among their peasants. Having been treated with dignity, the latter protected their lords, and then saved them, the château, and all its contents from the wave of destruction that swept across France from 1789 to 1794.

Much that is boldly original can be found at Tanlay, but not in the essentials of its plan and organization. Commenced in 1559–69 but concluded in 1643–48 by the court architect Le Muet, Tanlay rises, in the familiar way, from a quadrangle of medieval foundations. Above ground, it follows the equally familiar U-shape of a centrally placed main block, or *corps de logis*, flanked at right angles by twin subsidiary extensions that advance parallel to one another on either side of a *cour d'honneur*. One-storied and arcaded, the wings terminate in juxtaposed rectangular pavilions and plump cylinder towers capped by lantern domes. Where the *communs* commence, however, novelty too begins to reveal itself, in corner stair towers whose polygonal forms join the lateral service buildings to the main façade. Freshness of vision then becomes dominant in the approach to the château, which leads along an avenue of houses and trees and through a welcoming *petit château* to a green, heavily turfed

right: The most astonishing feature at Tanlay may be a fresco on the vault in the upper chamber of the tower terminating the château's left wing. It dates from the tenure of the Coligny family, who embraced the Reformation and made Tanlay a center of Huguenot worship and politics. The tower is named for the League, because the fresco depicts Jupiter presiding over a scene in which the League, or reactionary Catholic party, is represented as the warlike and licentious court of Catherine de' Medici (with Diane de Poitiers and the Duc de Guise personifying Venus and Mars) and the Huguenots as peaceful and virtuous, led by Admiral de Coligny as Neptune and his brother François d'Andelot as Hercules. The two-faced Janus symbolizes the French crown, smiling at the perfidious court and frowning at the Protestants.

left and *below:* The sheer breadth of the conception at Tanlay makes the château seem as much Baroque as Mannerist. The waterworks designed by Le Muet are extensive, and include not only the wide moat but also the grand canal that takes its "source" from a château d'eau—really a beautifully designed triumphal arch that is blind and flanked by blind arcades. This edifice conceals the storage tower by which Tanlay's waters are kept fresh with supplies from the Quincy and Baon rivers. Reflected in the waters are the château's "flaming grenade" chimney pots and, on the garden side, its double-recessed, pagodalike towers.

forecourt. A sharp turn to the left brings the great house suddenly into full view, guarded, however, by a pair of sentries in the form of rusticated obelisks, by a narrow bridge spanning a wide, deep moat, and ultimately by a two-story gatehouse designed as a triumphal arch. Here a vigorously rusticated, engaged colonnade helps to support a roof shaped like a truncated pyramid. But touches of genius are to be found everywhere, in the virtuoso command of Renaissance stylistics, in the extensive scheme of waterworks, which includes a "grand canal" and a *château d'eau*, and the double lanterns of diminishing scale that make the corner towers on the garden side look like Chinese pagodas. Inside as well, masterful hands show themselves, especially in the grand gallery, where a vast program of sculptural decorations has been carried out entirely in *trompe-l'oeil* painting. For the almost precious nicety of detail and the gloriously idiosyncratic use of the classical vocabulary, Tanlay is a masterpiece of Renaissance Mannerism. But for the largeness of its forms and the breadth and totality of the ensemble, the château belongs among the monuments of the French Early Baroque.

In the 13th and 14th centuries the site at Tanlay was occupied by a fortress under the command of the house of Courtenay, whose feudal lords could claim three Emperors in the Latin East. In 1535 Louise de Montmorency, the sister of the constable of France and widow of Maréchal Gaspard I de Coligny, purchased the domain of Tanlay. Twenty-five years later she gave it to her fourth son, François d'Andelot, who thereupon began to rebuild the dwelling, as well as to construct the large entrance pavilion now called the "Petit Château." Along with his two brothers—Admiral Gaspard de Coligny and Cardinal Odet de Châtillon, Bishop of Beauvais—François d'Andelot converted to Protestantism and became a leader of the Huguenot faction. Indeed, he made Tanlay a center, both political and religious, of the Reformation in France. A memento of the time is the fresco that, in a pure School of Fontainebleau style, decorates the vault of the upper chamber in the tower to the right of the *cour d'honneur*. The structure itself is called the "League Tower" because the painting allegorizes the conflict between, on the one hand, the Protestant forces of virtue and reform and, on the other, the court and the League, seen as joined in vice and war. In 1569, however, all work ceased at Tanlay, for the Wars of Religion had broken out, and François d'Andelot was forced to flee. He perished the same year, in exile at Jarnac. Cardinal de Châtillon sought refuge in England, where he died at Hampton Court in 1571, possibly by poisoning. Admiral de Coligny, having become the real figurehead of the Huguenot cause, was the first to be struck down in Paris on August 24, 1572, in the infamous Saint Bartholomew's Day Massacre.

In 1574 Anne de Coligny, the daughter of François d'Andelot, married Jacques Chabot, Comte de Charny and Marquis de Mirabeau. Eventually Chabot became the King's lieutenant general in Burgundy, and by 1610 he was able to complete the Petit Château, which probably had not risen above the basement level when his father-in-law died.

In 1642 the daughter of the Chabots sold Tanlay to Michel Particelli, seigneur d'Émery and the son of a Lyonnais banker with origins in Italy. During the regimes of Richelieu and Mazarin, Particelli experienced a spectacular rise, beginning as the King's own treasurer and concluding as superintendent of finances. Fabulously wealthy, he could well afford to finish Tanlay in the most sumptuous manner, and it was then that Pierre Le Muet took charge. Beginning in 1643, he endowed the château not only with a triumphal entrance, the water gardens, and the grand gallery, but also with a fine staircase, superb paneling and chimneypieces, a "Hall of Caesars" in the foyer, and a magnificent wrought-iron grille. In 1648, however, Particelli issued ordinances so antagonistic to the Parlement of Paris that they helped to provoke the Fronde, that rebellion of nobles against the royal authority. Particelli then retired, and two years later he was dead. After his son-in-law, Louis Phélypeaux de La Vrillière, became châtelain and then France's secretary of state, the Tanlay fief was elevated to marquisate.

In 1704 Jean Thévenin, governor of the royal abbey at Saint-Denis, bought Tanlay, and it remains the property of his descendants, the Comte and Comtesse de La Chauvinière.

The most spectacular part of the interior at Tanlay is the ground-floor grand gallery, where Italian artists executed a vast program of "sculptural" decorations entirely in trompe-l'oeil *painting, by means of the monochromatic technique known as* grisaille. *Now measuring twenty-six meters, the room was originally still longer, before being damaged by a fire in 1761.*

Pontchartrain

The Château de Pontchartrain took its name from a bridge long located on the route linking Paris and Chartres. This fact serves well to suggest the remarkable harmony of the ensemble at Pontchartrain—a long, low silhouette of a building so integrated with its environment as to seem a perfect abstraction of the lake and hillside forest on either side. The sheer quality of the château's design has given rise to a tradition that attributes the formal conception to the great Louis XIII architect François Mansart (1598–1666). Still, the fame of Pontchartrain is owing less to its beauty than to the residence there of one of the 19th century's most notorious adventuresses—La Païva.

Pontchartrain had thoroughly respectable beginnings. In 1614 Paul Phélypeaux acquired the domain while serving as secretary to Marie de' Medici and then as secretary of state. However, it was his son, France's chief auditor, who put into effect plans thought to be by Mansart, bringing about the totally brick structure with a succession of advancing and receding planes and tall as well as low elevations, all dominated by a precise symmetry. At this time the main or central wing was entered not through a prominent, pedimented bay but by means of an exterior horseshoe stairway. Then under the founder's grandson Louis, now Comte de Pontchartrain, the château gained its park by Le Nôtre and took on what La Bruyère described as a "fine and noble simplicity." As both controller of finances and chancellor, Louis achieved genuine distinction, inspiring Saint-Simon to note: "He was very small and thin, bristling with fire and wit."

Saint-Simon seemed to detest Louis's son Jérôme as cordially as he loved the father, maintaining that the new Comte de Pontchartrain retained royal favor and became naval minister mainly "for the malicious amusement" it created in Paris. At the death of Louis XIV, Jérôme was kept on in the royal council solely "to clean the candles." If worse were possible for the Pontchartrain dynasty, it arrived in the person of Jérôme's son, Jean-Frédéric Phélypeaux, Comte de Maurepas—called *le faquinet* ("the little cad"). Replacing his father at the naval ministry, Maurepas also became, unaccountably, a confidant of Louis XV—until his passion for dangerous foolery ran afoul of Mme de Pompadour. A song, in which he saluted the royal favorite as *petite bourgeoise, élevée à la grivoise, mesurant tout à sa toise,* earned him exile at Pontchartrain in 1749. The estate was the beneficiary, for the Count amused himself by giving the *corps de logis* its central lantern-capped pavilion, which replaced the original double flight of exterior stairs. Maurepas also addressed himself to the interior and the gardens, bringing elegant paneling to the one and the English manner to the other. Then Louis XVI made one of his terrible mistakes and recalled Maurepas to court; he even named the old man prime minister! This did little but teach the luckless monarch to make do without advice.

Upon the death of Maurepas, Pontchartrain went by marriage to the Duc de Brissac, the governor of Paris who died by assassination at Versailles in 1792. Following the Revolution, the estate was owned by the Osmond family. Finally, in the ripest years of the Second Empire, the notorious Païva descended upon Pontchartrain and became its châtelaine. Born Thérèse Lachmann, in Russia of Polish-Jewish parents, this *grande horizontale* set out at age twenty-two to conquer Paris, with her "fatal beauty" as an invincible weapon. After vanquishing Lord Stanley and the Dukes of Gramont and Guiche, she married in 1851 the Portuguese Marquis de Païva. But a great house on the Champs-Elysées seemed inadequate when the immensely rich Prussian Count Henckel von Donnersmark, ten years the courtesan's junior and a cousin to Bismarck, offered Pontchartrain. Redecorating and remodeling lavishly and serving exquisite food, La Païva made Pontchartrain a magnet not only for the "fast set" but also for such intellectuals as Taine, Sainte-Beuve, and Renan. With an avarice equal to her largesse, she set traps—it was said—

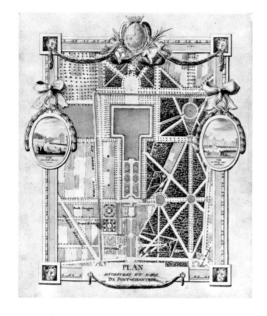

above: A late 18th-century drawing shows the plan of the gardens at Pontchartrain, laid out with the inventive geometry familiar at Versailles and characteristic of Le Nôtre.

opposite: Set against a heavily wooded hillside precisely subdivided by a long, straight allée *typical of Le Nôtre, Pontchartrain becomes the focus of a grand perspective scheme. Viewed from across the large artificial lake, the château takes on a floating quality, as romantic and visionary as it is serene and classical. The great Mansart is credited with the design, consisting of a wide* corps de logis *broken at the center by a lantern-capped, pedimented entrance bay, and flanked successively by tall, narrow pavilions and long, low wings, which finally terminate in small pavilions. Despite its horizontal extension, the façade enjoys perfect success, thanks to a sensitive arrangement of volumes, planes, and elevations, and the submission of all to the strictest centrality and symmetry. An unusual feature is the complete reliance upon brick, even for quoins and window enframements, where stone normally was used in the 17th century.*

for anyone likely to pick a fruit or a flower, imposing heavy fines on those found guilty. After the Franco-Prussian War of 1870, La Païva, now a Prussian Countess, found it expedient to leave France for a no less sumptuous life in Silesia.

Since the splendor of La Païva's reign, Pontchartrain has known some dark moments, but it now survives in the caring hands of Mme Lagasse.

Sceaux

In the early 18th century the Château de Sceaux provided the lavish setting for some of the most frivolous and costly regalements of the *ancien régime*—the "Nights of Sceaux" organized by the Duchesse du Maine. But the greatest folly to beset this magnificent 17th-century ensemble was its wanton destruction, not by the passions of the Revolution, but by the calculating ignorance of a tradesman who bought it in the aftermath of that upheaval. The creative geniuses behind Sceaux were the very ones who also contributed so substantially to the realization of Versailles—the architect Claude Perrault, the painter-decorator Charles Le Brun, the sculptors Coysevox and Girardon, and the landscape designer André Le Nôtre. Furthermore, the sponsoring Maecenas was none other than Jean-Baptiste Colbert, the great statesman who managed France's economy under Louis XIV and thus made it possible for the King to have Versailles. Given these conditions, plus Colbert's eagerness to establish his own country seat, Sceaux could scarcely have been anything but a château and park of supreme quality, indeed a veritable paradigm of French High Baroque classicism. Tragically, all that remains to suggest the actual achievement at Sceaux is the tiny, but perfect, Pavillon de l'Aurore, and the restorers' interpretation of Le Nôtre's park.

When Colbert bought the domain on the outskirts of Paris in 1674, there stood on it a 16th-century revision of a 15th-century manor house. He immediately set about to enlarge and modernize the dwelling. Perrault, the architect in charge, was at the peak of his powers, having just completed his collaboration on the design for the new Louvre's great colonnaded east front, that triumphant formulation of the French Baroque. The plan was the classic one of a central *corps* terminating in lateral pavilions, with subsidiary wings extended to form a *cour d'honneur*. But the styling, with its monumentality, stately proportions, and Greco-Roman vocabulary, all conceived as an integrated

left: The sole fragment to survive from Colbert's great château at Sceaux is the little Pavillon de l'Aurore, which, although small, is a clear demonstration of Perrault's style of architecture: a drum inscribed within a cube, set upon a platform, crowned by a hemispherical dome, extended laterally by two brief wings, and finished on all four sides with a highly simplified temple front. With its monumentality, stately proportions, and classical vocabulary, the Sceaux pavilion is part of a totally integrated ensemble of architecture, painting, sculpture, and landscape environment. The estate now serves Paris as a public park.

ensemble of architecture, painting, sculpture, and landscaped environment, would have swept away whatever lingered of the Gothic traditional to France. Once all was ready, Colbert invited the King, taking care, however, to show a characteristic economy in the festivities, lest he risk the fate of Fouquet at Vaux-le-Vicomte!

After the death of Colbert in 1683, his son, the Marquis de Seignelay and France's naval minister, enlarged the park and added the "grand canal." He also commissioned the *orangerie* from Jules Hardouin-Mansart, an architect much more directly associated with Versailles than Perrault. In 1680 Sceaux was purchased by the Duc du Maine, the legitimized son of Louis XIV and Mme de Montespan. The real occupant of the château, however, was the Duchesse du Maine, as vital and ambitious as she was diminutive in stature. At Sceaux Mme du Maine reigned like a queen, over a realm of the literary and the artistic, with Voltaire as one of the chief courtiers. Unfortunately, the Duchess's "Nights of Sceaux," being overt extravagances, may have created more scandal than entertainment.

The next important châtelain was the Duc de Penthièvre, du Maine's nephew and the heir as well to Anet and Rambouillet, among other estates. This cultivated gentleman also maintained a literary salon. Moreover, he was a person of such natural generosity that during the Revolution he and his properties remained unmolested. Confiscation came, however, after his death in 1793. This resulted in the 1799 sale to M. Lecomte, the commercial vandal who demolished the château and chapel and ploughed up the park. His son-in-law, the Duc de Trévise, proved more civilized and later did what he could to repair the damage. But with the château totally lost, he could only build a new one, a Louis XIII historicizing pastiche typical of the 19th century. The Seine *département* has now bought Sceaux, restored the park as a public garden, and in the Trévise château installed the museum of the Ile-de-France.

above: A precious remnant of Le Brun's vast decorative scheme for Sceaux is the illusionistic scene painted upon the curved interior surface of Perrault's cupola over the Pavillon de l'Aurore. It shows the goddess of dawn "about to illuminate the universe." Like all such works of the period, the painting contains a metaphor, this one subtly flattering Louis XIV, whose sunlike brilliance is being announced by "dawn"—Colbert, France's finance minister and the châtelain of Sceaux. A formula of simplicity within richness, here beautifully displayed, lay at the heart of Le Brun's great success as a 17th-century court painter-decorator.

opposite below: The park at Sceaux, one of the grandest ever designed by Le Nôtre, consists of an ingenious and geometric organization of allées, parterres, a "grand canal," pools on graduated terraces, and basins asplash with fountains and waterfalls. In the winter the large clumps of leafless trees simply emphasize the linear structure and mathematical precision of the design.

As a platformed, moat-cinctured assemblage of pavilions, each with its own separate, steep roof, Vaux-le-
Vicomte adhered to an old and native French tradition.
However, in its pervasive classicism, in the Italianism
of its central, two-story, dome-capped oval salon, and
in the grandeur of the overall conception, which placed
a great mansion as the focus of a vast, integrated system
of park and waterworks, Vaux-le-Vicomte constituted
a harbinger of the brilliant new tradition of French
Baroque classicism. Nicolas Fouquet commissioned the
château, the finest in France outside the royal domains,
from the architect Le Vau, the painter-decorator Le
Brun, and the landscape gardner Le Nôtre. Essentially
unknown when discovered by Fouquet, these young artists accomplished their task in a mere five years—from
1656 to 1661. They then went on to create Versailles
for Louis XIV, who even adopted Vaux's "sun palace"
theme and called himself le roi soleil.

In this portrait of Nicolas Fouquet, Marquis de Belle-Île (1615–80), Sebastien Bourbon captured the intelligence, warmth, and malicious wit of his subject. Along with the finance minister's fine features and sensuous mouth went an eye for talent, taste for beauty and pomp, and the love of pleasing women, poets, and other important persons. Fouquet's charm and generosity continued to dazzle his friends—especially the creative ones, La Fontaine, Mme de Sévigné, Molière, and Madeleine de Scudéry—long after the disgrace at Vaux sentenced him to life imprisonment. Having discovered and put together the team of Le Vau, Le Brun, and Le Nôtre, Fouquet's monument extends beyond Vaux to include Versailles and the whole of French Baroque classicism.

Vaux-le-Vicomte

France's *grand siècle* may have reached maturity at Versailles, but it was born at Vaux-le-Vicomte, sired not by Louis XIV but by his prodigally gifted, and ultimately unwise, superintendent of finances, Nicolas Fouquet. Fouquet had everything—genius for high finance, friends, and women, unfailing taste, a connoisseur's eye for talent, and incredible flair in marshalling all these assets into a brilliant spectacle. To give scope to his capacities, Fouquet made up a domain from land originally occupied by several villages in an area south of Paris, on the right bank of the Seine opposite the Forest of Fontainebleau. There he set to work legions of men and animals whose task it was to clear away the old settlements—one of which was called Vaux-le-Vicomte—fill in the valleys, and level the hills until the terrain had been made as flat as a drafting board. Here would be prepared an ideal order to supplant the randomness of nature. And those who would accomplish this were Louis Le Vau for the *maison de plaisance*—as Fouquet called his great country mansion—and André Le Nôtre for the immense surrounding spread of park and waterworks. For the interior Fouquet discovered the painter-decorator Charles Le Brun, and, to make sure the young master did his best, set him up with a complete atelier and staff in the nearby village of Maincy. What these artists achieved at Vaux is probably the finest French château outside the royal domains. Incredibly, it took only five years, from 1656 to 1661.

The dwelling and its *cour d'honneur* rest upon a high stone platform whose base is bathed on three sides by the waters of a moat. U-shaped and broken up into pavilions, with their roofs, French fashion, reflecting the divisions, the château is nonetheless wonderfully unified by its monumental compactness as well as by the consistency and sophistication of the Renaissance-classical styling. It is also pulled into centrality and symmetry by the vast lantern dome that hovers over the oval space of a two-story grand salon, from which the whole of the interior takes its organization. All about, the garden was laid out in the box hedges and *parterres* traditional since the Renaissance, but vastly extended by geometry into vistas of trees and canals, and enlivened by statues, plots planted *en broderie*, and ponds as well as jets and fountains of an incredible invention and variety. When all was ready on the interior, Le Brun had combined virtually every visual art practiced at the time—painting, sculpture, tapestry, stucco, gilding, cabinetmaking—to create a total ensemble whose richness, grandeur, and harmony constituted the definitive formulation of French classicism in its High Baroque phase.

Altogether, Vaux-le-Vicomte was fit for a king, and Fouquet invited Louis XIV, along with leading members of the royal family and court, to attend the inaugural celebration scheduled for August 17, 1661. Having saved La Fon-

125

taine, the fabulist, from drink, Fouquet could call upon him for a tribute in verse. Molière too was there, with a new comedy, *Les Fâcheux,* commissioned for the occasion and performed by his troupe on an open-air stage set up before a curtain of water. A ballet was danced, and a concert given by Lully and his twenty-four violins. The dinner, prepared by M. Vatel, then France's most besought chef, came forth in dishes of gleaming vermeil. Mme de Sévigné and the novelist Madeleine de Scudéry attended the banquet, and in the opinion of La Fontaine, "Vaux would never be more beautiful." The evening concluded with fireworks—some four hundred exploding like *fleur-de-lis,* others arranged to sail in the form of a galleon on the "grand canal," and, at the climax, a burst of flames all over the château's dome. The royal suite, to the right of the entrance, had been made ready for the King's rest that night. But before Louis could retire to it, he stormed away from Vaux-le-Vicomte, outraged that a subject, however highly placed, had dared to appear so rich and clever as to outshine the monarch himself. Nineteen days later, at Nantes, Fouquet was arrested on charges of embezzlement. He never saw Vaux-le-Vicomte again.

Fouquet's spectacular advancement had been made possible by Mazarin, who, as prime minister of France during Louis XIV's minority, was grateful for the younger man's loyalty at the time of the Fronde crisis. But once the old Cardinal was dead, Colbert, his successor, saw Fouquet as a rival in the struggle for power under the new regime. Thus, he had prepared Louis to see Fouquet's ostentation as an affront to both taste and morals. Not until 1664 was the disgraced minister brought to trial, and although little evidence could be produced to incriminate him, Fouquet was imprisoned for life at Pignerol. The court put seals on the château, while Louis seized a number of art works and the entire team who had created the dazzling success of Vaux-le-Vicomte. Le Brun's studio at Maincy was moved to Paris and expanded into the famed Gobelins tapestry works. And the next assignment for Le Vau, Le Brun, Le Nôtre, and the sculptor Girardon would be to envelop Louis XIV in the same kind of gloriole that they had prepared for Fouquet. What they produced was Versailles, calling it the "Palace of the Sun" for *le roi soleil.* Even the solar theme came from Fouquet, for it was in these terms that Mlle de Scudéry had characterized Vaux in her novel *Clélie.* Fouquet's unique éclat was long remembered and memorialized. After watching from a window as the accused was being returned to the Bastille in the course of his trial, Mme de Sévigné wrote: "My legs trembled, and my heart was pounding until I could bear it no more." Finally, Louis's most enduring favorite came from Vaux—Mme de Maintenon, who, before becoming the King's second, but morganatic wife, had been married to the poet-actor Scarron, a member of Molière's troupe. Mme Scarron in particular benefitted from the Fouquets' love and patronage of the theatre.

Only in 1673 did Louis XIV allow Mme Fouquet to repurchase Vaux with her own personal fortune. But when her son, the Comte de Vaux, died childless in 1705, she sold the estate to the Duc de Villars, Marshal of France. Although calling the domain Vaux-Villars, he considered it "too beautiful and . . . expensive. . . . Too many waterfalls and fountains." He also seemed to find his wife—a good twenty-two years younger—too attractive for his comfort, and possibly too literary and social, for now Voltaire and Fontanelle became regular guests. But in 1731 Louis XV arrived to view the Marshal's paintings of battle scenes.

In 1763 the Villars's son sold Vaux to César-Gabriel de Choiseul, Duc de Praslin, which resulted in a new name for the château—Vaux-Praslin. In keeping with the 18th century's taste for intimacy, the Duc de Praslin subdivided some of Vaux's large rooms into smaller suites. Although untouched by the Revolution, Vaux survived without extensive or severe damage. However, tragedy and scandal came in 1847 when Duc Théobald de Praslin committed suicide after murdering his wife in their Paris town house. Abandoned for almost thirty-one years, the château and park were in poor condition when bought in 1875 by M. Alfred Sommier. The Sommiers carefully restored the entire domain, including its original name—Vaux-le-Vicomte. It is now maintained by Comte Patrice de Vogüé.

At Vaux-le-Vicomte the great house, its moats, and the surrounding park and waterworks all come together to form a scheme of grandiose, ideal coherence. The conception climaxed at Versailles but dominated the design of French châteaux as long as they were built. It placed a classical monument at the center of a precise and geometrical layout of paths and trees, all aligned in vastly extended vistas and perspectives separated by boxwood parterres and plantings en broderie. While sheet ponds, canals, basins, falls, and fountains brightened this perfected realm, statuary humanized it. The great success of Vaux meant that the achievement transcended its immediate purposes and came to seem a materialization of some universal dream of happiness, an experience in which aspiration might soar without ever exceeding the bounds of decorum. The artistic, mathematical, and engineering genius who created the gardens at Vaux was André Le Nôtre (1613–1700).

left: The most lavish of Le Brun's decorations at Vaux-le-Vicomte were reserved for the royal suite—where the outraged Louis XIV refused to sleep. Above a cornice embellished with squirrel motifs the ceiling seems almost to burst with its wealth of classical imagery, all executed in gilded stucco reliefs and trompe-l'oeil *painting. Le Brun himself would have produced the paintings, but the stucco work probably came from the hand of the sculptor Girardon—like Le Brun, Le Vau, and Le Nôtre, soon to be fully employed at Versailles.*

below: The central feature around which all else at Vaux was organized is the huge salon located under the great dome and just behind the château's garden façade. The conception here is Italian—oval in shape, two stories high, and articulated throughout in the language of classicism. Dividing the ground-floor level are bays marked by composite pilasters and opened by keystone arches, which become windows on the park side and mirrors on the interior side. At the second level, above the entablature, the bays are signaled by stucco caryatids personifying the twelve signs of the zodiac. The busts of the Caesars atop the tall column-plinths are 17th-century copies that once adorned Prince Napoleon's "Pompeiian" villa. Upon the surface of the salon's crowning cupola, Le Brun was to have executed a fresco depicting the realm of Apollo the sun god. Instead, the idea went to Louis XIV and the gallerie des glaces at Versailles, once the King had imprisoned Fouquet for alleged embezzlement of public funds.*

Saint-Fargeau

Saint-Fargeau is the most important château of Burgundy's Puisaye district, a rose and white pentagonal structure of large Baroque forms, blue-slate roofs, and lantern crowns set off by an exceedingly fresh and leafy landscape. Although devoid of the stylistic unity and equilibrium of design seen at neighboring Tanlay and Ancy-le-Franc, Saint-Fargeau is a more historic château, an edifice whose disparate elements were compounded into compelling beauty and coherence by the great Louis Le Vau—the author of Vaux-le-Vicomte and Versailles itself. That Louis XIV's own architect would venture into the provinces is explained by the presence in Burgundy of La Grande Mademoiselle, the King's first cousin and one of the age's most commanding personalities. A lady in love with high adventure—a so-called *amazone*—La Grande Mademoiselle had suffered rustication for having joined the Fronde rebellion (1648–53)—indeed, for having personally fired the Bastille's cannon upon a contingent of royal troops! If she could not live at court, which she adored, then La Grande Mademoiselle would create her own court and a setting suitable to it. And the life that developed at Saint-Fargeau was brilliant, for the châtelaine had the genius not only to lure Le Vau away from the Île-de-France but also to discover among her minions a musician destined for glory—Jean-Baptiste Lully.

The site of Saint-Fargeau was first settled in 900 by relatives of Hugues Capet. The family bearing the name Saint-Fargeau arrived in the 13th century and remained until marriage conveyed the estate to Thibaud, Comte de Bar. In 1450 the Bar heirs sold Saint-Fargeau to Jacques Coeur, the great merchant prince and banker of Bourges who financed France in its struggle against England during the Hundred Years War. But scarcely had Coeur been able to complete the largest of Saint-Fargeau's six fat towers when, in 1453, he was arrested and stripped of all possessions by his principal debtor, Charles VII. The domain then went to Antoine de Chabannes, who, after serving with Joan of Arc, became the King's chief prosecutor against Jacques Coeur. Under Chabannes, the reconstruction of Saint-Fargeau continued until the château gained its present plan and overall shape.

By 1575 Saint-Fargeau had passed to François de Bourbon, Duc de Montpensier, for whom the fief itself was made a duchy. François's granddaughter, Marie, Duchesse de Montpensier, married Gaston d'Orléans, the brilliant and restless brother of Louis XIII. The indulged child of this union was La Grande Mademoiselle, the Mlle de Montpensier of song and legend. But when the great lady arrived in Burgundy to commence her exile she found Saint-Fargeau in a parlous state—the bridge broken, the doors and windowpanes gone, and grass knee-high in the courtyard. Always great of heart, Mademoiselle suffered further royal displeasure in order to remain constant in her devotion to the would-be military hero Antonin, Duc de Lauzun. In 1681 she even gave Saint-Fargeau to Lauzun, who retained it after their quarrel and separation in 1684. Lauzun remained châtelain of Saint-Fargeau until 1714, when he sold it to that great financier and Maecenas of the arts, Antoine Crozat. A year later Crozat sold the estate to the parlementarian Michel-Robert Le Peletier des Forts. A fire in 1752 made it necessary to rebuild one wing, unfortunately in a rudimentary manner totally unrelated to the design of Le Vau. After 1778 the châtelain was Louis-Michel Le Peletier, who followed family tradition and entered the Parlement of Paris. Elected to the Revolutionary Convention, he voted on January 19, 1793, for the death of Louis XVI, only to be assassinated the next day while dining in a restaurant in the Palais Royal. This made him a hero-martyr of the Revolution. But after the tide turned against Robespierre and his Reign of Terror, Le Peletier's body was shifted from the Paris Pantheon to the chapel at Saint-Fargeau. Jacques-Louis David memorialized Le Peletier in a celebrated posthumous portrait, which, once peace returned, the regicide's daugher bought and suppressed, some say by immuring the canvas in the walls of Saint-Fargeau.

Saint-Fargeau's highly irregular plan, generally pentagonal in shape with fat round towers defending every corner, was in part established as early as the 10th century. Reconstruction leading to the present ensemble commenced in the 15th century, under Jacques Coeur, the great banker of Bourges who financed the French cause in the Hundred Years War. From this campaign dates the heaviest of the towers, which measures no less than thirty-six meters in diameter. Saint-Fargeau's great beauty—its pink and white coloration, the wall summit that is continuous from tower to logis, the splendid façades of the interior court, the elegance of the tall lanterns crowning the towers—came in the 17th century from designs prepared by Louis Le Vau, the architect of Vaux-le-Vicomte and Versailles. The châtelaine powerful enough to commission such a master was La Grande Mademoiselle, first cousin to Louis XIV. From 1809 dates the green and leafy park, laid out in the informal English manner.

opposite: *In marked contrast to the heavy double towers of Saint-Fargeau's entrance châtelet, which dates from the mid-15th century, is the Baroque grace of the interior court executed in the 17th century from designs prepared by Louis Le Vau. The glory of this work is the drum-shaped, projecting vestibule placed at the corner juncture of two of the château's main wings. Preceded by a circular flight of steps and crowned by a lantern dome, the vestibule is felicitously integrated with the adjacent façades through its rose-white coloration and its arcaded bays marked off at the attic level by square windows alternating with stone reliefs. Originally these plaques bore the arms of Louis XIV's rebellious cousin, La Grande Mademoiselle.*

below: Much mutilated during and after the Revolution, and with its two wings joined by a dome-capped pavilion that was commenced in the 17th century but not completed until the 19th, the Château de Luzun enjoys a fame more by reflection from the Paris exploits of its 17th-century châtelain—the somewhat notorious Duc de Lauzun—than by virtue of its architecture. The latter, however, is beautifully Flamboyant Gothic in the left logis and octagonal stair tower and classically Renaissance in the facing structure.

opposite: Born at Lauzun in 1633 was Antonin-Nompar de Caumont, later famed as the Duc de Lauzun, whose ambitions for a great military career were destined to be pursued more in the boudoir than on the battlefield. About sixty years old in this portrait, Lauzun wears the Order of the Garter, bestowed upon him by James II in gratitude for the Duke's service in escorting the Stuarts out of England at the climax of the Glorious Revolution. A hectic life at court allowed the Duke little time at Lauzun.

Lauzun

Built in the Aquitaine by an ancient family—the Caumonts—Lauzun boasts a Gothic wing with stair tower and a Renaissance wing, both of them fine, as well as a series of splendid, monumental fireplaces composed of marble columns, friezes richly carved in relief, and classical caryatids. The château's greatest fame, however, derives from the 17th-century career of a younger son of the house—Antonin-Nompar de Caumont, Duc de Lauzun—whose attempts to rise at court and win an army command occurred more often in the boudoir than on the battlefield, making him the great hero of gossip mongers in the time of Louis XIV.

The Caumonts were at Lauzun from the outset of the 13th century, claiming ancestry in a companion of that mythical man of strength, Hercules. The family earned the additional name of Nompar, meaning *nonpareil* ("without equal"), after 1160, when Richard de Caumont vanquished a pair of widely feared giants, Estulagas and Golias. At the end of the 13th century, Anissant II de Caumont married Jeanne d'Albret, from one of the region's most powerful families. Meanwhile, Jean-Adam-Nompar took as wife Jeanne de Goth, the presumed daughter of Bertrand de Goth, who became Clement V and the first

The glory of Lauzun is its white stone fireplaces, all magnificent architectural assemblages, classical in style, richly carved, and lavishly encrusted with colored marbles. They are attributed to Pierre Souffron, the 17th-century architect of the choir of Auch Cathedral. The fireplace in the guardroom **(below)** *is composed of two stories of alternate black and white marble colonettes. Above, the vertical members enframe a cross motif and support a rinceau frieze of sumptuous complication. In the "royal chamber"* **(opposite)** *the colonettes are supplemented by canephores and majestic female statues. The subject of the 18th-century painting on the wall is "The Presentation in the Temple."*

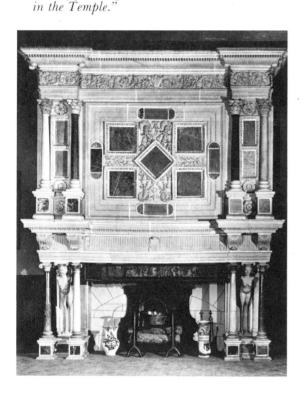

Pope to reside at Avignon. In 1565, while on a royal progress through France, Charles IX stayed at Lauzun and dubbed François-Nompar de Caumont Comte de Lauzun. Eleven years later another royal caller was Henri de Navarre, the future Henri IV of France.

So eventful was the life of the gentleman who became Duc de Lauzun that only a few of the more sensational exploits could be touched upon in a brief account, all of them recorded by the subject's brother-in-law, that irascible but compulsive chronicler of Louis XIV's reign, the Duc de Saint-Simon. Born at Lauzun in 1633, Antonin-Nompar de Caumont was sent to Paris as a youngster to make his way under the patronage of a relative, the Maréchal de Gramont. As the Marquis de Puyguilhem, the youthful aspirant excelled in both horsemanship and the handling of arms. Introduced at court, he soon made himself noticed by the slightly younger Louis XIV, who provided commissions and even promised a major command. But when this prize failed to materialize, Antonin-Nompar undertook a desperate—indeed mad—effort to discover why. First he engaged the interest of Mme de Montespan, the King's mistress, and then went much further. By seducing La Montespan's personal maid, he gained access to the favorite's private chambers and hid under the bed, where he overheard all—including the revelations of the enmity borne him by Louvois, the King's first minister. Hours later, in the light of day, Antonin-Nompar violently confronted first the Marquise and then the King and so shocked them with his seemingly clairvoyant knowledge of the situation that he ended up in the Bastille. Incredibly, a month later he was free and named, among other things, governor of Berry and commandant of the King's own household!

In 1670 Antonin-Nompar became the object of a blazing passion on the part of La Grande Mademoiselle, the first cousin of Louis XIV who had refused the hands of half the monarchs of Europe. When the King granted permission for the couple to marry, Mademoiselle immediately made over the greater part of her estate to Antonin-Nompar. But Louis, shaken by the court's scandalized reaction, withdrew permission and once again sent Antonin-Nompar to prison. Only in 1681 did La Grande Mademoiselle succeed in gaining her lover's release, at the cost to her of the benefits originally granted to Antonin-Nompar but now reassigned to the Duc du Maine, the King's favorite son, whose mother was Mme de Montespan.

It was at this time that the Marquis de Puyguilhem returned to Lauzun for his first visit since childhood, remaining there only a few days but long enough to commission a start on the château's connecting pavilion. It was also about this time that he and La Grande Mademoiselle seem to have married secretly, only to quarrel, over his infidelity and her jealousy, and finally to separate in 1684.

Available for service, Antonin-Nompar rendered it to the crown in 1688, when James II and his family needed an escort out of England at the climax of the Glorious Revolution. In 1689–90 the hero commanded the Stuarts' Irish expedition that ended in disgraceful failure at the Battle of the Boyne. No matter, Antonin-Nompar de Caumont was made Duc de Lauzun in 1692. A year later La Grande Mademoiselle died, bringing her estranged husband to an unexpected display of genuine grief.

Still ambitious, the sixty-three-year-old Lauzun married the fifteen-year-old daughter of Maréchal de Quintin, in the hope of succeeding to his father-in-law's army command. The marriage failed, in that Lauzun never did gain the King's favor but lived another twenty-eight years, growing more difficult and cynical all the while that his child wife had assumed she might quickly become a wealthy young widow.

At the death of Lauzun in 1723 the ancestral estate went to the husband of his sister, Charles-Armand de Gontau, Duc de Biron. Both this châtelain and the next, his son, received the baton of a marshal. Succeeding them at Lauzun was a nephew, the "beau Lauzun" who recovered the status of duchy for his estate. When the Revolution conveyed "beau Lauzun" to the guillotine, his father, the Duc de Gontau, inherited the château. In 1805 his heir sold the property to Jean-Nicolas Becquey-Beaupré, who demolished the crumbling *donjon.* Restoration commenced after 1837, when August Charrié acquired Lauzun. Following a new period of neglect, the Château de Lauzun found a caring owner in Comte de Folchi de Lattre and sustained a new restoration.

Le Champ-de-Bataille

Le Champ-de-Bataille takes its name from an epic contest that, according to tradition, occurred on this site in 935, between the army of Riouf, Comte de Cotentin, and that—numbering 40,000 knights—of Guillaume Longue Épée (William Longsword). The confrontation came about as William struggled to gain control of the entire territory granted in 907 to his father, Rollo, by Charles the Simple. William would win and thus consolidate a region that became the province of Normandy. However, the victory at Le Champ-de-Bataille was made possible by the military leadership of Bernard the Dane, who founded the Harcourt line of dukes. This clan still holds Le Champ-de-Bataille, and in 1966 its members gathered there to celebrate the first millennium of their family.

For all the antiquity of the family owning Le Champ-de-Bataille, the present château did not rise until 1686–1701, and then from the design of an architect whose identity has never been established. By that time the estate had passed, by way of numerous marriages, to the Comte de Créqui. The château this lord commissioned is one of the most thoroughly Baroque and strikingly original in all of France, made so mainly by the arrangement of the *communs* or utility buildings. Rather than form twin subordinate wings flanking the *corps de logis*, the secondary structures come together on a single axis to make one long building that all but duplicates the main dwelling, brick for brick and stone for stone. Aligned in parallel order, the two structures are like mirror reflections of one another, each a full forty-eight meters long, with the dependent one distinguishable only by slightly less rich embellishment. Linking the pair are an iron grille at one end and a stone and brick wall at the other, resulting in an enclosure that, by its resemblance to a garrison, seems an evocation of the site's ancient military past.

The château at Le Champ-de-Bataille had scarcely been completed when the Comte de Créqui died, leaving the estate to his nephew, the Marquis de Mailloc, whose wife was Lydie d'Harcourt, sister of the Duc d'Harcourt, governor of Normandy and marshal of France. When the Maillocs died childless in 1750, Le Champ-de-Bataille passed to the Countess's nephew by marriage,

below: Le Champ-de-Bataille is unique among French châteaux for the strongly Baroque quality of its forms and for the curious relationship of the main and subsidiary buildings, which are almost mirrorlike duplications of one another on opposite sides of the cour d'honneur. *The* corps de logis *is distinguishable, however, by its slightly richer embellishments, which include a grillework balcony and, on the exterior façade, busts mounted on consoles in the manner of Versailles. The game-rich forests of Normandy spread about the château on all sides.*

right below: At Le Champ-de-Bataille both the main logis *and its mirrorlike* communs *are brick and stone structures whose great length and strict symmetry are saved from monotony by the rhythmic placement of the component elements. At the center of each rises a tall, narrow pavilion that supports both round and triangular pediments and a square dome with crowning lantern. Terminating the ends are low, broad, projecting pavilions whose outside corners sprout decorative pepper-pot watchtowers. On the side of the main approach a balustraded wall, penetrated at the center by a triumphal arch, links the twin châteaux. On the opposite side the enclosure is completed by a grillework fence. There the gate has the interesting form of a broken arch lightened by corner niches and decorated with Doric pilasters and personifications of the Four Elements.*

Anne-François d'Harcourt, Duc de Beuvron and brother of the third Duc d'Harcourt. The new châtelain had married the daughter of the Comte de Jouy, who was minister for the navy and then foreign minister under Louis XV. But in his own right the Duc de Beuvron succeeded in a career that made him lieutenant general of the King's armies and governor of Normandy. A great amateur of the theatre, he built a performance hall in the *communs*, some remains of which have survived.

The Beuvrons abandoned Le Champ-de-Bataille during the Revolution, when it was sacked, and then sold the domain to the Comte de Vieux. After several subsequent sales, the property was acquired in 1903 by the Comte d'Harcourt, a descendant of the Duc de Beuvron and uncle of the present Duc d'Harcourt. This tenure lasted until 1936, when, following a new sale, the château entered a difficult period. First it became a home for the elderly of the town of Neubourg, and then, at the time of the Liberation, a prison. What remained was abandoned in 1947. Finally, a year later, the Duc d'Harcourt repossessed the estate through an arrangement whereby Le Champ-de-Bataille became compensation for the Château d'Harcourt in Calvados, which had been destroyed in 1944. Since that time the twin buildings, the enclosure, and the grounds have been systematically and completely restored, and the interiors of the *corps de logis* invested with a magnificent collection of historic furniture, objets d'art, paintings by such major masters as Fragonard, and important memorabilia.

below left: A major painting long in the Harcourt collection is Fragonard's portrait of the third Duc d'Harcourt, represented as a member of the Italian comedy.

below right: Le Champ-de-Bataille's main floor vestibule was redesigned in the late 18th century to have a noble, antique simplicity. It makes a pure and monumental setting for a choice set of 17th- and 18th-century furnishings.

Vayres

The grand salon at Vayres boasts a fine French beam ceiling, mullioned windows with deep embrasures, and a monumental stone fireplace dating from the late 16th century. Some of the Louis XV furniture even retains its original tapestry covering. In the château's main vestibule the portals are structured with moldings of a massiveness to evoke the forms of a Baroque alterpiece.

There is something of the fabulous and the fantastic about Vayres, an amalgam of disparate stylistic parts that, in defiance of all logic, fit together and achieve a harmony as real as it is original. Grandly sited upon a terraced promontory overlooking the Dordogne River, Vayres is pure symmetry on its river façade and total asymmetry on the side of the *cour d'honneur*. But from every approach it displays the combination of ancient, medieval, Renaissance, and Baroque elements that, by some marvelous chemistry of genius, have been combined to give the Gironde district its most sumptuous and anachronistic château.

The lords of Vayres appear in records dating back to the 11th and 12th centuries, and the stronghold had great importance during the Middle Ages, when the King of England was the Duke of Aquitaine, much resenting his vassalage to the King of France. In 1287 the domain passed to the Albrets of Gascony, who in 1326 allowed Edward II of England to strengthen the fortifications at Vayres. The Hundred Years War, however, left the château in a ruined state, which prompted Henri de Navarre—an Albret-Valois on his mother's side, a Bourbon on his father's side, and the future Henri IV of France—to sell Vayres to Ogier de Gourgues, Bordeaux's minister of finance. The châtelain immediately undertook a vast new campaign of construction, placing the project under the supervision of Louis de Foix, one of the greatest builders at work during the French Renaissance. While retaining the medieval structures on the right side of the *cour d'honneur*, he lightened them with Renaissance windows crowned by classical, triangular pediments. At the front of the court appeared a wall penetrated by three monumental, Italianized portals. On the left side, however, Louis designed a new *corps de logis* and in it made such free and monumental use of the Greco-Roman vocabulary as to place Vayres in the vanguard of the emerging Baroque style.

Destructive hands again set upon Vayres in the mid-17th century, when Marc-Antoine de Gourgues, Baron de Vayres and president of the Bordeaux parlement, joined the Fronde against the crown during the minority of Louis XIV. Not until 1695 did reconstruction begin, sponsored by Jacques-Joseph de Gourgue, Bishop of Bazas. Now Vayres received its beautiful, somewhat Palladian-style front with its cascading steps down the terraced slope to the river's edge. The Gourgue family held the estate until 1905. But it is the present owners, M. and Mme Paul Dubost, who are responsible for the splendid *parterres* laid out and planted on the garden side.

left: From the portico at Vayres, where certain of the column drums have been carved in the vermicule ("wormy") manner of the Late Renaissance, the terraced garden descends to the very banks of the Dordogne River. Although the parterres have been reconstituted by the present owners, the yew trees and the design date from the 17th century.

below: On its river façade Vayres would seem to belong more to the Brenta in northern Italy than to the Dordogne in southwestern France, so Palladian Renaissance or Baroque do the forms and their organization seem. The Middle Ages linger in the fortresslike platform and in the crenellated parapet crowning the main mass of the building. Meanwhile, classicism of a liberated, Baroque order expresses itself in the balustrades, pediments, and colonnaded portico, in the domed and lantern-topped central pavilion, and, most of all, in the fantastic, double-ramp, alternately angular and hemicyclical stairs that ascend to the château, terrace by terrace.

Bussy-Rabutin

From the exterior the Château de Bussy-Rabutin is sobriety itself—a moat-cinctured complex of medieval towers connected by Renaissance-Baroque wings that form a courtyard open on one side to a park spread out in the carpetlike manner of Le Nôtre. Scarcely could this harmonious ensemble suggest that within reigns the impertinent spirit of one of the 17th century's most notorious scapegraces. The family and fief of Bussy go back to distant and obscure origins in the Middle Ages, but the château that survives acquired its fame from Roger de Rabutin, Comte de Bussy, who, born in 1618, could count among his relations Mme de Sévigné and the lords of Sully. A respected military man and ultimately an academician, Comte Roger is best known for his libertine ways and for his attempts to relieve tedium at Versailles with scandalous tale-telling, an activity that first earned the amusement of Louis XIV and then a long life of exile from a court that he actually adored.

At age twenty Comte Roger became suddenly fashionable by creating just the sort of stir that could titillate a bored, high-born world. Quite simply the young man abducted the woman he loved—Mme de Miramion, a widow as noted for her piety as for her wealth and beauty. To make matters worse, the abduction took place with the aid of the loved one's own confessor, a priest who, in exchange for a handsome settlement, had persuaded the grandee that Mme de Miramion fully consented to the plot as the best means of achieving a marriage that her family would be certain to oppose. When the lady's screaming resistance made it evident he had been duped, Comte Roger proved gallant and returned his victim to her home. After paying a heavy fine, he married Louise de Rouville, while Mme de Miramion became known as the "mother of the Church," for her charitable work among the poor and the sick.

In his military career, Comte Roger gained distinction as a trusted friend of the great Condé, taking part in several of the major sieges of the Thirty Years War. But during the Fronde (1648–53)—a revolt of nobles led by Condé against royal authority during the minority of Louis XIV—Comte Roger remained faithful to the monarchy, only to dissipate the favor he enjoyed by irreverent roistering in the course of Holy Week. This resulted in his first retirement to the château in Burgundy, where he entertained himself and his mistress, Mme de Montglas, by writing the infamous *Histoire amoureuse des gaules,* a satiric account of erotic infidelities among the well-known courtiers then alive—and active—at Versailles. Meant to be circulated and enjoyed privately, the manuscript found its way to Holland and finally to publication. This precipitated an immense scandal and caused one outraged victim—the Prince de Condé himself—to commission another pamphlet, from a professional poison pen, that would seem to be also by Comte Roger, and that this time would embarrass none other than the King in his affair with Mlle de La Vallière. The ruse succeeded, transforming what had been royal amusement into official wrath and bringing a thirteen-month sojourn in the Bastille for Comte Roger and then some fifteen years of exile at the Château de Bussy.

The château in its present form can be traced back to the early 16th century, when it was rebuilt by the descendants of Agnès de Châtillon, who through marriage conveyed the estate to Pierre de Rochefort, also known by the name Chandio. Thanks to Antoine de Rochefort, who accompanied Seigneur de Bayard in the Franch campaign to dominate Italy in rivalry with Spain, the Renaissance came almost as early to Bussy as it did to the royal estates along the Loire. Having demolished one of the four sides of the square *enceinte,* so as to provide access from the *cour d'honneur* to the park, Antoine de Rochefort then opened the lateral wings at the ground level. There he built facing arcaded galleries, whose upper walls sculptors embellished with reliefs designed with all the freshness of France's Early Renaissance. In 1592 the château, although far from complete, was dignified by a visit from Henri IV, but only a few years later René de Chandio found himself forced to give the estate to one of his debtors, François de Rabutin, Baron de Vaulx et d'Épiry.

opposite: *Long the possession of the Rabutin family, which could trace its origins to the 12th century, the Château de Bussy-Rabutin acquired its present defenses—a cincturing moat and four cylindrical, corner towers—in the 15th century. Linking the towers are two lateral wings, built soon after the arrival of the Renaissance in France, and a main, central wing (above) whose sober weight and mass reflect the Baroque style current when construction was undertaken in the second quarter of the 17th century. The design of the surrounding park is thought—by virtue of its long vistas and ordered patterns—to have come from André Le Nôtre. The interior décor, the park, and the completion of the château itself were all supervised by Comte Roger de Rabutin, more famous for his scandal-mongering than for his military service during the Thirty Years War, or for the distinguished writing that brought him a chair in the French Academy.*

The new owner razed the old keep and replaced it with the central or main wing, the façade of which was not completed until 1649, now in a style touched by the emerging Baroque. The decoration of the interiors, as we know them, became the obsession of the exiled Roger de Rabutin, the grandson of Comte François. His scheme consisted mainly of arranging some three hundred pictures like panels in serried ranks, tier upon tier, the full height of the walls. In the Salon des Grands Hommes are portraits of major military leaders; in the Salle des Devises a collection of views of the royal residences. In his own room (curiously named for Mme de Sévigné, who stayed at Bussy, but probably not in this particular space) the ever-robust Roger surrounded himself with the portraits of some twenty-six comely women, many among them courtesans. The most notable of the interiors is the Tour Dorée located in one of the original defensive towers. Here, Roger installed the images—in paintings claimed by the Count to have been affectionate gifts from their subjects—of the most beautiful ladies at the court of Louis XIV. Once again acceding to the allure of irony, Comte Roger inscribed the frames with legends suggesting the contrast of character that lay behind each of these aloof and stately poses.

The chapel at Bussy, which also fills one of the château's four corner towers, was the scene of a clandestine marriage in 1681 between the Marquise de Coigny, the beloved daughter-companion of Comte Roger, and a charming but impecunious adventurer who concealed a very common, even shady, past under the title of Henri-François de La Rivière. Comte Roger, shaken with rage, sought legally to dissolve what he considered an irregular and unfit alliance, pursuing the case to such lengths that his parental concern won the admiration of the formerly offended Louis XIV. These misadventures brought from Comte Roger another book, *Discours à ses enfants*. But before dying at Bussy, the author also produced a set of *Mémoires*, the *Histoire abrégée de Louis le Grand*, and a prolific correspondence, much of it with that great mistress of the epistle, his cousin Mme de Sévigné.

In 1733 the children of Comte Roger sold Bussy, causing the property to pass through a number of hands until 1929, when the state acquired it.

opposite: Exiled from the court of Louis XIV, Comte Roger de Bussy-Rabutin used his time of rustication in Burgundy to decorate the interior of the family château. His scheme was an intensely personal one, and nowhere is this more evident than in the Tour Dorée, a drum-shaped room fitted out in one of the corner towers with paintings aligned in serried ranks, tier upon tier, from floor to ceiling. Accompanying the images, mainly portraits of handsome, sumptuously dressed ladies, are rather surprising legends inscribed upon the gilded frames. One inscription reads thus: "The most beautiful woman of her time, but less famous for her beauty than for the use she made of it."

below: In 1520 Antoine de Rochefort commenced to rebuild the Château de Bussy in emulation of the Renaissance he had learned to love during his participation in France's Italian campaigns. After demolishing one side of the quadrilateral enceinte, to open the cour d'honneur to the surrounding park, he had the lateral wings penetrated by open, flattened arcades at the ground level and the upper surfaces covered with classical motifs rendered in sculptural relief.

Dampierre

above: Designed by Le Nôtre, the majestic perspective at Dampierre includes the entrance drive and the park stretching into the distance, its thick woods creating a lush background for the château below. The communs bordering the cour d'honneur survive from the 16th-century dwelling that occupied this site. Rare archaisms in the work of Hardouin-Mansart are the corner towers, also the brick and stone masonry.

opposite: On the garden façade at Dampierre, superimposed Doric and Ionic columns rise like a stone fanfare. They support a triangular pediment carved with the Luynes arms and bring great emphasis to the façade's central bay. The magnificent triple flight of steps spans the moat and links the château to its gardens. Glowing in the sunlight, rose-hued brick and golden-warm stone find a perfect foil in the coolness of the blue-slate roof, whose double slope is a signature of the great 17th-century architect, Jules Hardouin-Mansart.

The Golden Age (1842–49) by Jean-Auguste-Dominique Ingres.

A classic ensemble of symmetrical, temple-fronted château set harmoniously within a thick wood contained by precisely drawn, geometrical borders, Dampierre in the Chevreuse Valley would hardly suggest that on this terrain dwelled one of the most tempestuous and revolutionary personalities of the 17th century. The beauteous Marie de Rohan-Montbazon, Duchesse de Chevreuse, joined the Fronde of aristocrats against the monarchy during the minority of Louis XIV, pouring into the conspiracy such torrents of passion that she, like La Grande Mademoiselle, became known as a great *amazone*. Such activity won her a long exile at Dampierre, and once she had lost her conquering looks and charm as well as her liberty, the old Duchess unfortunately became an object of ridicule for that ungallant ironist, Bussy-Rabutin, who wrote: "Chevreuse is an ancient fortress, now completely in ruins—the citadel has been destroyed by many sieges. They say it often surrenders unconditionally."

And indeed little remains of the actual château in which Marie de Rohan lived. The estate at Chevreuse had a *château fort* as far back as feudal times, but it largely perished when Richelieu ordered a dismantling so as to disarm the Amazon. In the early 16th century, for the benefit of a favorite, François I had made Chevreuse a duchy, but when the luxury-loving Cardinal Charles de Lorraine, son of the Duc de Guise, acquired it in 1552, he found the dwelling there so austere that he abandoned it in favor of totally new construction on a different site. The residence that came forth was a sumptuous one in the manner of the French Renaissance. Charles left his estate to a nephew, the Duc de Guise who died at Blois in 1588, a victim of an assassin's hand at the height of the Huguenot conflict. And the Château de Dampierre that he inherited at Chevreuse would not last long, for in 1675 the new Duke, who descended from Marie de Rohan and her first husband, the Duc de Luynes, razed the Renaissance structure and undertook to rebuild from plans provided by the most accomplished French architect of his time, Jules Hardouin-Mansart. Perfectly integrated with the park designed by André Le Nôtre, the result is one of the major 17th-century achievements in architecture outside the royal or public domains. The fortune that paid for this came in part from the Duke's wife, whose father was Colbert, Louis XIV's great economic minister, as well as from the Duke's position as tutor to the Duc de Burgogne, heir to the throne of France.

The 18th-century Duke received Queen Marie Leszczynska at Dampierre, wrote memoirs that provide an interesting account of life at the court of Louis XV, and redecorated much of the interior with beautiful white and gold carved paneling typical of the period. During the Revolution his grandson remained at the château in complete safety, thanks to his habitual generosity toward the tenants on the Chevreuse estate. After the fall of Robespierre the Duke and his family returned to Dampierre, triumphantly escorted by all the villagers.

During the Napoleonic regime the Duchesse de Chevreuse went into exile at Lyons rather than serve as jailor to the captive Queen of Spain. Her son, Duke Honoré, became a distinguished archaeologist and numismatist and after the revolution of 1848 entered the National Assembly as deputy for the Oise. He also undertook a major restoration of Dampierre, a project that engaged the painter Ingres to fresco two large compositions, *The Age of Gold* and *The Age of Iron*. After two years, however, these important works from a major master were abandoned, with one of them not quite completed and the other barely sketched out.

The present Duc de Luynes and lord of Dampierre and Chevreuse serves as president of the Society for the Preservation of French Historical Monuments.

Champs

The Château de Champs, high over the Marne, is a monument to the remarkable fact that in the 18th century even parvenus—generally thought to be vulgarians—had the infallibly elegant taste characteristic of their age. It also provides a measure of the power increasingly gained throughout the last century of the *ancien régime* by the professional financiers, which allowed them to build and behave in general like royalty itself.

Toward the end of the 17th century a luxury-loving tax collector responsible for financing French war efforts—Charles Renouard de La Touanne—bought the domain at Champs from the Faure family. La Touanne immediately engaged Jean-Baptiste Bullet de Chamblain, an important disciple of Jules Hardouin-Mansart, to replace the old manor house with a new château, a structure splendid enough for a king but styled and scaled with the lighter, more refined touch then emerging, even at the Versailles of Louis

After 1739 Claude Desgots laid out the gardens at Champs in the familiar manner of his uncle, André Le Nôtre, creating magnificent parterres *that descend in geometric sequence toward the right bank of the Marne.*

right: *A forerunner of the age of elegance, Champs was built by parvenus, which proves that in matters of taste the 18th century could do no wrong. Designed by J.B. Bullet de Chamblain, and constructed between 1699 and 1709, Champs is everywhere touched by a delicate and discriminating hand. What results is a calm, highly unified, even compact white-stone ensemble of two stories capped by a dormered Mansart roof. The central bay on the garden façade, a semicircular exedra with a light pediment and sculptured consoles, is typical of the fresh and subtle manner in which the language of classicism has been employed at Champs. The quality of this façade would receive the tribute of frequent copying.*

opposite: *An original feature of the entrance façade is the open vestibule or atrium that one enters through a colonnaded and pilastered portico, which projects no farther than the central bay itself. The deep shadows of the recess are in rich contrast to the overall simplicity and low relief qualities that are nowhere more evident than in the plain, unadorned pediment. In lieu of the traditional moat, balustrades enclose the* cour d'honneur.

XIV. But ambition drove La Touanne beyond his considerable means, and while some four hundred workmen swarmed over the building site, the châtelain went bankrupt and perished in 1701—according to Saint-Simon, of a stroke suffered at Champs when he saw officers arrive to confiscate the property.

Another tax collector and army supplier—Paul Poisson, also known as the Baron de Bourvalais—was at the ready and acquired the assets at Champs. A particular attraction for him was the château's location, near a village where he and his wife had begun life as domestic servants. With origins somewhat lower than those of La Touanne, Poisson now aimed higher and ordered Bullet to enlarge the plans to create the château we now see. The dwelling completed between 1703 and 1707 is a calm, highly unified, even compact, white-stone ensemble of two stories capped by a Mansart roof containing a dormered attic. Like the whole of the classical styling, the overall rectangular volume is inflected only by the subtlest variations—slight projections for the lateral pavilions flanking the *corps de logis*, and at the center of this form a bay that on the garden side is a semicircular exedra and on the *cour d'honneur* a predimented portico of columns and pilasters. The last feature serves as main entrance and gives access to an interior atrium, which may be the freshest departure made by Bullet in his design for Champs.

The interior must have been particularly lovely, if one is to judge by what survives from this time—the grand salon with its two majestic marble basins and overdoors painted by Desportes and Oudry. Bourvalais, a great host of fashionable society, kept an equally grand establishment at his Paris *hôtel* in the Place Vendôme. It all prompted an envious former master to remind Bourvalais that he had once been a valet, to which the Baron retorted: "True, but if you had been my valet, you would still be one." Bravado, however, could not save the would-be Maecenas when his immense fortune was discovered by the Regency government to have been amassed largely through embezzlement of public funds. Seizure and imprisonment resulted, with Bourvalais dying in the Bastille in 1719.

Champs was then acquired "for nothing" by the Princesse de La Vallière. In 1739 it passed to the Princess's nephew, the Duc de La Vallière, who engaged Claude Desgots to lay out the gardens in the familiar manner of his uncle, André Le Nôtre, creating magnificent *parterres* that descend in geometric sequence toward the right bank of the Marne. The Duke managed Mme de Pompadour's theatre at Versailles and installed one of his own at Champs. Such high style proved too costly for La Vallière, and in 1757 he rented the estate to the royal favorite. A cultivated woman of exquisite taste, the Marquise undertook a major revision of the interior, not only having Huet paint the *chinoiserie* on the paneling in the salon and carve the reliefs in the boudoir, but also ordering many modifications for the sake of convenience and comfort. The latter included a kitchen next to the dining room and—the most daring of all—a bathroom for each of the bedrooms upstairs. She also had the gardens redesigned by Jean-Charles Garnier de L'Isle. But La Pompadour soon tired of Champs and gave it up even before she died in 1764.

By the time of the Revolution Champs had passed to the Duc de La Vallière's daughter, the Marquise de Marboeuf, who died on the scaffold during the Reign of Terror. After inheriting the estate, the Duc de Lévis-Ventadour allowed the gardens to be partly destroyed and the park divided up. What remained was purchased in 1830 by M. Grosjean, who replaced the high roof with a flat one and finished the top of the façades with a balustrade in the Italian manner. In this form the château passed to Ernest Santerre, a lateral descendant of the Revolutionary commander of the National Guard, remaining in this family for thirty-seven years.

Not until 1895 did Champs come into the hands of an owner able and willing to restore it to something like its original splendor. This was a physician, the Comte Cahen d'Anvers, who returned the roof to its original Mansart state and restored the gardens according to the plans of Desgots. He also created the effect of a *cour d'honneur* by adding outbuildings on either side of the main façade. In 1934 his heirs donated Champs to the French government, which now uses it as a guest house for visiting heads of state.

opposite: The perfect symmetry of the grand salon at Champs prepares one for the classical geometry of the gardens beyond. Much of this room, including the monumental marble basin imported from Italy, survives from the original early-18th-century décor. The nobly theatrical character of the flower-filled basin is continued in the crystal chandelier and in the Chinese jars on marble columns at either side of the tall window hung with red velvet draperies.

below: After taking a lease on Champs in 1757, Mme de Pompadour set out to redo the château in her own exquisite taste. From that era survive the delightful chinoiseries that cover the paneling in the main drawing room. They were executed by Christophe Huet, known for comparable work at the Château de Chantilly and in Paris's Hôtel de Rohan. The little Oriental figures disporting themselves at hunting, fishing, gardening, and flirtation were exotic enough, for all the Frenchness of the Rococo setting, to satisfy a superficial desire to escape from the mounting problems of the 18th-century world.

Lunéville

The splendor of Louis XIV's Versailles had its intended effect, which was to impress the world with the power and glory of the French monarchy. A somewhat unexpected result was the Versailles-itis that spread like contagion to virtually every court in Europe, however large or small. Of all the attempts to emulate the creation of Le Vau, Hardouin-Mansart, Le Brun, Le Nôtre, and their munificent royal patron, the one that came closest to the original—in form as well as in substance—was the garden-set palace commissioned by the Duke of Lorraine. The duchy of Lorraine east of the Meuse had enjoyed semi-independence of both France and the Holy Roman Empire for over a thousand years, beginning in the mid-6th century. Hard-pressed during the Thirty Years War and occupied by French troops during the War of the Spanish Succession, the Lorraine made a dramatic return to prosperity in the early 18th century. This enabled Duke Léopold I to initiate an ambitious new building program (1703–20) for his country seat at Lunéville, just outside the capital city of Nancy. To approach the prototype as closely as possible, Léopold engaged Germain Boffrand, the great follower of Jules Hardouin-Mansart, Louis XIV's own architect, to design a vast new château, and Yves des Hours to create huge gardens with *parterres,* canals, and fountains laid out with all the geometric invention of Versailles's André Le Nôtre. A grand and monumental ensemble, Lunéville, when finished, constituted a triumph for the French classical style, with all its nobility, clarity, and somewhat severe elegance.

A lighter, gayer, Rococo, and even intellectual note sounded after 1737. It was then that Stanislas Leszczynski, the deposed King of Poland who also happened to be the father-in-law of Louis XV, replaced François III, the successor to Léopold I, Duc de Lorraine. François had just married Maria-Theresa of Hapsburg, daughter of the Holy Roman Emperor and heiress to the throne of Austria, creating an alliance that threatened to upset Europe's balance of power. To hold the Lorraine within the orbit of France, diplomacy brought about an exchange, whereby the duchy of Lorraine would go to Stanislas, while François III would become Grand Duke of Tuscany, then a Hapsburg fief. A debonair 18th-century prince, Stanislas completed the interior at Lunéville, filled the gardens with fanciful pleasure pavilions—designed by Héré of Nancy and Mique of Versailles—and the château with a brilliant company, which included Voltaire, the poet Saint-Lambert, and their great friend Mme du Châtelet. Festivals, balls, theatre, opera, concerts, and good conversation dominated life at Lunéville until 1766, when Stanislas died and the Lorraine reverted to France, becoming integral with that nation. No longer the residence of a sovereign, the great château lost not only its significance but also its furnishings, gardens, and pavilions—even the lead sculptural groups decorating its fountains, which were purchased by the Elector Palatine Karl Theodor for the park at Schwetzingen.

In 1801 Lunéville received the delegates to a peace conference between France and Austria. Otherwise, it suffered long neglect and even abuse, as a barracks and riding center. Only since 1939 have the château and park been under restoration. The main buildings now house a municipal museum.

right: No less than the Château de Lunéville, the park surrounding it provides a variation on the theme pronounced at Versailles, with its geometrical organization of parterres, canals, and fountains. During the reign of Duke Stanislas (1737–66), the gardens were filled with fantastic pleasure pavilions and a crowd of courtly and gay, but also philosophical, people.

Guermantes

The name Guermantes is unforgettably linked to Marcel Proust and his great novel, *A la recherche du temps perdu*. The very mention of the château evokes, with true Proustian free association, the Duchesse de Guermantes, whose beauty, privilege, and elegance can be imagined as she strolled through the grand gallery or the gardens, a proud figure with a "birdlike profile" and a distant expression. Ironically, Proust knew nothing of the actual château or its inhabitants and adopted the name for the aristocratic heroine of his narrative only because the sound of it captivated him. Not until the end of World War I did he visit the estate, and then only to allay his anxiety that offense might be given by the use of a name whose real bearers had no relation to his fictional characters. Proust could rest secure because the last of the Guermantes had died in 1884, almost forty years before the *Le Côté de Guermantes* episode was published in 1921.

The château itself dates from the reign of Louis XIII in the early 17th century, when it was built by Claude Viole, counselor to the Parlement of Paris. His son, who became President Viole, enlarged and embellished the dwelling before falling into disgrace for having joined the Fronde against the crown during the minority of Louis XIV. After his death the estate went to a great-nephew, who in 1698 sold it to Paulin Prondre. This rich financier could afford to arrange new suites at Guermantes and to have them designed by such a master to royalty as Claude Robert de Cotte. He also had the park replanted from a scheme composed by André Le Nôtre. When a splendid *fête* was held in 1710 to inaugurate the new features, the guest list included many of the period's most illustrious names. Despite fines for questionable financial dealings, the Prondre family succeeded in having Guermantes elevated to marquisate. The last of the clan was Ernestine, Comtesse de Dampierre. It was this lady who died in 1884, after a very long life made famous by her vicious tongue and by the lavishness of the receptions she gave at Guermantes.

After the death of the Comtesse de Dampierre, Guermantes passed first to the Marquis de Lareinty, then in 1928 to M. Maurice Hottinguer. Having restored the château and park, the Hottinguers now maintain them with impeccable care.

above: Guermantes, even after much remodeling, retains the strong, common-sensical simplicity of a château built by a parlementarian, Claude Viole, during the reign of Louis XIII (1610–43). Not until the 17th century, while owned by the rich financier Paulin Prondre, did Guermantes become a marquisate. It was then that Le Nôtre prepared a new design for the park. In modern times the name Guermantes was immortalized by Marcel Proust, but the name only, for the great novelist knew neither the château nor its inhabitants.

opposite: Luxury came to Guermantes in the 18th century, brought there by the wealth of its new owner, the unscrupulous tax collector Paulin Prondre. Nowhere is it more evident than in the grand gallery, sumptuously decorated from a design of Robert de Cotte. Executed by Hanard, the gilded molding enframes, on the walls, copies of paintings by such Old Masters as Raphael, Correggio, and Poussin and, on the ceiling, an original painting by Andrieu, student of the 19th-century master Delacroix.

Raray

above: In the Porte de Diane, leading from Raray to the surrounding forest, the native medieval tradition of symbolic bestiaries is joined to the Italian Baroque tradition of realistic representation observed in the wall friezes of the château's cour d'honneur. Thus, it is the unicorn that the barking dogs hold at bay.

top and opposite: At Raray the château and its decorative bestiaries give effect to the full spirit of the Bourbons' grand siècle, which produced the somewhat chilly, classical formality of Versailles, along with the humor and wit of a fantasist like Antoine de La Fontaine, whose animal Fables constitute a masterpiece of world literature. The stag reliefs in the pediments above the château's end pavilions are beautiful enough, but the extended hunting scenes that crown the two walls on either side of the cour d'honneur exceed in energy, spirit, and charm the Italian tradition of realistic representation that inspired them.

Northeast of Paris, in the old duchy of Valois, lies a château of such fantasylike charm that Jean Cocteau chose it as the setting of *La Belle et la bête*. In the journal he kept while making the film the great Surrealist poet wrote: "Under an equinoctial sky, surrounded by slate-colored villages, sulfurous lakes, pink forests . . . the spectacle of the walls of Raray is sublime." These marvelous galleried walls, whose summits reproduce in stone sculpture packs of hounds chasing, on one side, a stag and, on the other, a wild boar, are a product of the early 17th century, that era when the Baroque art of Italy proved so liberating for the European imagination. The two main bestiaries, which flank the *cour d'honneur*, seem all the more vivid and vital for being attached to a dwelling of extreme, classical sobriety, a quality that was no less characteristic of the Baroque age than the delightful inventions of the *animaliers*.

The story of Raray begins about 1600, when Nicolas de Lancy—royal counselor, military treasurer, and chamberlain to the Duc d'Orléans—purchased the domain of Raray. There, next to an older *château fort*, he had built a new *maison de plaisance*, rectangular in form and terminating in pavilions with advanced façades. Leading out from these are the two startling and unforgettable walls. Each of them is penetrated by a centrally placed portal and by a sixteen-bay arcade whose interstices shelter niched busts carved in the antique manner. Even here humor inserts itself, for the particular combinations of hats, helmets, laurel crowns, and beards constitutes nothing so much as a delicious mockery of an old and rather stagey tradition. Above them a riot of pure joy breaks out in the hunting scenes, where stone urns alternate with hounds mounted on scroll plinths, all of which center upon either the recumbent stag or the charging boar. In Italy, animals often inspired the decorative ensembles of gardens designed during the Renaissance and Baroque eras, but none ever captured in so witty a fashion the liveliness and energy of animal life as the series at Raray. And the château comes by its Italianism honestly, for Mme de Lancy was originally Lucrezia di Lanchisi, the daughter of a Florentine banker established in Paris. But the style of realistic representation that she would have brought from the south was integrated at Raray with the native medieval tradition of animals used symbolically to represent moral values. This can be found in the Porte de Diane, which originally served as the main access to the game-rich forest that surrounds the Château de Raray. Here the several sculptures combine to illustrate the legend of the fabulous unicorn, that romantic symbol of feminine chastity so sacred to the age of chivalry.

In 1654 Louis XIV elevated the Raray fief to marquisate. Just over a century later the property was sold to the Marquis de Barres, who added a large pavilion to the château's south side. At the same time, he raised the 17th-century structure by an attic story, preserving, however, the beautiful round-headed pediments that, with their stag reliefs, adorn the front façades of the two end pavilions.

In Napoleonic times Raray passed by legacy to Charles de La Bedoyère, whose son was shot for having supported the deposed Emperor during his Hundred Days. Today Raray belongs to the present Comte de La Bedoyère.

Craon

The entire history of the Lorraine seems to be embodied in the form and fabric of the Château de Craon. Here the delicacy of 18th-century classicism graces an elevation that rises above a medieval moat and from foundations ancient enough to preserve the plan of the typical defensive *enceinte*, square in shape with corners reinforced by round, pepper-pot towers. As early as the 13th century, the site—Haroué on the Madon, a tributary of the Moselle—was fortified to protect a strategic point on the route between France and Germany. As late as the early 19th century the château received a suite of exquisite furnishings from the household of Louis XVIII, who in his sad old age found solace in a charming relation of the princely family of Beauvau-Craon. The prevailing style at Craon, however, is that of the French Rococo. It derives from the architect Germain Boffrand, famed for his work at the Hôtel de Soubise in Paris and at Lorraine's ducal palace in Lunéville, as well as from the sculptor Guibal and the ironsmith Jean Lamour, two masters whose artistry helped to make the Place Stanislas in Nancy one of the glories of Europe. But the Craons, like the duchy of Lorraine itself, had strong connections with the throne of France; thus, none other than Jean Pillement and Hubert Robert, two of the painter-decorators most favored at Versailles, brought to the château's interior the touch that made their age the very acme of elegance and refinement.

The fief at Haroué took its name from the Harouels, the feudal lords who assumed charge of the French position at this outpost in the Lorraine. All that remains from the first *château fort* are a pair of outbuildings and one stout entrance portal. Eventually the Bassompierre family succeeded the Harouels and in the late 15th and early 16th centuries replaced the original structure with a much larger and more important one, the foundations of which support the present building. The new edifice would reflect the early French Renaissance, in its styling if not in plan, and in it was born François de Bassompierre (1579–1646), who at age nineteen charmed the court of Henri IV and gained access to the King's innermost circle. Steadily rising in favor, François became a marshal of France and the ambassador from Louis XIII to England in the time of Charles I. Under Richelieu, however, François suffered disgrace and even imprisonment in the Bastille. While there the château in the Lorraine fell victim to the Thirty Years War and was sacked. Its condition was such that by the time lawsuits incident upon the succession were settled some seventy years later, the château was in ruins.

Finally, in 1720, the relative to receive the estate at Haroué was Marc de Beauvau, whose Angevin ancestors included Louis de Beauvau, the confidant to whom René d'Anjou, King of Naples, had assigned the governorship of Lorraine when the latter relinquished the duchy in favor of his son. Not only was Marc de Beauvau a close childhood friend of Léopold I, Duc de Lorraine, but his wife, Anne-Marguerite de Ligniville, became the Duke's favorite. The honors this brought included the positions of master of the ducal horse and tutor to the ruler's son, as well as the title of Marquis de Craon. At Duke Léopold's request the Holy Roman Emperor made Marc a prince of the Empire in 1722 and a grandee of Spain in 1729. By 1739 Louis XV found it possible to grant the Beauvau-Craon family the title of cousin to the monarch,

opposite: A moat, corner towers (not visible here), and a square plan attest to the ancient origins of the Château de Craon. In all other respects, however, Craon is a monument to 18th-century French classicism, derived as it is from a design by the Rococo master Germain Boffrand. On the garden side shown here the approach leads up a grand flight of steps and across a stone bridge to a façade whose central bay is articulated by two superimposed stories of Ionic and Corinthian columns and pilasters enframing arched doorways. The crowning pediment, the freestanding figural groups, and the decorative grillework are from the sculptor Guibal and the ironmaster Jean Lamour, both Lorrainers.

Although shaped by the late-medieval tower that houses it, a corner drawing room at Craon is pure 18th-century Rococo. The chinoiserie wall decorations by Jean Pillement, an artist who pioneered this curvilinear style in France, are beautifully integrated with the cylindrical space and serve to lighten the effect of the massive walls and heavy vaults. Also surviving from the room's original décor are the chair and console table.

In the green drawing room seen here, as in the dining room at Craon, the furniture is by Bélanger, a great master of the early 19th century. The pieces come from the Pavillon de Saint-Ouen, established in 1820 by Louis XIII for the companion of his lonely old age, Mme du Cayla, whose daughter married the Prince de Beauvau-Craon. The upholstery is original, in pale green silk brocade threaded with gold. On the wall hangs a portrait by Baron Gérard; it shows the old Bourbon monarch in his study at the Tuileries, seated before the simple, unpainted wooden table that had served as his desk throughout the exile brought on by the Revolution and the Napoleonic regime.

"in consideration of the fact that the Prince de Craon comes from the same stem as Isabeau de Bavière, eighth ancestor of His Majesty."

Such status required a new château at Haroué and resulted in the structure we now see. Only the exterior had been completed when Léopold I died in 1729, leaving the duchy of Lorraine to his son, François III, whose mentor had from birth been the Prince de Beauvau-Craon. And it was the latter who bore the major responsibility for negotiating the marriage between the new Duc de Lorraine and Maria-Theresa of Hapsburg, daughter of Charles VI, Holy Roman Emperor, and heiress to the throne of Austria. The union took place in 1736, but only after France had been satisfied in its objection to the transfer of the Lorraine to Germanic Europe. The satisfaction occurred through an exchange whereby Stanislas Leszczynski, dethroned King of Poland and father-in-law of Louis XV, would become Duc de Lorraine, while François III would receive, in compensation, the grand duchy of Tuscany. Having steered the interests of his charge through these difficult waters, the Prince de Craon went to Florence as viceroy, a post he held until 1747. He then returned to the Lorraine and died in his château at Haroué in 1754.

Of the twenty children fathered by the Prince de Craon, the son to inherit his titles and dignities was Charles-Juste, who achieved a brilliant military career and became marshal of France. A popular figure, he had the honor in February 1778 of crowning Voltaire during a triumphal performance of *Irène* at the Comédie-Française in Paris. At the death of Charles-Juste the estate passed to a younger brother. During the Revolution the Château de Craon was saved by the simple act of removing the crowns that had been woven into the decorative ironwork. In the 19th century the Prince de Craon married the daughter of the Comtesse du Cayla, who had been the favorite of the widowed Louis XVIII, the brother of Louis XVI who received the crown of France when the monarchy was restored in 1815, following the defeat and exile of Napoleon. This accounts for the presence at Craon of the fine portraits by Gérard of the King and of Mme du Cayla, as well as the superb furniture the old Bourbon had ordered from Bélanger for the pavilion he arranged for his companion in the village of Saint-Ouen outside Paris. The château belongs to the present Prince de Beauvau-Craon, who faithfully continues the restoration that began at Haroué in 1921.

In the cour d'honneur *at Craon, Germain Boffrand continued the superimposed Ionic and Corinthian orders seen on the garden façade and flanked the projecting entrance bay with colonnaded porticoes reminiscent of the Palais Royal in Paris. These support open terraces at the upper level, where the graceful grillework handrails, like those elsewhere at Craon, are by the Lorraine ironmaster Jean Lamour.*

An 18th-century engraving records the splendor of the festivities staged on the occasion of Louis XV's visit to Strasbourg in 1744, when the sovereign occupied a royal suite on the river side of the vast Château des Rohan. Except for the loss of its furnishings during the Revolution, the château-palace has remained virtually unchanged since its completion in 1731.

Le Château des Rohan

The so-called "château" built in the early 18th century by the Cardinal-Archbishop of Strasbourg, the Prince de Rohan, could be more accurately described as a palace, conceived as it is on royal rather than mere princely lines. Moreover, it is not a country house but a town dwelling, placed at the very heart of Alsace's capital city. Facing Germany across the Rhine, it is France's easternmost outpost. Often it has served as a way station for emissaries intent upon bridging or widening the historic division between western and eastern Europe.

The Château des Rohan could hardly have been anything but regal, given the circumstances of its commission and construction. Alsace, like the Lorraine, had long been in dispute between France and Germany, and during the Reformation a majority of its citizens had sided with Luther and Zwingli. Not until 1681, at the time of the expansionist conquests of Louis XIV, did the Catholic rite return to the great Cathedral of Strasbourg, and only since 1697 had the province been fully possessed by the French crown. It seemed urgent, therefore, that these historic changes be signaled in some emphatic way. Periodic appearances in Strasbourg by the sovereign would make the necessary political point, while the right kind of permanent representative could press the religious one, since the chief civil authority in Strasbourg, as in many Rhenish cities, had traditionally been the Bishop. And how better to express the new presence than to endow Strasbourg with a new episcopal palace, an edifice that would emulate, if not actually copy, the grandeur of Versailles, which itself had been inspired by the classicism of the Renaissance and Baroque palaces of Rome.

The career opportunity posed by Strasbourg was perceived at the French

opposite: Rising majestically upon a bank of the Ill River, the château of the Cardinals-Princes de Rohan in Strasbourg established the French Catholic presence in the capital of a formerly Protestant and German Alsace. To Lutheran Germany across the Rhine it also presented an image of grandeur, emulating the High Baroque manner of Versailles and papal Rome. The plans of Robert de Cotte, the architect favored by Louis XIV at the end of his life, guaranteed a palatial, urban dwelling suitable for the royal visits that would ensue.

159

On the façade opposite Strasbourg's towering cathedral, the Château des Rohan consists of a low, concave, hemicyclical structure linking a pair of large corner pavilions and providing an entrance porch. It is surmounted by a balustrade, which in turn supports decorative urns and stone sculptures representing children at play and the personifications of religion and clemency, the latter carved by Robert Le Lorrain.

court, by none more dramatically than the Princesse de Soubise, eager for the advancement of her son, Armand-Gaston de Rohan (1674–1749). That the young man would provide the most intimate link possible between Louis XIV and his new Alsatian subjects could not have been doubted, since it seemed granted by all, including the King, that Armand-Gaston was the issue of an affair between the Princesse de Soubise and His Majesty.

Officially, Gaston-Armand was the fifth son of François de Rohan, Prince de Soubise, and Anne de Rohan-Chabot, an auburn beauty clever enough to hold the King's favor even after his ardor had cooled. To win Strasbourg for her son, she mounted a major campaign, which, to begin with, had to prevail over the college of canons traditionally elected by Strasbourg's most aristocratic families. At the outset only four of the twelve canons were French. Soon, however, virtually the entire body would support the candidate from France. Of considerable help was Armand-Gaston himself, who had inherited all of his parents' astuteness. "Everything favored the Abbé de Soubise," wrote that great chronicler of the age, Saint-Simon. "Avenues to fortune opened on every side. From the Sorbonne he came forth a marvel of knowledge, and from the seminary a miracle of piety and of purity in manner. The Oratorians, the Jesuits, the faculty of the Sorbonne . . . everyone exclaimed in admiration. Such pronouncements delighted the mother, and they scarcely failed to please the King, with whom every care was taken to share the rejoicing over the Abbé de Soubise. Meanwhile, the latter's sweetness, courtesy, spirit, and grace—not to mention his patience and talent in making himself loved—confirmed more and more a reputation already well established." Almost as if foreordained, therefore, Gaston-Armand de Rohan mounted the episcopal throne of Strasbourg in 1704. Six years later he received a Cardinal's hat, and a year after that the title of Grand Almoner of France

It was in 1727 that Cardinal de Rohan commissioned a design from Robert de Cotte, the architect preferred by Louis XIV at the end of his life. Completed in 1731, the palace occupied a site just opposite Strasbourg's majestic cathedral, with its principal façade raised upon the west bank of the Ill River, a tributary of the Rhine. On the water side it contained suites scaled and decorated to make a monarch comfortable, and on the *cour d'honneur* slightly more domestic chambers for the Cardinal and his household.

Consecration of the palace came in 1744, when Louis XV arrived on a state visit. Having survived a serious illness at Metz, the King seemed a miraculous apparition, truly the anointed of God. Strasbourg reacted properly and staged the most splendid of festivities. Thereafter it was in the Château des Rohan that the Germanic princesses destined for the sons of royal France would spend their first nights on French soil. Marie-Josèphe de Saxe slept there in 1747, followed in 1770 by Marie-Antoinette, Archduchess of Austria. The tradition continued even during the Empire, bringing to Strasbourg Catherine de Wurtemberg, the bride of Jérôme Bonaparte, and the Archduchess Marie-Louise, Napoleon's second Empress.

Rohan princes succeeded one another in Strasbourg throughout the 18th century, until the Revolution, which the inglorious Cardinal Louis-René de Rohan helped to trigger. Already in Vienna, as French ambassador, he had behaved in such a worldly manner that Empress Maria-Theresa asked for his recall. This also incurred the displeasure of the Empress's daughter, Marie-Antoinette. To curry favor with the latter, Louis-René, now Cardinal de Rohan, became involved in the notorious "necklace affair," a fraud that brought scandal to a beautiful, innocent, but unwise Queen. Although Louis-René was deprived of his office of grand almoner and banned from Paris, the damage done to the royal family could never be repaired. As the Revolution engulfed France, Cardinal de Rohan sought refuge in the German section of his diocese at Ettenheim, where he died in 1803.

The Revolution deprived the palace of its sumptuous Louis XV furnishings and converted it to a town hall. The ensuing Empire refurnished the great suites, which were then occupied at various times by Napoleon and Joséphine, succeeded after the Restoration by the Duc de Berry, the Duc d'Angoulême, Charles X, and Louis-Philippe. Since 1899 the Château des Rohan has been a public museum.

Originally a fortified manor house, but substantially aggrandized within a century after 1640, La Baume on the exterior looks tough and hard-bitten, like the Grolée family who built it. The near wing, with its heavy corner pavilion and machicolated parapet, is in striking contrast to the far, parallel wing. Like the entrance gate, this section has a Mansart roof, which adds elegance to the château and softens its somewhat martial air. Still, the dwelling remained old-fashioned for the early 18th-century, when this, the newest, wing was constructed.

La Baume

Like the history of the family that built the château, La Baume has something tough and hard-bitten about it. The form is that of a fortified manor house, a distinctly provincial mass built entirely of granite—even the roof is stone—and set in a countryside that the writer Jean Lartéguy, a native of the Gévaudon, characterized as a "land of granite and heather." It is also a region full of pines, running streams, and family feuds that last for generations.

Records as early as 1275 mention a *mas,* or "farmhouse," at La Baume, the property of Comte Laval, who probably was a bastard of the lord of Peyre, the castle seat of the local barony. In 1532 the last of the Peyres died childless and left the estate to a grand nephew, Antoine de Cardaillac. His two sons, in their time, settled respectively at Peyre and at La Baume. By the close of the 16th century, La Baume had become more than a mere *mas,* really a seigneurial château.

Indeed, the story of the barony throughout the 17th century is that of repeated suits brought by the junior branch at La Baume against the senior line at Peyre. Aiding the junior branch, which won and took everything, was the marital status of the heiress at La Baume, while the heiress at Peyre remained a spinster. Then the former's husband, Antoine de Grolée, found an ally in the policies of Richelieu, who was eager to strengthen the royal authority at the expense of the old feudal powers. Awarded Peyre and a bonus for destroying it, Antoine de Grolée—now Comte de Peyre—set about to enlarge and en-

left: As La Baume became more important in the 17th century, it received a grand new staircase, carved in granite and vaulted overhead. Although constructed in 1708–10, the sober, even severe massiveness of the design reflects an older taste.

hance La Baume. In the next generation, only César, the eighth child of Antoine, inherited his father's acquisitiveness, which emboldened him not only to pension off his siblings, in exchange for all rights to the Peyre-La Baume estate, but also to sue for the return of all properties sold since his great-grandfather's day by the heirs of Peyre. This time, judgment favorable to César may well have been determined at Versailles, where an intimate friend of César's—Angélique de Scoraille, Marquise de Fontanges—had recently engaged the affections of Louis XIV. As rich appointments now flowed to César—lieutenant general of the King's armies in Languedoc (1690) and bailiff of Le Gévaudan (1708)—La Baume grew more important also. Soon it became known as the "Versailles of Le Gévaudan," with its somewhat primitive and provincial, but wonderfully brilliant, polychrome interior décor.

About 1850 Casimir Mayran, senator from Aveyron, acquired La Baume from the remote descendants of César de Grolée. The estate then passed to the new châtelain's son-in-law, Comte de Las Cases, whose family now maintains the dwelling—along with its collection of imperial memorabilia, left by Comte Émmanuel de Las Cases, Napoleon's companion on Saint Helena.

La Baume became known as the "Versailles of Le Gévaudan" for its suites of sumptuous interiors, all commissioned by César de Peyre. Rare and beautiful is the Count's study, richly decorated— walls, beams, and ceiling—in the polychrome style favored in the provinces of 17th-century France. The delightfully archaic quality no doubt derives from the skills of local artisans.

Bagatelle

A Flemish jewel in Picardie is Bagatelle, whose very name means something small and delightful. Built in its first stage between 1751 and 1754, Bagatelle was intended to be a kind of *folie*, a place on the outskirts of Abbéville where a Dutch cloth tycoon, Abraham van Robais, could entertain his clients and business associates. Initially the structure consisted of a single story surmounted by a balustrade *à l'italienne*. Around 1763 van Robais ordered an attic, and shortly thereafter he crowned this with another floor, dormered within a Mansart roof. Thus completed, Bagatelle is like a miniature château, built of brick trimmed in stone and styled with a Rococo opulence more Flemish than French. On the ground floor of the interior a "winter" salon and a dining room flank the projecting central bay, which contains a "summer" salon on the garden side and a vestibule on the entrance side. Once the upper stories had been added, a graceful, hairpin-curve, double-ramp stairway was cleverly fitted into the small vestibule. All in tulip-fresh colors, Bagatelle's carved wall paneling, period furniture, and fine china bring to perfection a complete 18th-century ensemble. The architect of this enchanted realm remains unknown.

Abraham van Robais became one of the first of the modern industrialists. His family had emigrated to Abbéville from Holland in 1665, at the invitation of Colbert, Louis XIV's great minister, who wanted France to rival the English and Flemish in the manufacture and export of cloth. By the time of Abraham, the van Robais enterprise had more than one hundred looms and as many as three thousand workers. The family fleet, with a flag ship named *The Golden Fleece*, sailed to Bilbao for wool and to Germany, Spain, and Italy—even to the Levant and India—with finished cloth. To attract and retain the energetic van Robais, the French state granted economic assistance, a guarantee against future competition, and the right to practice—in secret—their Protestant religion. Even after the revocation of Edict of Nantes (1685), the van Robais kept their own chaplain and private cemetery.

Until the Revolution, Bagatelle was an essential way station for any important figure traveling northwest from Paris. In 1793 the van Robais sold Bagatelle to the uncle of Boucher de Perthes, the founder of studies in prehistory. After 1810, the château belonged to the Wailly family. In the early 20th century Bagatelle heard many concerts, organized by Paul de Wailly, a pupil of César Franck, and attended by such musical greats as Saint-Saëns and Vincent d'Indy. It was at this time that the dwelling received the low, lateral wings that terminate in two-story pavilions. The estate is now owned by M. Jacques de Wailly.

To reach the attic stories added after the initial construction, the rather small vestibule on one side of the central, apsidal bay was cleverly invested with a double-ramp stairway, its graceful hairpin curves embellished further with Rococo handrails in the kind of wrought-iron work that made Abbéville artists famous.

Occupying the garden side of the hemicyclical, central bay is the "summer" salon, where the carved wood paneling was painted in the manner of Salembier, a Rococo mesh of flowers, vases, and decorative arabesques.

opposite: The pastrylike richness of the exterior decorations at Bagatelle reflect the Flemish or Dutch taste of its builders, the van Robais of Holland. A perfect and homogeneous ensemble, Bagatelle belies the successive stages in which this exquisite miniature of a château was constructed. Initially, it consisted of a single story, arranged as two rectangular bays on either side of a projecting, hemicyclical bay, but the structure was subsequently enlarged by first one attic and then a second, the latter set with dormers in a Mansart roof. Varying the formal symmetry of the block and its garden
setting are the oeil-de-boeuf ("bull's-eye") windows entered above the tall fenestration of the ground floor, where the round-headed arches on the central bay change to anses de panier, or low "basket-handle" arches, on the flat façades. Quoins, window "draperies," stringcourses, a caryatid-supported cornice, and vase pinnacles—all carved in white stone—form a rich icing on the "devil's-food" red of the brick walls. The lateral extensions, with their terminating two-story pavilions, date from the early 20th century, when Bagatelle also acquired a rich musical life.*

165

Beychevelle

Too valuable for its production of the world's finest red wine, the rocky, sandy soil of the Médoc cannot be given over to the construction of vast châteaux. Thus, the dwellings built there, even seigneurial ones, tend to be modest in scale, but a few, like Beychevelle, make up in style for what they lack in size. Pragmatism also informs the very name of Beychevelle, which means "lower sail" and refers to a medieval practice, wherein the lords of the domain exploited their position on the banks of the Gironde to exact tribute money from ships making their way to Bordeaux. In those days a small keep provided a lookout from which a sentry would cry the order as each vessel approached. So sacrosanct was the custom that the Plantagenêt legate permitted it to continue right through the English occupation of the Aquitaine.

Apart from its wine, Beychevelle became known to the world only with the accession to the estate of Jean-Louis da La Valette, the Duc d'Épernon so favored by Henri III. Disgraced under Henri IV, Jean-Louis withdrew to Cadillac, leaving Beychevelle to his son, who as governor of Guyenne (the Aquitaine) found the means to replace much of the old château with new construction. From this era survive the two lateral pavilions of the present dwelling. After 1661 the domain passed from the Epernon family, and by the mid-18th century it belonged to the Marquis de Brassier. Finding the château in a pitiable state, he proceeded to rebuild it in an elegant variant of the Louis XV style.

During the Revolution, as soon as the Brassiers emigrated, the government confiscated Beychevelle. In the aftermath of the upheaval Mme de Saint-Hérem, *née* Brassier, bought the estate but sold it in 1800 to a Bordeaux shipping magnate, M. Jacques Conte, who subsequently left the property to his nephew, Pierre-François Guestier. Orleanist in their sympathies, the Guestiers were regularly hosts to members of Louis-Philippe's court during the July Monarchy (1830–48). In 1875 Mme Armand Heine purchased Beychevelle, and it is her grandson, M. Achille-Fould, formerly France's minister of agriculture, who presently owns the estate. The château, now a splendid residence filled with fine art objects, has attracted visits from many, including the Count and Countess of Paris and the crowned heads of Belgium.

above: The sumptuousness of the interior at Beychevelle becomes immediately apparent in the entrance hall. The historiated tapestries hanging before walls covered with 18th-century paneling were woven in Brussels about 1709, probably from cartoons by Louis Van Fhoor. Upon the Regency gaming table rests a Louis XIV clock flanked by Chinese porcelain horn vases dating from the 18th century. The bronze in the foreground is a small version of an heroic equestrian portrait statue of Louis XIV that once stood either in the Place Vendôme or in the Place des Victoires in Paris.

opposite: Since its reconstruction in 1757, Beychevelle has been one of the most attractive dwellings within the district around Bordeaux. The foundations of the medieval enceinte became a balustraded terrace. Between the high, dormered end pavilions, which survive from the 17th century, the old medieval structure was replaced by a new three-bay corps de logis, whose long, delicately classicizing white-stone façade fronts onto a formal garden adorned with yew trees and statuary. Flanked by a balustraded flat roof—a tradition local to the Médoc—the central bay is crowned by a pediment decorated both on its face and its sloping sides with Rococo motifs.

Champlatreux

The creation of an old parlementary family, rather than a feudal one, Champlatreux would naturally be among the first châteaux built in the mid-18th century to reflect the new sense of restraint, the sober need to cleanse the Late Baroque of its Rococo excesses. Still, Champlatreux was built under the *ancien régime*, and, for all its anticipations of the forthcoming Neoclassicism, it has the period look of a pleasure palace for the privileged, with its setting related less to actual nature than to a depiction by the painter Watteau of what idyllic, arcadian nature should be. But quite apart from its stylistic affinities, Champlatreux is a splendid dwelling, noble in scale, beautifully proportioned, and typically French in its elegance and refinement, in its harmonious integration of decorative richness into an overall clarity of form.

For more than two centuries Champlatreux belonged to the Molés, a family with origins in Troyes. Mathieu Molé was attorney general to the Paris Parlement when he bought the domain in 1618, and by 1641 he had become president of that body. A man of absolute probity, President Molé played an important conciliatory role during the Fronde (1648–53), that revolt of nobles against royal authority during the minority of Louis XIV. Mathieu died in 1656, but not until a century later, in 1757, did a descendant undertake to demolish the old château and replace it with the one we know. This châtelain, Mathieu-François Molé, had also achieved the rank of president of the Paris Parlement. In addition, he enjoyed the fortune brought to him by his wife, whose father was the financier Samuel Bernard. The commission for the château went to Michel Chevolet, best known for his design of the Hôtel de Hanouvre in Paris. But not only did Chevolet design the mansion, he also laid out the park, with its beautiful, long perspectives.

Mathieu-François Molé died in 1793, by which time his son, Édouard-Mathieu had become president of the Paris assembly, as well as the son-in-law of President Lamoignon de Malesherbes. The Revolution had also erupted. It transformed Champlatreux into a military hospital and sent Édouard-Mathieu to the guillotine. After calm returned, his son followed family tradition and entered public service. As Comte Molé, Louis-Mathieu realized one of the most brilliant political careers of his time: director of highways and bridges at age twenty in 1809; chief justice in 1817; naval minister and then colonial minister in 1817; foreign minister in 1830; and council president in 1836. Chateaubriand, Joubert, and Fontanes all went to Champlatreux, as did King Louis-Philippe, the later to preside over a meeting of the council of ministers. This was the age of Romanticism, which Comte Molé acknowledged in redesigning the gardens after the English manner. The mood expresses itself in Comte Molé's *Mémoires:* "After lunch . . . I entered the park at Champlatreux with Chateaubriand and Chênedollé. . . . The conversation was immediately about women and love. Chateaubriand well knew my lack of experience in such matters. And it made him impatient: 'You will fall in love, my grave Mathieu,' he said, 'in your own way, you will be in love, and passionately so!' " The great poet-diplomat proved right about his friend, for only a few years later Comte Molé would confess, again in his *Mémoires:* "I have fallen in love to the point of delirium, and it exalts my qualities both good and bad. I am jealous to excess; I demand back all that I give; I give all that I can imagine. . . . I love glory. . . . I feel born for the best!"

Comte Molé retired to Champlatreux and died there in 1855. The last to bear the Molé name, he left the estate to his granddaughter, who married the Duc de Noailles. The poet Anna de Noailles frequently stayed at Champlatreux and found much inspiration there. The Noailles still own Champlatreux, and in 1930 they restored the gardens and *cour d'honneur* to their original 18th-century design.

above: For all its 18th-century elegance and refinement, Champlatreux has a grave and sober look that not only expressed the character of the parlementary family that built it in 1757, but also anticipated the purified forms of the forthcoming Neoclassical style. The château is all of a piece, a single, rectangular block subdivided into slightly projecting pavilions at either end and a tall, temple-fronted pavilion at the center, with each unit crowned by a separate, dormered Mansart roof. On the entrance façade here, reached along an extended perspective, the triangular and arched pediments are smooth, but discreet enrichment occurs elsewhere—in the superimposed Doric and Ionic colonnades of the central pavilion, and in the sculptural treatment of window keystones and dormer enframements. Furthermore, round-headed and rectangular windows alternate between the façade's projecting and receding walls.

opposite: On Champlatreux's garden façade, the central pavilion is less formal, really a flat-fronted hemicycle, soberly Doric on the ground floor and elegantly Ionic on the upper story. The sculptural embellishments are rich, but discreet by virtue of their restriction to keystones, flower-filled urn-finials, and the central, quarter-circle pediment. Here the work is particularly interesting, dropped below the broken cornice and beautifully carved in a bas-relief of Diana surrounded by putti and dogs.

Kergrist

Charmingly candid in expressing the periods during which it was built, Kergrist (*ker* means "house" in Breton) is pure Late Gothic on its court side and in its corner towers and equally unalloyed in the Baroque of its main and garden façades. The earlier portions date from the mid-15th century, when the châtelains were Jean de Kergrist and his wife Gillette le Cozic. Their direct descendants kept the domain, a marquisate, almost to the end of the 18th century, gradually enlarging, adapting, and improving the château and its gardens. Finally, in the absence of male heirs, the property passed through marriage to the Kergarious, the Barbier de Lescoëts, and ultimately, in 1860, the Huon de Penansters, who today maintain the estate in an exemplary fashion. Only the exterior is generally accessible to visitors.

above: A classical façade terminating at either end in corner pepper-pot towers, this aspect of Kergrist speaks forthrightly for the château's origins in the mid-14th and mid-18th centuries. But despite the disparity in styles, a remarkable harmony prevails at Kergrist, extended and enhanced by the surrounding park.

opposite: At Kergrist a splendid rise of stone steps, laid out in sawtooth pattern, links the garden to the château by way of a terrace and a double flight of entrance stairs. The latter, adorned with an iron handrail wrought in the graceful arabesque of the Rococo manner, lead to the main floor, where the tall windows are broken up into small squares framed in white. Carved in relief upon the plane of the central pediment is the device of a marquis.

left: The cour d'honneur at Kergrist remains entirely Gothic, the defensive towers intact and the dormers elaborated with a fanciful array of stone crockets, hooks, and finials.

Caradeuc

Like most of the châteaux of Brittany, Caradeuc is modestly scaled. And while clearly a product of the 18th century, the dwelling expresses the Rococo in a sober and much-chastened form. This makes Caradeuc seem peculiarly Breton, a reality that robs it of neither charm nor elegance. A genuine enhancement is the surrounding park, since the late 19th century a herbaceous bower adorned with stone statuary and clipped yew trees.

The Château de Caradeuc was commissioned by Nicolas de Caradeuc, counselor and dean of the parlement of Brittany. However, it was during the tenure of the builder's son—Louis-René de Caradeuc de La Chalotais—that a certain fame accrued to the Caradeuc family and estate. Voltaire himself expressed it when he wrote to d'Alembert: "Imagine how my blood boiled when I read that statement written with a toothpick—a toothpick that engraves for immortality. To hell with anyone who reads such a message and feels no fever!" The statement Voltaire referred to had been composed by La Chalotais, then attorney general to the Breton parlement but imprisoned at Saint-Malo for behavior considered by the crown to be subversive. According to the author, he wrote "on a chocolate wrapper, using a toothpick as pen and ink mixed from soot, vinegar, and sugar." Such desperate bravado marked the culmination of a long struggle between the parlement of Brittany and the royal authority as represented by the Duc d'Aiguillon.

La Chalotais had entered the public consciousness and the esteem of the *philosophes* when in 1762 he issued a report on the French Jesuit Order. In effect, it condemned the order and recommended its suppression. The following year the Breton attorney general aroused further controversy when he published a treatise on public education. From a modern perspective, La Chalotais could hardly seem a revolutionary, since he recommended against general instruction for the poor. Voltaire, the great luminary of the Enlightenment, stood firmly behind La Chalotais, declaring: "The ignorant brothers . . . teach reading and writing to those who need only to draw a line and handle a plane or file, and who don't ever want to do anything else."

The imprisonment of La Chalotais, however, came from quite a different matter. The central government wanted to level additional taxes, but rather than acquiesce, the parlement in Rennes resigned, all but twelve members. Then the crown began to receive insulting letters, which, although unsigned, seemed to be the work of La Chalotais. Louis XV thought he detected a plot and ordered that arrests be made. And on his part, La Chalotais believed himself to be the victim of a plot hatched by the threatened Jesuits. Thus, the "toothpick" report came as a violent attack made by La Chalotais against his presumed enemies. But with the whole of the Breton assembly in resignation, no judicial body existed that could hear a trial. Finally, the King became exasperated and decided in December of 1766 to cancel the legal proceedings, "His Majesty not wanting to find guilty parties." Still, La Chalotais had to go into exile at Saintes. In 1774, however, the more liberal Louis XVI authorized his return to Rennes, where he made a triumphal reentry. Five years later the monarch made Caradeuc a marquisate. La Chalotais died in 1785, leaving the estate to his son, who had shared his father's official duties as well as his exile. The second Marquis perished on the guillotine in 1794.

In 1841 the last direct descendant of the Caradeuc family married the Comte de Falloux, an eminent member of the liberal Catholic party who, as minister of public education, proved true to the memory of his wife's ancestor. He introduced free public instruction through a project that has borne his name ever since. The Château de Caradeuc now belongs to the Marquis de Kernier, an indirect Caradeuc descendant.

right: Furnished with restraint and elegance, the reception rooms at Caradeuc fill with sunlight from windows that open onto the park.

The charm of the 18th century is especially present in the overdoor paintings of pastoral scenes framed in Late Baroque moldings.

opposite: The Château de Caradeuc is typical of Brittany and the 18th century in its modest scale and gracious lines. More specifically Breton is the sobriety of its Rococo classicism. The entrance bay is especially handsome—a tall, narrow pavilion capped by a truncated pyramid and fronted by a high pediment and a stone portico. Here, paired free and engaged Tuscan columns support a balustrade terminating in stone blocks topped by spheres resting on volutes.

below: On its garden façade, the long, low profile of Caradeuc is saved from monotony by the relatively tall projection of the pavilions that punctuate the building at either end, as well as at center, and thus establish its essential symmetry. A curvilinear, balustraded stairway provides a pleasing and harmonious transition from the château terrace to the park below.

The old 15th-century château at Le Marais survives only in the moats, which have been transformed into canals and a vast, oblong sheet of water aligned on axis with the dwelling built just after 1770. An early expression of Neoclassicism—that highly purified, almost archaeological or Platonic approach to Greco-Roman forms—the edifice has the monumental simplicity of a single block, utterly devoid of communs or secondary buildings. Stressing the central entrance pavilion is a low attic surmounted by a square dome, but instead of the usual strong projection, the unit actually shelters an alcove, or recessed portico, which cuts into the main mass of the building.

Le Marais

opposite: *The monumental simplicity achieved by the new purified classicism at Le Marais is nowhere more apparent than in the entrance pavilion. As at Champs, the portico is recessed, but here the forms are heavier, grander, and more spare, and the whole pavilion projects less. The plainest of the orders—Tuscan—is used for the colonnade, and balusters are limited to the windows or to the double-ramp stairway. The pediment is bare, and sculptural embellishment not only sparse but isolated within the entrance alcove. Even so, sensitive, impeccable handling saves Le Marais from coldness or academic aridity.*

The desire to return to classical gravity and grandeur, after the decorative lightness of the Rococo, brought the architectural orders to the interior of Le Marais. Still, crystal, gilt, stucco reliefs, and the trompe-l'oeil marbling combine to give an effect of great luxury, and make a proper setting for the splendid entertainments that for many years were offered in these reception rooms.

If the French court and nobility failed, in the second half of the 18th century, to adopt the moral and socioeconomic reform demanded by the Enlightenment, they did not hesitate to embrace its aesthetic counterpart—Neoclassicism. In this style the Greco-Roman ideals that had dominated European art and architecture since the Renaissance found a great new lease on life, mainly through a process of rigorous, even radical, purification. The inspiration came not only from the *philosophes,* but also from the rediscovery of those long-buried cities of ancient Rome—Pompeii and Herculaneum. Thus, while purging the Rococo or Late Baroque of its delightful but "decadent" graces, the exponents of the new order also attempted a classicism so strict and proper as to become almost archaeological in character. Now, the search was no longer for charming invention or picturesque complexity, but rather for grandeur and learnedly austere exactitude—or for a geometric, even Platonic purity of form. Still, this was the 18th century, and no real architecture built then could ever come forth without those hallmarks of the age—elegance and refinement. Le Marais, whose plans date from 1770, is chaste, correct, and very grand—and saved from coldness or academic aridity by the designer's innately discriminating touch.

The architect at Le Marais was Barré, one of the most able form-givers of his time, and the commission came from M. Le Maistre, who had made a fortune as treasurer of the French artillery. The estate is located just north of Paris on the right bank of the Seine opposite Marly. A manor house had been on the site since the 15th century, put there by another handler of military funds, Jacques Hurault. In 1706 the decision had been made to build entirely anew. And so great was the desire to achieve antique, monumental dignity that the classical orders themselves—columns and pilasters upon high bases and capitals supporting architraves, cornices, and coffered ceilings—were brought inside to form the decorative theme throughout the interior.

And the interior at Le Marais is important, for it has served as the setting of an incredibly long series of splendid entertainments. In the last years of the *ancien régime,* Mme de La Briche, Le Maistre's niece and heiress, was a concerned châtelaine who even mounted great Rousseau type festivities for the workers on her estate. Having thus been decent, she and Le Marais survived the Revolution unmolested. After calm returned, Mme de La Briche renewed her summer "seasons"—mainly theatrical—for the benefit of her daughter and son-in-law, to distract the one from her marital unhappiness and to advance the other—young Mathieu Molé—in his political career. The effort succeeded, for Comte Molé became prime minister under Louis-Philippe.

After passing through the female descendants of Mme de La Briche—Comtesse Molé, Comtesse de La Ferté-Meung, and the Duchesse de Noailles—Le Marais was purchased in the early 20th century by the American heiress Anna Gould, who had married Comte Boni de Castallane, one of the period's great dandies. Now the receptions at Le Marais became sumptous indeed. In 1908 the Comtesse de Castallane married the Duc de Talleyrand, and it is their daughter, the Comtesse de Pourtalès, who maintains the château and continues to restore it.

Bénouville

top: *For the sober severity of his main façade at Bénouville—a triumph of late-18th-century Neoclassicism—Ledoux modified his original conception **(above)**, changing from six columns on the portico to four freestanding columns flanked by two engaged ones. More unfortunate is the replacement of the low, centralized, blind attic with a higher attic extended full measure and opened by tall windows. This rather crushes the finely tuned balance of the mass below.*

opposite: *A masterpiece of spatial manipulation, Ledoux's grand staircase at Bénouville rises in a single flight to the intermediate landing and then repeats itself to complete the ascent. The illumination from the oculus set in a coffered, quadrangular vault serves mainly to articulate the monumental purity of the classical forms and their arrangement in a well of whiteness.*

Bénouville, on the outskirts of Caen in Normandy, is a château whose architectural pedigree is superior to any social or cultural value that may attach to it. This is because the architect, Claude-Nicolas Ledoux, here essayed some of the ideas that would make him France's greatest form-giver in the second half of the 18th century. It was Ledoux, more than anyone else, who cleansed the classical vocabulary of its Late Baroque excesses and brought about the Neoclassical style—or *style Louis XVI*—making it an expression of the new, sober, Revolutionary spirit of moral rigor and reform.

A château existed at Bénouville from the 14th century onward, but the estate—which became a marquisate as late as 1715—entered history only in 1768. It was then that the Marquis de Livry inherited Bénouville from his father-in-law, Antoine Gillain, and with his wife determined to replace the old château with a structure to be designed in conformity with the most recent "modern" taste. A naval officer with a distinguished war record, the new Marquis de Bénouville had traveled in Italy and Greece, which in part accounts for his interest in the emerging vogue—a white Greco-Roman temple accommodating the latest domestic comforts and dominating a green and natural park. The commission went to Ledoux, whose fame was then on the rise, thanks mainly to the now-destroyed Hôtel d'Uzès in Paris. It made Bénouville something of a prototype for Louveciennes, the pavilion in the Île-de-France that the architect designed two years later for Mme du Barry, the favorite of Louis XV.

At Bénouville, Ledoux took his commission seriously and transformed the requested "small" château into something quite grand. So important were the ideas that the architect illustrated them in his treatise, *Architecture considérée sous le rapport de l'art, des moeurs et de la législation,* which now provides a significant record of how Bénouville was initially conceived and then developed. Begun in 1768, the work had largely reached completion by 1777, when Ledoux assigned the decoration of the interior to his associate, J. F. E. Gillet of Caen. The Revolution stripped the château, but the splendid central staircase survives, a masterwork built from designs provided by Ledoux himself.

On the very eve of the Revolution, the Marquis de Bénouville died, leaving his creditors unpaid and the Marquise insolvent. A forced sale conveyed the estate to François-Marie Mesnage de Pressigny, a former tax collector. This owner perished on the guillotine, but his daughter, Mme d'Aubigny, managed to recover Bénouville. After passing through a variety of owners, the château was purchased in 1927 by the *département* of Calvados, which transformed Ledoux's "country house" into a maternity hospital.

La Lorie

Although devoted to the "sport of Kings"—as the Prix La Lorie at Longchamps's racetrack confirms—and invested with a marble interior almost as rich as those at Versailles, La Lorie has never been a royal residence. Rather, it remains as it was when erected in the mid-17th century—a private estate. The first châtelain was René Le Pelletier, provost marshal of Anjou, who commissioned the small Louis XIII style château on the right bank of the Oudon River, somewhat northwest of Angers. True to the period, this dwelling was built of red brick finished in white stone and consisted of a central *corps de logis* with twin subsidiary wings facing one another on either side of a *cour d'honneur*. Around 1660 depleted finances forced the founder to sell La Lorie to his son-in-law, Gabriel Constantin, who himself had taken the post as Anjou's provost marshal. A full century later Charles Constantin married a rich American heiress. It was now, therefore, that La Lorie acquired its stud farm, in addition to the left and right extensions of the *logis*, one of which houses the chapel and the other the spectacularly beautiful marble *salon de musique*. Still furnished with the original chairs and settees made and signed by Pluvinet, this room constitutes one of the most remarkable Louis XVI ensembles to be found anywhere. The brilliant society who gathered there included a number of those great horse lovers—the English—as well as the elite of Angevin nobility.

The Revolution put both royalist and republican troops in the château, which in the 19th century necessitated a vast restoration effort. Since Charles Constantin, the estate has been owned by the Comte de Marmier, Constantin's son-in-law, the Duc de Fitz-James, and then the Marquis de Saint-Genys, whose grandson now maintains the estate.

above: *La Lorie in Anjou reveals its Louis XIII origins in the tripartite, symmetrical arrangement of its buildings around a central, open forecourt, in the red-brick masonry finished in white stone, and in the high, separate roofs, with their pedimented dormers and blue-slate sheathing. The lateral extensions of the* corps de logis *were added after the middle of the late 18th century, one for a chapel and the other for a resplendent* salon de musique.

opposite: *For the brilliant company they gathered at La Lorie in the last years of the* ancien régime—*many of them horse lovers—the Constantins designed one of the château's new extensions as a grand* salon de musique. *After fifty years of the Rococo taste for carved wooden paneling, a shift occurred back to the soberly classical but richly polychrome marble veneers favored at Versailles in the time of Louis XIV. Such a revival heralded the advent of the Neoclassical style that began to develop toward the end of Louis XV's reign. At La Lorie, Italian artisans prepared the walls, while the French* ébéniste *Pluvinet made and signed the chairs and settees for this very room. Originally the straight-back pieces (*sièges meublants*) would have been aligned against the walls and the curved-back pieces (*sièges courants*) placed in a circle at the middle of the room. Such an arrangement is reflected in the pattern of the marble floor inlay and in the balustraded cupola overhead.*

left: *At La Lorie the ground floor of the main* corps de logis *is given over entirely to a grand entrance gallery, an arrangement created in the 19th century from what originally had been two separate rooms. Tuscan piers—freestanding but aligned close to the walls—support a series of low "basket-handle" vaults, leading at either end to a stately flight of stairs. Also marking the space's division into bays are porcelain vases mounted on tall marble plinths and high-back armchairs upholstered in velvet with petit-point borders.*

179

Royaumont

The "château" at Royaumont originated as an abbot's palace, but the form is that of a villa on the order of the north Italian country houses designed by the 16th-century master Andrea Palladio. So completely at odds stylistically with monastic Royaumont, the domestic dwelling dates from 1783, when a rather wordly abbot commissioned it from Louis Le Masson, a pupil of Claude-Nicolas Ledoux. Typical of the Palladian style is the château's symmetry, the purity of its classical forms, and the light-reflecting, uniform whiteness of all the surfaces.

opposite: Something of the beauty of Cistercian Royaumont can be discerned in this buttressed ruin of a wall, which originally enclosed the chapter hall on the ground floor and the monks' dormitory above. A project close to the heart of Louis IX, France's royal saint, Royaumont was built at the very climax of medieval civilization. The heroic proportioning and the monumental simplicity of the ogival arches reveals Royaumont's kinship in form and style to the Sainte-Chapelle in Paris, as well as to the great cathedrals of Chartres, Amiens, Beauvais, and Bourges.

Louis IX, the sainted King of France and the greatest monarch of the High Gothic age, founded the Cistercian abbey at Royaumont in 1228, when he was but thirteen years old. During a reign that lasted forty-five years, from 1226 to 1270, Louis saw the triumph of French medieval architecture in the great cathedrals of Chartres, Amiens, Beauvais, and Bourges, led several Crusades, attended to the political and economic consolidation of France, curbed private feudal warfare, extended justice to all, simplified administration, and made taxation more equitable. He was also pious and charitable, yet manly and affable, all personal qualities that made it possible for this busy monarch to join personally in the physical effort to build Royaumont, whose name means "royal mountain." Throughout his life Louis remained close to the monastic foundation, virtually transforming it into a crown residence, a place as intimately associated with him as that ravishing jewel, the Sainte-Chapelle in Paris. And with medieval civilization at its climax, Royaumont inevitably blossomed as Gothic at its finest. Only in a much later age, however, did Royaumont become what could be called a "château." This occurred in 1783, on the eve of the Revolution, when a socialite abbot commissioned a new abbatial "palace" for Royaumont. What came forth was a Palladian villa as perfect in its small-scale, 18th-century classicism as the neighboring monastery—in ruins since the Revolution—is exemplary of the monumental High Gothic.

The Life of Saint Louis, written by the Queen's confessor, described the holy monarch at Royaumont, assisting the chapter and with his own hands feeding a leprous monk. But the Hundred Years War (1337–1453) proved disastrous for the great royal abbey. The English held it for ransom on several occasions, during which the community dwindled to thirty monks and the buildings deteriorated from neglect. With the Renaissance the abbot became a royal appointee, instead of a leader elected by the brotherhood. Still later, Cardinal Richelieu used it as a residence whenever the king, Louis XIII, stayed at nearby Chantilly. And it was to Royaumont that Richelieu summoned the conference of abbots, from Cîteaux, Clairvaux, Pontigny, and Morimond, to consider how to check the decline of the Cistercian order. Cardinal Mazarin, Richelieu's successor as prime minister of France, took Royaumont for the "living" it provided. And the same was true of the next "abbot," Alphonse de Lorraine, a Harcourt prince who was only ten years old at the time of his appointment. The monument to this regime is Prince Alphonse's tomb at Royaumont, by Coysevox and one of the masterpieces of French Baroque sculpture.

Thereafter the secularization of the Royaumont abbacy simply accelerated, until the time of Abbot Henri Éléonore Le Cornut de Balivière, whose grand social life—among the likes of Diane de Polignac, Paul I of Russia, and Gustave III of Sweden—justified the erection of the new Palladian "château." It was also during Balivière's tenure that the Revolution broke out, expelling the community, reducing the great abbey church to rubble, and dispersing Royaumont's rich collection of medieval manuscripts. First one industrialist installed a cotton-spinning factory in the conventual buildings, and then a second—a Belgian named van der Mersch—acquired the property, only to separate the communal structures from the abbot's palace and in 1832 sell the latter to the Marquis de Bellissens.

The whole estate became one again in 1905 after both parts had been bought by M. Jules Goüin. M. and Mme Henry Goüin effected a restoration, endowing monastic Royaumont with a vast, new library and inviting the creative and the scholarly to come and work there. Among those who have participated in the old abbey's vital, 20th-century life are the artist Jean Lurçat, the architect Le Corbusier, the writer Merleau-Ponty, the philosopher Gabriel Marcel, and the composers Arthur Honegger and Georges Auric. During the summer concerts are held on Sunday afternoon. As for the palace, it went to Baron and Baroness Fould-Springer in 1923.

Louveciennes

After 1750, so pervasive was the mood of reform, in reaction against the decadence of life under Louis XV, that one of the major symbols of the new spirit is the little freestanding pavilion at Louveciennes. The irony is that the structure was commissioned by none other than the Comtesse du Barry, Louis XV's last mistress and the archsymbol of all that contemporaries considered effete and self-indulgent in France's *ancien régime*. No one could have been less interested in moral regeneration or the politics of revolution than Jeanne Bécu du Barry (1743–93). Kind, good-humored, and devastatingly beautiful, she existed solely to amuse a bored and aging monarch, who, in gratitude for the services she rendered, all but suffocated her with favors. One of these was the gift of Louveciennes, a small château built in 1681 by Louis XIV for Arnold de Ville, the Liègois who had designed the famous Marly machine for pumping water to the King's fountains. Mme du Barry had none of the intellectual ambition of her predecessor at court, the Marquise de Pompadour, but she was a lady of fashion and eagerly followed the new trend just as soon as it set in. This was Neoclassicism, a fresh, highly purified interpretation of Greco-Roman forms designed to purge the Rococo, or Late Baroque, of its soft, curvilinear graces, and thus to parallel in art and architecture the rigor and rectitude then being urged in the socioeconomic dimension of life. When the latter got out of hand, it exploded into the violence of the French Revolution. As always in a time of crisis, the arts did just the opposite. Instead of destroying, they yielded an absolute plethora of enduring masterpieces. Among the first of these was Mme du Barry's pavilion at Louveciennes.

Delighted with her new toy—the château—La du Barry immediately commissioned a restoration from Jacques-Ange Gabriel, the great exponent of the *style Louis XV* at its most elegant and refined. But the dwelling remained small, and so the châtelaine turned to Claude-Nicolas Ledoux, then largely unknown, and asked him to design a supplementary pavilion consisting of nothing but a few reception rooms. What the young master produced is so simple, severe, and elementary that it borders on pure abstraction, and more than a palace of sensuous delight, it seems a temple for the votive rites of Vestal Virgins. In this crisply articulated, oblong box, not even a pediment, but merely a balustrade, crowns the central bay; thus, hardly a diagonal or an arabesque obtrudes within a realm derived directly from those most primary of forms, the cube and the sphere. Paradoxically—and characteristically—Mme du Barry called it a "folly." Still, when it came to the exterior décor, she rejected the true follies—and gorgeous ones at that—painted by Jean-Honoré Fragonard and ordered a whole new cycle of murals from Joseph-Marie Vien. Although a lesser artist than Fragonard, Vien was one of the first of the Neoclassicizing painters and the teacher of the style's greatest master, Jacques-Louis David. Gouthière prepared bronzes and Pajou sculptures. Once completed, the Louveciennes pavilion caused a furor, for clearly the new age had arrived. No one could have recognized it better than Louis XV, whose own Pompadour had already said: *Après nous le déluge!* Thus, when Mme du Barry marked the inaugural with a great banquet, the King attended.

After Louis XV's death of smallpox in 1774, when she personally attended the King despite the risk of her own infection, Mme du Barry suffered many indignities, beginning with a period of confinement in a convent—where she managed to make the nuns like her. Too faithful to the memory of Louis XV to emigrate, she became the butt of the most rabid Revolutionary hatred. Finally condemned, the former royal favorite mounted the scaffold on December 8, 1793, and at age fifty submitted to the guillotine.

Much later, after the ground had shifted under the Ledoux pavilion, threatening its structure, M. F. Coty moved the edifice, stone by stone, to another site. Unfortunately, he also added an attic story and installed a swimming pool in the basement. The interior décor was reconstituted from old engravings. Louveciennes remains a private estate, owned by M. V. Moritz.

above: *The chief interest at Louveciennes is the small freestanding pleasure pavilion commissioned in the late 18th century by Mme du Barry, Louis XV's last mistress. But even in this "folly" the emerging mood of reform expressed itself through the almost Platonic purity of the Neoclassical design prepared by Claude-Nicolas Ledoux. Devoid of Rococo classicism's curvilinear graces and soft, decorative transitions, the Louveciennes pavilion is little more than a crisply articulated, oblong box. A simple balustrade, rather than a pediment, crowns the central bay; thus, hardly a diagonal or an arabesque obtrudes within a realm derived directly from those most primary of forms, the cube and the sphere. The interior (below), when finished, was sumptuous but no less Neoclassical in its styling. Long after the Revolution, an attic story was added to the Louveciennes pavilion (opposite), which somewhat spoiled Ledoux's reductive proportioning.*

For its contents alone, Montgeoffroy is one of the most precious châteaux in France. From the damask on the walls to the silver on the table, the furnishings are complete, original, and verifiable against an inventory drawn up in 1775. Even the arrangement is that made by the dwelling's builder, Maréchal Louis-Georges-Érasme de Contades.

opposite: Serenely set back and patrician, but modest in design and scale, Montgeoffroy is a rare 18th-century country house in a region—the Loire Valley—known mainly for the grandiose royal castles built there during the Middle Ages and Renaissance. The entrance through an exquisitely Rococo gilded grille leads to a simple, three-story, cream-colored stone block sprouting red-brick chimney stalks through a blue-gray slate roof. The arrangement of a pedimented central bay and projecting lateral pavilions crowned by pyramid roofs is ordinary for the time of construction (1757). Exceptional, however, is the incorporation of 16th-century towers—round, low, and cone-capped—as terminals to the communs on either side of the cour d'honneur. This last feature is closed on its "open," semicircular side by a balustrade and a dry moat.

Montgeoffroy

Not far from Angers lies one of the rarest gems in France, the Château de Montgeoffroy, which, while little more than a large country house, retains every last fragment of its original 18th-century furnishings, from the damask wall covering to the silver candelabra. Everything is of the finest quality and can be checked against an inventory of contents made in 1775. Many pieces of furniture are signed, by Gourdin *père*, Durand, or Garnier, and each remains in the very place assigned by the château's builder. The dwelling too is rare for being an unpretentious 18th-century structure located in the Loire, a region favored in the Middle Ages and the Renaissance by monarchs who built, not economically, but with truly royal grandeur. On a low hill somewhat away from the valley, and approached by a triad of converging avenues, Montgeoffroy stands serene and patrician, a three-story, cream-colored stone block with red-brick chimney stalks sprouting from the gray slate of its modestly steep roof. The arrangement of a pedimented central bay and projecting lateral pavilions is standard for the period in France, as are the separate roofs over the end pavilions. Exceptional as well as charming, however, are the round and low, cone-capped towers that, like the chapel, were retained from a much earlier château. They function as terminals to the service buildings on either side of a *cour d'honneur*. The architect was Barré, better known for his work in Paris and at Le Marais and Le Lude.

Montgeoffroy survives intact because its builder, the Maréchal Louis-Georges-Érasme de Contades, chose not to emigrate during the Revolution. Instead, he disciplined himself to serve France impartially through its several regimes, from Louis XV to Napoleon. Although the château he commissioned dates only from 1773, the domain itself can be traced back to 1209, when Montgeoffroy belonged to one Geoffroy de Chateaubriand. The owners in the 16th century were the La Grandière family, from whose château survive Montgeoffroy's two low defensive towers and the chapel with its Flamboyant window filled with the original stained glass. Érasme de Contades acquired the estate in 1676. The Duc de Saint-Simon, writing in the early 18th century, tells us that this ancestor of a long and still enduring line was "familiar to the King [Louis XIV] by his several gifts of very fine and well-trained setters." Of the next Contades, Georges-Gaspard, lieutenant general of the royal armies, Saint-Simon wrote: "Rather handsome with a pleasant face, he spoke with courtly language and in a manner suitable to women, who found him attractive. . . . He knew . . . how to make his way honestly, and how to live in Paris, at the court, and in the army among the best, most useful, and worthwhile company." Then with characteristic ferocity, the Duke added: "The miracle in all this is that he was scarcely intelligent and never even learned how to write a letter."

It was in the next generation, however, that the Contades acquired a great reputation. After distinguishing himself in Corsica from 1737 to 1740, Louis-Georges-Érasme was made marshal in 1758 and commander-in-chief of the army in Germany during the Seven Years War. But he lost favor following a defeat at Minden, only to serve for twenty-five years as governor of Alsace. Because of the assignment in Strasbourg, it was the Marshal's daughter who took charge of completing the interior at Montgeoffroy. The old soldier died in 1795, at age ninety-five! His descendant, the Marquis de Contades, maintains the château and its precious contents with utter devotion.

below: *The main façade of the single logis completed at Le Bouilh consists of an arcaded ground floor whose projection supports a balustraded terrace upon which rises a giant, two-story colonnade, which itself supports a crowning balustrade. Behind this the Mansart roof houses a dormered attic. So abruptly did work cease at the Château de Bouilh that the column capitals were never carved and remain simply stone blocks. The entrance, with its grand staircase, is through the side wing. Outside are the famed vineyards of the Côte du Bourg.*

left: *The entrance at Le Bouilh, with its monumental, straight-line stairs and severe, impeccable classicism, is modeled after Victor Louis's masterpiece in Bordeaux's Grand Théâtre.*

opposite: *Potentially the grandest château of the Louis XVI period, but arrested by the Revolution, Le Bouilh was planned by the Bordelais architect Victor Louis to have twin logis linked by a raised colonnade passing around a centrally placed peristyle. The form conceived for the latter is that of a rotunda, like Rome's 2nd-century, low-domed Pantheon. It would have been a splendid ceremonial entrance to the château, with double-ramp stairs wrapped around the temple's circular base.*

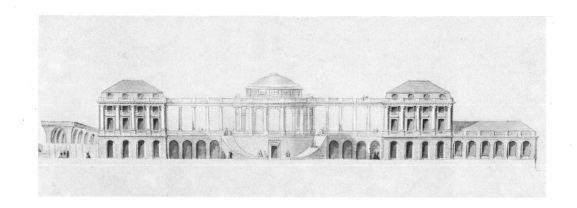

Le Bouilh

Le Bouilh could very well have become the finest château of the Louis XVI period, had it been commenced somewhat earlier than that fateful year, 1789, in which the fall of the Bastille set off the French Revolution. Work at Le Bouilh immediately came to a halt, leaving realized only a fragment of the grandiose plans drawn up by Victor Louis, the master architect who had made the Grand Théâtre in nearby Bordeaux one of the supreme monuments to the new Neoclassical style. In its present form, shaded by large, old trees and surrounded by the Côte du Bourg vineyards on the north bank of the Gironde, Le Bouilh bears a strong resemblance to the plantation architecture surviving from the antebellum era in the American South.

Le Bouilh was commissioned by Jean-Frédéric, Marquis de La Tour du Pin-Gouvernet, who, following a brilliant military career as provincial commander, had just been named minister of war by Louis XVI. No sooner did he accept the appointment than the Marquis ordered work to cease at Le Bouilh, the better to avoid the impression that his personal château was being constructed at public expense. From the enormously ambitious scheme, calling for two main *logis* linked by a raised colonnade passing through a centrally placed peristyle, only one *logis* with its lower wing and a vast hemicycle of service buildings were ever completed. The peristyle would have had the low-domed, rotunda form of Rome's 2nd-century Pantheon. But so abruptly did the builder withdraw that the capitals atop the giant, two-story columns on the single pavilion's main façade remain simple blocks, uncarved with the intended volutes of the Ionic order. But the interior did receive its Louis XVI paneling, and that survives. In lieu of the great circular, double-ramped entrance planned for the center of the complex, a staircase modeled after that in Victor Louis's Grand Théâtre was inserted into the low side wing.

The Marquis de La Tour du Pin was guillotined in 1794. To save themselves, his son and daughter-in-law emigrated to the United States. On their return to Le Bouilh in 1796, they found the château decimated. In her *Mémoires,* the Marquise wrote: "I had left this house well furnished, and while it contained nothing elegant, everything was convenient and abundant. I now found it absolutely empty—not a chair to sit on, not a table, not a bed." Although Napoleon named the Marquis imperial prefect in Brussels, the latter joined the Bourbons upon their restoration in 1815. He then became counselor of the French embassy in Vienna, minister at the embassy in The Hague, and finally ambassador to the house of Savoy in Turin. His son, after the July Revolution that brought the Orleanist Louis-Philippe to the throne, joined the plots hatched by the Duchesse de Berry to force a restoration of the senior branch of the Bourbon line. This resulted in his being condemned to death in absentia. It also caused the La Tour du Pin family to sell Le Bouilh and emigrate to Lausanne.

The new châtelain was M. Hubert de L'Îsle, whose daughter-in-law possessed such beauty that it was immortalized in verse by the great Romantic poet Alphonse de Lamartine. Her daughter, Noëline, married Comte Edouard de Feuilhade de Chauvin, and it is the descendants of this couple who own Le Bouilh today.

La Dame Blanche

The domain of La Dame Blanche is so ancient that the name of the château is ascribed to a legend dating back to the 8th century, when the Saracens from North Africa made their incursion into France and for a brief period occupied the region of the Médoc north of Bordeaux. These Islamic forces, or Moors as they have often been called, penetrated as far north as Poitiers and Tours before being driven back over the Pyrenees by the armies of Charlemagne (in a campaign that inspired the epic poem *The Song of Roland*). As the Moslems evacuated the Médoc, a dusky North African maiden was believed to have lingered in spirit so as to protect the life, property, and fortunes of the young French seigneur to whom she had given her heart. By the light of the new moon, her phantom presence, dressed entirely in white, could be seen and felt in the vineyards and woods surrounding the château on the site that came to be known as La Dame Blanche.

Something of the delicate feeling of this old story can still be sensed at La Dame Blanche, a chaste and white Louis XV château set in the shady expanse of an emerald green park. Long ago the domain was called Le Taillan and belonged to the viscounts of Lomagne. From this clan came Bertrand de Goth, who entered history as Clement V, the first of the Popes to settle at Avignon. At the end of the 14th century Jeanne de Lomagne, dame du Taillan, bore the estate to her husband, seigneur de Blanquefort, to create an alliance that itself could have produced the name of La Dame Blanche.

From the 16th century to the Revolution, La Dame Blanche belonged to the Lavie family, many of whose members served in the Bordeaux parlement. Armand de Lavie collected a great library of "rare and curious" works, all of which disappeared from the château during the Revolution.

In the 19th century the Marquis de Bryas became châtelain of La Dame Blanche and was followed there by General de Borelli, a great traveler who left a journal of his expedition into southern Ethiopia. The General's son became an established poet and playwright. *Alain Chartier* by Vicomte de Borelli was played by the great actress Julia Bartet in Bordeaux and at Paris's Comédie-Française. After several subsequent transfers, the estate now belongs to M. Jean Cruse of the great family of Bordeaux vintners. The vineyards at La Dame Blanche yield a white wine much appreciated for its dry, "sappy" qualities.

above: The present Château de La Dame Blanche adorns an ancient estate, but the building itself dates only from the second half of the 18th century. Giving ample evidence of this is the white simplicity of the Neoclassical styling, set in the bosky realm of a cool green park.

opposite: This salon at La Dame Blanche exemplifies the chastened classicism that developed in architecture and the decorative arts toward the end of the 18th century. Here symmetry is so important that false doors have been introduced to balance the real ones. The simple but graceful fan motif over the mirrors originated in England under the discriminating hand of the brothers Adam. In France such refined and attenuated classicism is associated with the Directory of the late 1790s. Bracketing this period are the rather more massive and rectlinear classicism of the gilded Empire chairs and the magnificent marquetry commode à la greque *executed in the earlier manner of Öben.*

Malmaison

In the hectic days of the Revolution and the ensuing regimes of the Directory, the Consulate, and the Empire—a period spanning from 1789 to 1815—France saw more destruction than actual building. And while the leading figure to emerge from these public dramas—Napoleon—was eager enough to erect monuments to his own glory, the sheer momentum with which this Romantic hero moved—from the victory of Arcole to the collapse at Waterloo and exile on Saint Helena—precluded the possibility of vast new châteaux bearing the stamp of Napoleonic taste. Even so, this stamp was a distinctive one, making itself felt powerfully, if not in complete châteaux, then in triumphal arches and urban layout, in painting and sculpture, and, above all, in furnishings and interiors, epecially those arranged within older structures. And just as the Napoleonic dynasty survived through the progeny of Bonaparte's first wife and Empress—Joséphine de Beauharnais, ironically rejected and divorced because she could not give the Emperor a child of his own—the chief witness to the Empire style is Malmaison, a modest 17th-century château northwest of Paris that Joséphine bought in 1799, rebuilt, retired to, and generally transformed into the only place to which her ill-fated Emperor felt a deep and enduring attachment. Aiding her at Malmaison were the architects Charles Percier and P.F.L. Fontaine, who became the official form-givers of the Napoleonic reign.

The very name Malmaison would suggest that here, far back in the Middle Ages, was once established a hospital, probably for lepers. In the 14th century the domain belonged to the Abbey of Saint-Denis, but by the early 17th century, during the Louis XIII era, it had become the property of Christophe Perrot, a

In 1807 François Gérard portrayed Joséphine de Beauharnais (1763–1814) at the height of her glory as Empress of France. After her divorce from Napoleon in 1809, Joséphine made Malmaison her special retreat. The old château had already been transformed into a triumphant expression of the Empire style.

Malmaison north of Paris is the château most intimately associated with the early 19th-century lives of Joséphine and Napoleon Bonaparte. The building—which is little more than a long corps de logis terminating in tall lateral pavilions—dates from the early 17th century and still possesses the severe dignity of the Louis XIII era. While Napoleon was away on his Egyptian campaign, Joséphine acquired the estate in 1799, commissioning Percier and Fontaine to modernize the château both inside and out. To reinforce the old structure, the architects added buttresses to the main façades. Treated as Doric pilasters crowned by vases or statuary, these vertical elements have a decorative effect and bring relief to the otherwise monotonous lengths of wall. A stone bridge, flanked by red marble obelisks and a pair of bronze statues (from the Château de Richelieu), leads to the entrance on the garden front. A few handsome trees and an artificial stream are all that survive to remind the visitor of the Empress's English garden, which was famous for its profusion of roses and its vast greenhouse fragrant with an immense variety of exotic flowers.

counselor to the Parlement of Paris who put up the essential structure that now survives. This consists of an unusually long *corps de logis* interrupted only by terminal pavilions with steep roofs. In 1771 the financier Lecoulteux du Moley acquired Malmaison and made it the setting of a brilliant salon, attended by such notables as the painter Vigée Lebrun, the mathematician-philosopher Condorcet, the naturalist Bernardin de Saint-Pierre, and the poet André Chenier. Then came Joséphine, the sensuous and irresistibly fascinating Creole from Martinique whom the impetuous Bonaparte, while still a freshly commissioned army commander, had married in 1796. In 1799 Napoleon was on his Egyptian campaign, and so from the outset Malmaison reflected the decisions and aspirations of Joséphine. First off, her architects had to reinforce the building structurally, which accounts for the famous defile of buttresses added to the main façades. Treated like Doric pilasters crowned with vases or statuary, these upright elements bring rhythm and decorative relief to what must have seemed boring and interminable lengths of wall. Moreover, Percier and Fontaine enlarged the dwelling by two small wings and embellished the entrance with a veranda painted in imitation of a military tent, a feature now long lost.

The two architects also took charge of the interior and, with the help of those great *ébénistes*, the brothers Jacob, made the prototype of the Napoleonic style. Sometimes called Directoire, but more often Empire, it had a long life in 19th-century Europe once the mode spread abroad under the rubric of Biedermeier. The forms still honored the classical antique in the purified, archaeological manner that had developed during the final years of the *ancien régime*. However, they reassumed some of the erotic quality of the old Rococo, while also taking on the heroic weight and force expressive of an age in love with martial conquest and Roman-like, imperial grandeur. Whether left smooth or worked in stucco, ceilings and walls were articulated with crisp Pompeiian motifs, forming rather chaste frames for scantily clad, dancing nymphs, motifs that often were set off by such male imagery as military trophies. Rooms could also be draped in imitation of campaign tents, the better to celebrate the Emperor's steady march across Europe's age-old frontiers. Instead of pastel-painted fruitwood, furniture was made of dark, highly polished mahogany and endowed with symmetry and clean-cut silhouettes. Rare but rich, embellishments came in the form of brass or ormolu mounts, with claw feet supporting pedestal tables a typical feature. Also characteristic were Egyptian themes and a type of furniture known as the gondola or sleigh bed. In Joséphine's time, and over the years since, Malmaison became a veritable dictionary of the full vocabulary of the Napoleonic style.

But, the marvel of Malmaison was its garden, designed in the English manner by the Scotsman Thomas Blaikie. It contained natural streams and artificial basins, whole populations of animals and stone statues—and roses, roses, roses of every known variety. The châtelaine served tea in a Temple of Love and in a vast greenhouse cultivated exotic flowers, such as the carnation, for the sweetness of their fragrance. Alas, nothing of this delicious realm survives from the plantings made by Joséphine and her gardener.

Under the Consulate Napoleon made Malmaison his preferred residence, but moved officially to nearby Saint-Choud once his self-appointed role as Emperor required more spacious quarters. But even after the divorce in 1809, which enabled Napoleon to marry the Austrian Archduchess Marie-Louise, Joséphine and Malmaison remained important factors in the life of France and Europe. The former Empress died in 1814, of exposure suffered during a reception she had given for the allied heads of state gathered in Paris to force the Emperor's abdication and exile to Elba. The following year, after Waterloo, Napoleon spent five days at Malmaison and then left for his second and final exile, this time on the lonely island of Saint Helena.

The widow of Eugène de Beauharnais, Joséphine's son, sold Malmaison, which brought about the dispersal of the library and furnishings. Napoleon III, Joséphine's grandson, acquired the estate in 1861 but sold it after his own abdication in 1871. Several subsequent transfers left the château largely stripped of both contents and land, but in 1903 the financier Osiris bought Malmaison and initiated a restoration that resulted in the establishment there, in 1906, of the Musée Napoleon.

In portraying Napoleon as First Consul, Isabey naturally placed his subject in the park at Malmaison, which was indeed his preferred residence in the period just before he became Emperor. The days Napoleon spent there may also have been his happiest, since it was to Malmaison that he returned prior to his final exile on the remote island of Saint Helena.

Napoleon's library at Malmaison was prepared in 1800 by Percier and Fontaine, who had to deal with a space complicated by the immovable presence of a kitchen flue. They solved the problem in part by introducing an arcade resting upon dark mahogany columns and supporting vaults decorated in the attenuated Pompeiian manner. The furniture, which includes the great "mechanical" desk signed by the Jacob frères, was originally made for the Tuileries Palace.

In this sumptuously imperial room and in the magnificent gilded bed, its swans and cornucopias carved by Jacob-Desmalter, Joséphine, Napoleon's first Empress, died on May 29, 1814. The chamber's décor—which with its crimson draperies suspended from gilded poles evokes the campaign tents used by the constantly warring Napoleon—has been reconstituted from contemporary documents. On the mantel the Three Graces clock is a work in Sèvres biscuit made after a model prepared by the Napoleonic sculptor Chauvet. The flanking vases in Paris porcelain bear the monogram of Joséphine.

Château Lafite

"In 1775, when the Maréchal de Richelieu was appointed governor of Guyenne," related Mme Denise Bourdet, "he consulted a Bordeaux doctor who prescribed the wine of Château Lafite as the best and most pleasant tonic." At the return of Richelieu to Paris, Louis XV said to him: "Marshal, I'm tempted to believe that you are twenty-five years younger than when you left for Guyenne!" To which the King's servant replied: "I have found the famous fountain of youth. I discovered that Château Lafite is a delicious cordial and comparable to the ambrosia drunk by the gods on Mount Olympus." Soon the wine was being consumed by the entire court at Versailles.

As early as the 14th century a squire of Lafite was called "prince of vineyards," but the present, much-remodeled château, in the Médoc district north of Bordeaux, appears to date from no earlier than the 15th century. The great staircase was built in the 17th century, while the paneling and plaster work in the suites are products of the 18th century. During the Revolution the owner of Lafite—Pichard, president of the Bordeaux parlement—lost first the estate and then his head. Subsequently a Dutch arms supplier named Vanderberghes acquired Lafite, only to have it managed by an English banker, Sir Samuel Scott. In 1868 complications resulted in an auction at which Baron James de Rothschild, founder of the French line of that great banking family, bought the château for the colossal sum of 4,140,000 gold francs. Baroness James—a beauty celebrated in a portrait by Ingres and a great salon hostess whose guests regularly included such immortals as Balzac, Meyerbeer, Rossini, and Heine—furnished the rooms at Lafite in the rich style of the Second Empire. Classified since 1855 as a "first growth" Médoc, Château Lafite is one of the world's premier red wines. The estate remains a possession of the Rothschild family.

above: The château at Lafite, with its oddly matched round and square towers (the square one flanked by a Renaissance bartizan), seems to date in part from the 15th century. However, much remodeling occurred at later periods, especially during the 17th and 18th centuries. A majestic, one-hundred-year-old cedar spreads a wonderful shade over the building's main façade.

opposite: The library at Château Lafite dates from the Second Empire and is characteristic of "the Rothschild style." Flowered carpet, walls hung with green silk brocade held by embroidered edges, oaken paneling and mantelpiece all serve as a setting for the sumptuous furniture, which includes a "comfortable" chair and ebony chests inlaid with ivory and fashioned in the 17th-century manner. The thoroughly Victorian "X-bench" in the foreground had its general inspiration in an 18th-century model.

George Sand (1804–76),
by Thomas Couture

Nohant

Neither the modest Louis XVI architecture nor the genuine aristocratic connections at Nohant can account for the magnetic charm of this country house in Berry. Devoid of moats, machicolated towers, and vast parks, Nohant is a rare château that attracts almost solely by the society that inhabited it. And what society! The very cream of 19th-century Romantic France—Musset, Liszt and Marie d'Agoult, Chopin, Delacroix, Théophile Gautier, La Malibran and Pauline Viardot, Balzac, Sainte-Beuve, Michelet, Alexandre Dumas *fils*, Flaubert, and Turgenev, to name only a few—all drawn by the châtelaine, who was none other than the passionate and prodigious novelist George Sand (1804–76). Having begun her long public life in scandal, Aurore Dupin, Baronne Dudevant, ended it—after some eighty novels—on her ancestral estate, adored by family, friends, and fellow Berrichons, as *la bonne dame de Nohant*.

George Sand inherited Nohant from her paternal grandmother, Marie-Aurore de Saxe, Mme Dupin de Francueil, who had acquired it as a place of retreat during the worst days of the Revolution. The natural daughter of Comte Maurice de Saxe, France's greatest military leader in the 18th century,

opposite: *Of Nohant, her country house in Berry, the novelist George Sand wrote: "The château, if indeed a château it is (since the house is nothing more than a mediocre structure from the time of Louis XVI), touches the hamlet and also borders on the adjacent fields. It is hardly more sumptuous than a cottage."*

Still, history came to Nohant, for there George Sand grew up—under the tutelage of an aristocratic, but liberal-minded, grandmother— raised her children, entered into the life of the village, wrote her greatest works, produced delightful theatre, and attracted the cream of 19th-century Romantic France.

Mme Dupin de Francueil raised George at Nohant after the child's father, a brilliant officer under Napoleon, died of a riding accident and her plebeian mother abandoned the country for life in Paris. Thus, it was in rural Berry that George Sand, educated by an intelligent, liberal-minded old lady and running freely in the fields with the children of the village, developed her profound sense of place. There she gathered the materials for her later masterpieces—the bucolic novels *La Mare au diable, La Petite Fadette, Les Maîtres sonneurs,* and *François le champi.* And there too, at age eighteen, after finishing her education in a Paris convent, she married Baron Casimir Dudevant, thereby entering an alliance so disastrous that, in 1831, it drove her, with her two children, to Paris and into an open alliance with the poet Jules Sandeau. In the garret world of impecunious bohemians, Baroness Dudevant became the male-attired, cigar-smoking George Sand (a pseudonym that simply abbreviates Sandeau) and accomplished her first professional writing, which included *Indiana* and *Lélia.* But in 1837 she was back at Nohant, making a studio of her grandmother's former bedroom: "This boudoir was so small that with my collections of books, herbs, butterflies, and rocks . . . no room was left for a bed. To rest, I strung up a hammock. With an armoire I made a desk that folded out like a secretary and that a cricket long shared with me once it got used to my presence."

Tireless and ever fluent, George Sand wrote all night to sustain her daily world of children, neighbors, servants, lovers, and, it would seem, the entire world of arts, letters, and even politics. After the poets Sandeau and Alfred de Musset, George Sand established her famous relationship with the tubercular Chopin, which lasted from 1839 to 1846. The painter Delacroix was a frequent guest at Nohant during this period. "At any moment in the garden," he wrote, "gusts of music can come through the window where Chopin works at [George's] side. It blends with the roses and the song of nightingales." On a typical evening Chopin would accompany Pauline Viardot as she sang for Delacroix, in a voice that Théophile Gautier described as "one of the most magnificant instruments to be heard anywhere. . . . Its ineffably sweet and compelling tones truly touch the heart." After 1846, for the betterment of life in general, George and her son Maurice built two theatres at Nohant, a conventional one and another for marionettes. George herself wrote the plays and sewed the costumes. "Yesterday," she recorded, "we had a splendid performance. A play . . . half-spoken, half-mimed, with surprises, devils, and explosions in every scene. About sixty people made up the audience. It got a bit out of hand, for we shouted and stamped. The actors were electrified."

Gradually the "lioness" of the Romantic movement became the "good lady of Nohant," who drew upon her richly experienced life to become the wise counselor of the boys and girls of Berry. The affair with Chopin ended sadly, in part because of jealousy felt by George's daughter, Solange. But love and joy were never long absent from Nohant. A late visitor was Flaubert, whom George characterized as "a great bear" hibernating in work. "We hop, we dance, we scold Flaubert, who wants to stop everything in order to talk literature. . . . But we are raucous, we make games, and play the fool with delight."

Three years later, at age seventy-two, George Sand died at Nohant in her room "tapestried in soft blue." After attending the funeral, Flaubert wrote to Turgenev: "I bawled like a calf."

Mme Aurore Lauth Sand, George's granddaughter and last descendant, preserved Nohant as the setting the great writer had created. She then deeded the château to the French state.

right: Here, at age seventy-two, George Sand—now la bonne dame de Nohant—*died on June 8, 1876. Shortly before, she had written: "I have tapestried myself in a soft blue, spotted with white medallions in which little mythological figures dance. It seems to me that pale tonalities and Rococo subjects are nicely conducive to a state of repose; in such an environment I should have sweet and beautiful thoughts."*

above: George Sand's salon at Nohant retains its handsome furniture signed by Jacob, as well as Pauline Viardot's harp. There after dinner gathered such guests as Viardot and her famous sister, La Malibran, Liszt and Marie d'Agoult, Musset, Chopin, Delacroix, Théophile Gautier, Balzac, Sainte-Beuve, Michelet, Dumas fils, Flaubert, and Turgenev. Of the evenings at Nohant, Chopin wrote: "George's eyes are veiled, they light up only when I play. Then the world becomes clear and beautiful. My fingers glide over the keys; her pen flies on the paper."

right: The bedroom at Nohant of George Sand's paternal grandmother recalls the ancien régime origins of this natural daughter of Comte Maurice de Saxe, marshal of France. The bed à la polonaise and the Louis XVI chairs are draped and upholstered in flowered chintz. In such a calm, simple, and old-fashioned environment were played out some of the Romantic age's most passionate scenes.

Ferrières

Ferrières, the 19th-century château of the French Rothschilds, was designed and furnished to be truly fit for kings and emperors. And when Napoleon III made a visit there, *Le Monde Illustré* (December 27, 1862) published a detailed account of the event and its remarkable setting. In the imperial party were, among others, Prince Metternich, the Austrian ambassador, Lord Cowley, who was then British ambassador to France, and the Prince of Moscow. Baron James, the great financier and founder of the French house of Rothschild, and his four sons met their guests at the railway station. They then drove the party to the château in carriages specially built for the occasion, each drawn *à la Daumon* (by four horses two of which were mounted). Midday dinner was served from Sèvres of the most magnificent kind. The shooting that followed yielded eight hundred pheasants, a few hares, and one snipe. None other than Rossini composed the hunting fanfare that accompanied the supper served in the main hall. As the Emperor departed, he found his passage lined from the steps of the château to the park entrance by the entire Rothschild household, all of them bearing torches to light the great man on his way.

As early as 1829 James de Rothschild had purchased the Ferrières estate from the descendants of the Duchesse d'Otrante, the widow of Fouché, the terrible minister of police under both Napoleon I and the Restoration. A person of grandiose vision, James had the château rebuilt and considerably enlarged from plans prepared by Sir Joseph Paxton, the designer of the Crystal Palace, then London's most famous monument. For the interior James engaged the talents of Eugène Lami, who adopted the boldest of Second Empire eclecticism to create a rich setting worthy of the vast Rothschild art collection.

With its columns, pilasters, pinnacles, balustrades, lanterns, and cupolas, Ferrières survives as a masterpiece of Second Empire eclecticism. The architect of the château was Sir Joseph Paxton, the former gardener to the Duke of Devonshire who gained immortality by perceiving in the traditional greenhouse the principles of modern prefabricated, steel-and-glass architecture. His fame arrived when he applied the principles to create the great Crystal Palace for London's 1851 Universal Exhibition.

right: Dazzling in its ornamentation and designed in the manner of great English country houses, the huge hall at Ferrières is two stories high and lighted only by windows in the ceiling. The generally Baroque installation offers a gallery whose supporting caryatids were inspired by an organ loft in Venice. From church façades came the notion of the statue-filled niches. Truly monumental and vaguely Renaissance in character, the fireplace is surmounted by a colossal, polychrome marble bust. The Gobelins tapestries that originally covered the walls disappeared during World War II and have been replaced by silk damask, its color—emerald green—chosen to harmonize with the chocolate and gilt paneling. Also set off by the fabric is the bronze in the room, as well as the marquetry furniture by Boulle. The opulence of materials, scale, and eclectic historicism is typical of the Second Empire.

While Paris was besieged during the Franco-Prussian War (1870–71) the Kaiser and his "Iron Chancellor," Bismarck, took Ferrières as their headquarters. So impressed was the German monarch by the grandeur of the estate that he ordered his staff not to do so much as the slightest damage. He even forbade Bismarck, an ardent huntsman, to shoot the game in the park. Still, Comtesse de Moustier wrote in a letter: "Rothschild told me yesterday that Bismarck was not satisfied with the pheasants at Ferrières, and that he had even threatened to thrash the manager of the estate."

The tapestry room became the scene of the peace talks conducted by Jules Favre in a series of meetings with Bismarck. When Prussia began to claim an enormous indemnity against France, it was Baron Alphonse de Rothschild who advised his government on a method of payment that eventually was accepted.

The greatest adornment of Ferrières was its first châtelaine, Baroness James. A celebrated beauty, Betty de Rothschild created a salon, both in Paris and at her country residence, and gathered to it the age's leading figures in politics, literature, and art. Heinrich Heine celebrated her in his poem *The Eagle*. Balzac, Meyerbeer, and Rossini were all her friends. The grace and elegance of Baroness James are with us still in her portrait by Jean-Auguste-Dominique Ingres.

In their recent restoration of Ferrières, the Rothschilds preserved all the rich anachronisms that make the château the most beautiful thing of its kind dating from the Second Empire. Now the family have conveyed Ferrières to the state, which intends to offer it to distinguished guests from abroad.

below: For the beauteous and beguiling Baronne James de Rothschild (1805–86) the great Ingres undertook one of his last portrait commissions. By balancing the sitter's face and form between the lushly folded, gleaming costume and the planar austerity of the background, Ingres—in the words of Robert Rosenblum—"transformed mid-19th-century material wealth into a timeless icon of aristocratic grace and beauty."

Groussay

above: Originally built in 1803, the Château de Groussay has been modified and extended laterally until it now seems a remarkably true evocation of the English Palladian sytle. The rotundalike central pavilion survives from the early 19th century. In the modern additions are found, on the left, a gallery, the drawing room, and the Louis XIII dining room and, on the right, the Goya gallery, the foyer, and the theatre. The latter is a dazzling creation of brocade-draped loges and crystal chandeliers and a central canopied box reminiscent of that in the Margravine's theatre in Bayreuth.

opposite: For the dining room at Groussay M. de Bestegui designed and prepared a décor that conjures the interiors of the time of Louis XIII. But in an inspiration entirely his own, now much copied, the châtelain combined bold checks and vigorous floral patterns, yet succeeded in resolving these warring schemes into a tense but harmonious whole. The brilliant red and blue floral design has been woven as heavy tapestry. It serves for tablecloth and curtains, as well as for the canopied, step-back sideboard, a type of furniture often illustrated in 17th-century engravings of banquet subjects. Paneled walls and a coffered ceiling complete an ensemble of a type that could be found as late as Louis XIV's reign.

Magnificent country villas and houses have been built in France since the Revolution, and many old castles restored, but no original structure has gone up with the scale, the grandeur, the self-assured aristocratic bearing—or the phyiscal durability—to compare with the indestructible and defensive bastions of old. Still, there is a marvelous country dwelling, put together mainly since World War II, in which the owner's sense of style and his love of the good life have produced a delightful and curiously modern evocation of a great château from the *ancien régime*. This is Charles de Bestegui's Groussay in the Île-de-France a few miles west of Paris.

The Groussay that Charles de Bestegui acquired in 1939 was a substantial country house built in 1802 for the Duchesse de Chârost, whose mother, as royal governess, had been an intimate of Marie-Antoinette when the Bastille fell in 1789. But even though the structure had existed for almost a century and a half, the interior remained untouched by the decorator's hand, save for one handsome lattice-design ceiling prepared during the Second Empire, probably for Princess Soltykov. In Groussay, therefore, de Bestegui found true scope in which to fulfill his genius for free re-creations of period interiors.

A huge, two-story-high, mahogany-lined library like those in great English country houses, a Louis XIII dining room, a Goya gallery, and a garden *à l'anglaise* filled with architectural "follies" are among the more spectacular inventions to be found at Groussay. But the most dramatic feature certainly is the theatre added by de Bestegui after World War II. The only private theatre now functioning in France, it opened with a play, *L'Impromptu de Groussay*, written for the occasion—a true *pièce d'occasion*—by the great playwright Marcel Achard and acted by members of the Comédie Francaise in roles based upon the host's own friends. This was followed by a performance of Marivaux's *Les Fausses confidences*, for which M. de Bestegui designed the costumes.

In the last thirty years the guest list at Groussay has included, among royalty and heads of state, the writers Jean Cocteau and Louise de Vilmorin and the musicians Georges Auric and Francis Poulenc.

Pierrefonds

If Gothic, fortified Pierrefonds seems too good to be true, that is exactly what it is—a superb *château fort* reconstructed to the point where it represents less the reality that it was than what a very great, and creative, 19th-century medievalist imagined the perfect 14th-century fortress-château should have been. This has brought considerable scorn upon Pierrefonds, from those who regard it as a mere pastiche, typical of Second Empire naïveté, pedantry, and presumption. But for that very reason, the castle fascinates twice over, since it does embody authentic medieval elements of the finest kind, at the same time that it offers an equally authentic display of French taste at another, but no less important, period—the age of Louis Napoleon.

The Gothic Pierrefonds came into being during the last decade of the 14th century, after Charles V gave the domain to his second son, Louis, Duc d'Orléans, husband of the famous Valentine Visconti and father of the poet, Charles d'Orléans. During the war between the Burgundians and the Armagnacs, Louis d'Orléans was killed by Jean sans Peur, Duc de Bourgogne, and Pierrefonds burned. Charles d'Orléans transferred the château to his son, the future Louis XII, and the site did not reenter history until the 1590s, when the Wars of Religion caused the Catholic League to occupy it. After a long siege, Pierrefonds fell in 1594 to the troops of Henri IV. The sons of the commander then put in charge of the fortress—the d'Estrées—became the leaders of the *Mécontents* ("Malcontents") after the accession of Louis XIII. This brought a new siege, and ultimately the dismantling of the castle. Three centuries later Napoleon I bought what remained for a few francs, and in 1822 Louis-Philippe found the ruin sufficiently romantic to arrange a feast there, celebrating the marriage of his daughter Louise to Leopold I of the Belgians. Only in the next regime, however, did reconstruction actually commence, in 1857, under the direction of Viollet-le-Duc. A romantically fervent medievalist as well as a gifted engineer-architect, Viollet-le-Duc rather let his imagination triumph over his scholarship, for while saving and restoring what he found at Pierrefonds, he also added a great deal more. The fruit of his labor, therefore, is less a reconstruction of the real Pierrefonds than a three-dimensionalization of the paintings by the Limbourg brothers in that wonderful book of the 14th century—*Les Très Riches Heures du Duc de Berry*.

overleaf and *below:* High-walled, towered, turreted, crenellated, battlemented, gabled, and dormered—Pierrefonds, in all its picturesque detail and asymmetry, seems the complete Gothic château, everything the modern, Romantic imagination would hope to find in a great royal dwelling from the age of chivalry. And that indeed is what it is, a monumental reconstruction of an authentic 14th-century château fort, so fancifully realized, however, as to be a product of Second Empire taste as much as it is a survivor of the High Middle Ages.

below: A 19th-century photograph showing Pierrefonds before Viollet-le-Duc rebuilt it.

Broglie

The domain at Broglie is one of the oldest in France, but far outweighing this distinction is the brilliance of the ducal line that arrived in the 18th century and gave the estate its present name. The château—vast, angular, ground-hugging, many-windowed, and fundamentally simple—dates only from the 17th century, but as early as 1071 a *château fort* occupied the site near the village of Chambrais, as Broglie was known until 1742. The family established there for four centuries were the descendants of Henri de Ferrières, who received the estate from William the Conqueror. Through marriage and legacy the property eventually passed to Eustache de Conflans, a grandee prominent at the court of Henri IV—and as noted for his free thought in religion as for his eccentric attachment to an unfashionably long and flowing beard.

In the second half of the 17th century Chambrais belonged to Simon Arnauld, Marquis de Pomponne, the nephew of the Grand Arnauld and Mère Angélique of Port-Royal, the Jansenist center near Paris. Much esteemed by Louis XIV, Pomponne served as ambassador to Sweden and then, without success, as France's foreign minister. It was he who abandoned the feudal fortress and began the present château.

Chambrais became Broglie in honor of the second Maréchal de Broglie whose Piedmontese grandfather, François-Marie, had entered the French military and there earned many laurels. Victor-Maurice, the son of François-Marie, obtained the rank of marshal in 1724, but it was the second François-Marie, the grandson of the first, who brought the Broglies their first real glory. After brave, even spectacular performances in several major sieges and battles, and after serving as ambassador to London, the Marshal took command of the Bohemian army during the War of the Austrian Succession and sustained the siege of Prague. This brought him the title of Duke, only for disgrace to ensue when the newly elevated peer had to retreat from Bavaria. After exile to Broglie, he died in 1745.

The Duc de Broglie's son, Victor-François, created a family tradition when he too succeeded as a military leader and then fell from grace. Despite his having scaled the walls of Prague, despite his victories at Sandershausen,

below: Stripped by Revolutionaries—even of its window casements and shutters—the Château de Broglie was magnificently restored after 1816. It is an immense edifice—long, low, and angular—that extends over 240 meters. Projecting pavilions and pedimented bays save the façade from boredom. Although great in its actual dimensions, the château retains a rustic, good-natured aspect, thanks mainly to the materials used—the ordinary ones of flint, "pudding" stone, and tile. Only a ruined tower and the moat survive to suggest that before the present 17th-century dwelling there stood on this site—originally called Chambrais—an ancient château fort dating back to the 11th century.

opposite above: Designed in the severe, clean lines of the early 19th-century Neoclassic style, the grand staircase at Broglie offers a double flight of steps that converge halfway before reaching the floor above. No less Neoclassic is the vestibule itself, with its stucco columns, palm frieze, and marble busts. The décor here derives from the massive restoration undertaken after the Revolution, when Broglie was all but demolished.

Bergen, and Munden, and despite the title of Prince bestowed by the Holy Roman Emperor, the Duc de Broglie suffered disgrace caused by a stupidity on the part of the Maréchal de Soubise—the favorite of La Pompadour. In retirement at the family estate, but still passionately supported by the public, the Marshal-Duke renewed building, the better to receive the great of his time, among whom could be found the brother of Marie-Antoinette, the future Joseph II of Austria. In 1789 Louis XVI summoned the Duc de Broglie to be minister of war, but it was too late—France had exploded in Revolution. The Marshal emigrated, then offered his services to the princes' army, but died in Germany in 1804.

The third Duc de Broglie, having espoused liberal ideas, participated in the American War of Independence, but was arrested in France and guillotined in 1794. His heir returned to find the château stripped of all its moveable parts—even the window casements and shutters. No less liberal than his father, the new Duke entered the diplomatic service and in 1816 married the daughter of Mme de Staël, the incomparable Albertine, whose salon became one of the most provocative of the Restoration period. The fortune she inherited from her maternal grandfather, the great Swiss banker Necker, made possible the complete restoration of the Château de Broglie. The Duke's ideas caused him to abandon the reactionary elder Bourbons and to support the Orleanists, who gained the throne with the accession of Louis-Philippe in 1830. After Napoleon III's *coup d'état* in 1849, he maintained his values by retiring from public life.

Albert, the fourth Duc de Broglie, adhered closely to his father's precedent. But following withdrawal from public life in 1849, he devoted his energies to major historical studies and produced *The Church and the Roman Empire in the 4th Century*, which won him election to the French Academy. In 1873 he was asked by Mac-Mahon to form a cabinet and prepare for the return of the Bourbon dynasty, in the person of the Comte de Chambord. When both the royalist and the conservative causes failed in 1877, the Duke retired to Broglie—much praised by Daudet, Gambetta, and many other of the age's major spokesmen.

In the 20th century the Broglies added new lustre to their line when Duke Maurice discovered the X-ray and subsequently the "Broglie ray," which could penetrate the atom. At age thirty-two, Prince Louis de Broglie published a revolutionary thesis on the quantum theory and formulated wave mechanics, all of which earned him the Nobel Prize in 1929.

The present châtelain of Broglie is Prince Jean.

overleaf: In the grand drawing room at Broglie, a fabric printed with a pattern of blue arabesques on a white ground uniformly frames the windows and serves as upholstery for chairs and couch. Although Second Empire in origin, the scheme blends well with the 18th-century paneling. This—together with the flower-filled vases, the family souvenirs, the large windows admitting light and a view upon the green park outside— makes a fresh and pleasant place for the gathering of intimate friends.

below: The portrait of Germaine de Staël dominates the library at Broglie, reminding us that her daughter Albertine became Duchesse de Broglie. It was the great fortune accumulated by Mme de Staël's father, the Swiss banker Jacques Necker, that made possible the restoration of the château. The early 19th-century taste for the antique—as well as for the exotic—is evident in Mme de Staël's Neoclassical attire, crowned by a turban. It is equally present in the gilt candelabra, in the bronze and marble clock, and in the mahogany pilasters framing the bookshelves.

List of illustrations:

Jacket:

Front — Chenonceaux photographed by Ami Guichard.

Back — Bussy-Rabutin by Claude Arthaud, Paris, assisted by Studio Richard Blin.